THE
ADULT
SON

THE ADULT SON

DALE MILLER
Drake University
Des Moines, Iowa

THE ADULT SON

Copyright 1974 by Dale Miller

Standard Book Number: ISBN 0-9600726-1-6

Library of Congress Catalog Card Number: 74-77418

Scripture quotations are from the Revised Standard Version of the Bible, copyrighted 1946 and 1952 by the Division of Christian Education, National Council of Churches, and are used by permission; or are privately translated by the author.

Printed and bound by Wallace-Homestead Co.
Des Moines, Iowa, U.S.A.

TABLE OF CONTENTS

INTRODUCTION

The meaning of the *Gospel of Mark* has been obscured since the first century because of the difficulty which the heirs of Greek culture have had in reading literature from Hebrew culture. The rediscovery of the distinction between Hebraic and Hellenistic thought has, in our century, unlocked the possibility of reading *Mark* as its author intended it to be read. The purpose of this present book is to make clear that intention of the author of the Gospel, whom I shall refer to as Mark.

Even after the Hebraic-Hellenistic distinction became known, the dominant trends in Gospel studies continued to be overly influenced by the assumption that much of the Gospel material originated in Greek cultural settings. This conclusion was consistent with two assured results of modern scholarship, one that the original Gospel materials came from many sources, and the other that the Gospels were originally written in Greek. It was also consistent with a basic assumption of Form Criticism, the leading twentieth-century methodology, that the author of *Mark* had not mastered all of the materials which he used—with the result that *Mark* is not built around a single organizing theme.

My own conclusion is exactly the contrary. I claim to have discovered a Hebraic flow of thought which runs throughout *Mark*. It depends upon having every unit of material (technically called a pericope) in its assigned location. It credits the author with an extensive use of literary symbols of a sophisticated nature and an appreciation of literary motifs from Jewish scripture. The result is a picture of *Mark* as a Jewish book in the classical biblical tradition, arguing Jewish questions with a presumably Jewish audience.

The method which has produced this result can be generally described as literary analysis. It is to be distinguished from historical methods which have dominated scholarship for the past century. Detailed notes about the methods of literary analysis are provided both in this Introduction and in the text at appropriate points.

Many of the interpretations of Jesus arrived at will seem radically new to most readers. Most of them have come as great surprises to me. I have been at the task of understanding *Mark* since 1954. Family and friends have become accustomed to my excitement as some new meaning emerged from application of the methodology. I know that this process is not finished, but it is far enough along that I must offer the book as the beginning of a conversation with other scholars. The resultant feedback will considerably enrich my own understanding of the subject.

1

A Description of Literary Analysis: Composition Criticism

The particular form of literary analysis used in this study is Composition Criticism, as distinguished from Form Criticism and Redaction Criticism. Both of the latter focus attention on the previously existing materials from which the Gospels were constructed. Form Criticism emphasizes the categories of material; Redaction Criticism, the process of editorial change in quoted materials. Composition Criticism centers on the author's creation of a book which has an integrity of its own without regard to the question as to whether some or all of his materials existed previously. Form Criticism and Redaction Criticism are interested in the history of the materials before they arrived at their present setting. Composition Criticism is interested solely in the meaning of the book in its present form.

It is important to note that adopting the methods of Composition Criticism does not invalidate historical methods of Gospel study. Historical methods have produced valuable results and will continue to do so. None of the assured results of historical studies are necessarily called into question. Nevertheless, it is likely to be one of the results of a rigorous use of literary analysis methods that many of the conclusions now taken for granted will be re-examined and some will be revised.

Historical studies of the Gospels have often committed two methodological errors which Composition Criticism can rectify. Both involve failure to limit historical studies to proper spheres. The first has been the tendency toward circular argument. Conclusions which were originally only logical deductions have been treated as factual data and have been used as the basis for arriving at other logically deduced conclusions.

Logical deductions are valid only as logical deductions. They must be distinguished from historical facts. Note the following collection of statements about *Mark,* each clause of which is a conclusion based only on logic.

John Mark, in whose home the Last Supper occurred, wrote his Gospel, under the influence of Simon Peter, to the church at Rome, in relation to the persecution which had occurred there, for the purpose of encouraging Christians to remain steadfast in the face of suffering.

Without challenging any clause in that paragraph, the problem is that none of it is known for sure, not even that John Mark wrote the book. There is no solid, first century, factual evidence for any of it. All of it is built upon logical deductions from the Gospel itself or from later interpreters who may or may not have possessed accurate information.

It is widely assumed, however, that such conclusions about *Mark* are sufficiently factual so that each clause can be used as a sound basis for drawing other conclusions about the book, e.g. that because Mark got his information from Peter the book is historically trustworthy, or that because Mark was writing to the Roman church the book was intended primarily for Gentiles. No such conclusion would be methodologically valid even if it turned out to have landed by coincidence upon what actually occurred in history. The fault is not with the conclusions, but with the methods which treats logical deductions as historical data.

The second error of historical method is much more important. It is the tendency to argue from the general to the particular and to accept the result as historically accurate. Assume, for purposes of understanding this point, that all of the assertions in the paragraph about John Mark above are both historically accurate and verifiable by evidence. The question then is: what conclusions about *Mark* can be drawn from them. This is a methodological question of prime importance. The art of writing history is the recreation of the past based upon particulars which are both accurate and relevant. The word "relevant" is as important to that point as accuracy is. Accurate information about the author of a book does not necessarily provide much help for interpreting the book. There is no necessary connection between one particular and another. It might be known, for example, that a modern author is an Iowan, a Harvard man, a politician, and an executive. That does not tell us whether he is a saint, a sinner, a liberal, a liar, or a crusader. The problem is one of relevance.

Likewise with the study of the Gospels. Certainty that the author's name was John Mark, that he received information from Peter, that he addressed his book to the church at Rome—none of this is relevant to questions concerning his concept of miracles, his view of crucifixion, or his stand on any other disputed concept in *Mark*. With rare exceptions, the only relevant historical evidence for the interpretation of a literary passage is the flow of thought of the total work of which it is a part.

But, you may well ask, what if the author has made a concrete statement about his intention in writing a book? Would not such a declaration be relevant to the interpretation of the book? It *may* provide helpful clues, but it is not in itself evidence. The author may have intended to communicate a particular message and failed to do so. Both MacLeish and Silone in our time have indicated as much by revising their original published versions of *J.B.* and *Bread and Wine*. In each case, the original book made sense even though it was not the sense which the author intended. It is that something-which-was-actually-said which it is the task of the literary analyst to identify. By doing that task well, one may learn something which the author did not consciously intend to reveal or discover meanings in the book which are there but which the author was not conscious of putting there.

Composition Criticism is thus a significant but limited method. It is significant in that it provides accurate information about books which is not otherwise available. It is limited in that it makes little contribution to the discovery of historical data surrounding the literature studied.

The ultimate criterion of truth in literary analysis is logical consistency. That interpretative scheme for understanding a work of literature is most true if it is the most logically consistent of all possibilities considered. External data does not enter in. Consider for example Mark's reference to Herod of Galilee as King Herod, a title which historical evidence indicates he did not hold. Historians spot this inaccuracy and properly draw conclusions from it. Literary analysis is not concerned with such an error. The only literary questions is whether the designation of Herod as king is logically consistent with the rest of the book. If it is, then for purposes of understanding *Mark,* Herod was a king.

Two Hypotheses to Be Tested

Composition Criticism tests two hypotheses each of which contradicts the assured results of Gospel study in our century. The first is that the problems involved in understanding the thought of Jesus and his associates are of the same nature as for any other ancient figure, such as a Roman emperor, a character in Greek tragedy, or a biblical prophet, and that these problems are not insurmountable. The second is that each of the four Gospels was written by someone who understood what he was doing and who wrote a book which makes sense when read as a whole. It is these hypotheses which will be tested in this book.

The first directly contradicts three of the most fundamental conclusions of modern Gospel scholarship. 1) Wrede saw the Jesus of *Mark* as a supernatural figure who knew his identity as Son of God but decided for some reason inexplicable to man to keep his identity a secret until he chose to reveal it. 2) Wrede also conceived of unclean spirits as actual beings who either knew Jesus' true identity as Son of God and sought to reveal it before he was ready to be publicly known, or who were sources of mental and physical disease in those whose bodies they inhabited, and who thus had to be exorcised. 3) Schweitzer saw Jesus as one primarily interested in the coming of a future Kingdom of God, which he thought at first to be at hand but later admitted to be farther away. The net result of these three conclusions was to make of Jesus and his associates people with such a strange view of life as to be largely incomprehensible to modern man. It was under the influence of that sense of Jesus' strangeness that scholarship turned to the kind of questions asked by Form Criticism and Redaction Criticism, thus studying the history of the materials rather than the history of Jesus and his accociates. My own hypothesis is that there are better interpretations of each of the three topics, interpretations which put Jesus back into the mainstream of human life.

The second hypothesis contests the widely accepted dictum of Bultmann that the author of *Mark* was not the master of the materials with which he worked. Form Criticism has adduced abundant evidence in support of such a claim. Against such evidence there is only one answer: either demonstrate that there is in the Gospel a hitherto unrecognized continuity which makes sense out of the whole, or accept Bultmann's assertion. It is with this challenge that this book is primarily concerned.

Principal Themes in The Gospel of Mark

The view of *Mark* which is assumed throughout this book is so different from popular opinions about *Mark* that a clear statement of the major themes will help alert many readers to the direction of the argument. *Mark* is centered around two motifs. The central one concerns Jesus' response to his baptismal experience of becoming aware for the first time that God loved him as a son. Jesus' responses move through three distinct stages: one in which he conceives of himself as a preacher-teacher of Jewish crowds, a second in which he focuses on training an elite New Israel, and a third in which he becomes a doer of deeds which do not require for his success any followers at all. This motif is thus developmental. Each of the stages is good; the problem is that they are not good enough until the final stage is climaxed by the crucifixion. Only crucifixion justifies Jesus' acceptance of the designation as God's beloved son.

A second motif in *Mark* is subsidiary to the first. It involves Jesus' specific responses to Jewish tradition. The book is written *as if* Jesus had consciously said to himself after his baptism: "My religion (Judaism) must tell me what it means to be God's son. Therefore I will search the scriptures and traditions of Judaism and try on for size each of the concepts of sonship which I find there." The author of *Mark* concludes that after Jesus had completed that quest he discovered that all but one of the traditional Jewish concepts was inadequate.

This secondary motif is quite extensive in *Mark,* making a literary impression on virtually every pericope in the book. Among the models from Jewish scripture which Jesus tested are the following: Elijah, Elisha, the sons of the prophets, the sons of Jacob, the sons of Levi, David and the sons of David, Ezekiel as son of man, *Daniel's* Son of man, the miracle worker tradition, Judah as betrayer of Joseph, Isaiah, Malachi, Nahum, Passover, the messianic Psalms, and Joshua the high priest. No one name or item on the list is overpowering in its significance, but taken as a whole the list is an impressive one. It indicates that Mark was thoroughly oriented toward Jewish traditions in his presentation of Jesus' responses to his awareness that he was the beloved son of God.

Stylistic Features in Mark

Some peculiarities of Markan style, such as his sandwich method of interrupting a story with another in the middle and his seemingly indiscriminate use of the word "immediately", have long been noted. Others, much more important to the interpretation of the book, are less obvious. Among the latter, the most important is Mark's use of narrative sequences with implied continuities. Stories are linked together without explicit clues as to their relationship to each other. This makes difficult reading for modern people who are accustomed either to essays or to narratives with complete continuities.

An excellent example of narrative style with implied continuity is found in the references to "wilderness" in the opening sentences of *Mark*. Mark first quoted from *Isaiah* in regard to a messenger in a wilderness. He then described John the Baptizer as a preacher in a wilderness. After John baptized Jesus in that wilderness, Jesus was sent into a different wilderness to be tempted. Nowhere does Mark comment on the relationship of these three references to wilderness. The task of interpretation cries out for implied continuities to make sense out of the whole.

A second example occurs in the same section. It was the Holy Spirit which sent Jesus out to be tempted. In the preceding pericope, the Holy Spirit had announced to Jesus that he was the beloved son of God. What is the implied continuity which explains what there was in the Holy Spirit's role in the baptism which led directly into a temptation episode? The central task of the Composition Critic in working with *Mark* is to recognize this particular feature of Mark's style, and thus to ask and answer such questions as the above.

A second major Markan stylistic peculiarity is the use of symbols, both individual word symbols and events as symbols. Quite commonly, numbers, key words, and the names of people and places have symbolic meanings. The number twelve symbolized Israel; town names such as Capernaum and Bethsaida were closely connected to events which occurred there; seeing and hearing were used as equivalents of understanding. Many of Mark's implied continuities are discoveed only after the meaning of his symbols becomes obvious.

Mark's use of events as symbols is a more striking feature of the book. Examples include the unchainable Legion as a symbol of greatly increased temptation in Jesus' early career, the half-healed blind man as a symbol of Peter's half-true recognition of Jesus as messiah, and the woman who put all her money in the temple treasury as a symbol of Jesus giving his all in the crucifixion.

In regard to events with symbolic meaning, it is important to note that some incidents in the book function in such a way as to affect the course of events, whereas others do not. This has nothing to do with whether the events actually occurred in history. It has only to do with their influence in the book. Symbolic events are those which in no way result in any change for any character in the book. The prime example begins in the fourth chapter where Jesus faced the dilemma of how to enable the newly called disciples to become fruit-bearers. His solution was to give them a task: row a boat across the lake. This led through a series of incidents to Jesus' return to his family's home town. Then in the next pericope after that one, Jesus proposed a solution to his dilemma: send the disciples out on a mission. *Mark* proceeds from that point as if the boat-home-town series of incidents had not occurred, but depends strongly upon the occurrence of the events which begin with the mission. For literary purposes within the book, the earlier series was symbolic, the latter one actual.

Another important Markan style deals with prediction. Mark pays careful attention to predictive details within the Gospel. A short list given at one point, such as the tasks assigned to the disciples at the time of their calling or the details of the three passion predictions, often becomes the outline of subsequent events. The passion predictions, for example, accurately predict the order of the trials of Jesus at the end of his career.

Hellenistic Galilee as the Setting for Jesus' Career

The importance of the name Jesus and the location Galilee have long been hidden in such plain sight that no one had paid any attention. I had long taken for granted the popular view that the name "Jesus" was merely a Greek version of the actual historical name of Jesus, that his real name had been Joshua or some Aramaic form of Joshua (Yeshua??), and that Aramaic was his language and the language of Galilee. This had seemed so historically likely that I had given no thought to it.

Mark presents Jesus as a Hellenized Jew from Galilee, a region with many Hellenized Jews, in contrast to Judea as the region of Hebraic Judaism. The difference between Galilee and Judea, as portrayed by Mark, seemed to be primarily one of language. Galilee was borderland where some people had Hebrew names, some Hellenized Hebrew names, and some Greek names. Note the following:

Hebrew Names in Mark	Greek Names in Mark	Hellenized Names in Mark
John	Andrew	Jesus
Jacob	Philip	Simon
Barabbas	Alphaeus	Judas
Joseph		Mary
Levi		

Jesus' family in particular showed the result of Hellenistic influence, with his mother Mary and his brothers Judas and Simon all bearing Hellenized names. In the sources available to me it is not clear whether Joses, a third brother, is a Hellenized version of Joseph or an entirely separate Hebrew name. The fourth brother, Jacob, carried a Hebrew name. All of the names were taken from Bible: Jesus (Joshua), Mary (Miriam), Simon (Simeon), Judas (Judah), Joses (Joseph), and Jacob. The family was strongly Jewish and strongly Hellenized.

It is likewise the case that some place names in Galilee bore Hebrew names and others Greek ones. From non-Mark sources we know of places with Roman names, but none appear in this Gospel. That fact may be of utmost significance in historical studies of *Mark* inasmuch as some of the larger towns bore Roman names, and the name of the author was a Roman name. Within the limits of literary analysis alone

7

it would appear that Mark was consciously describing a setting for Jesus' career which lay on the boarderline of Hellenization as distinct from one which lay in Galilee as an incidental area.

Strong support for such a Markan choice lay in the Greek translation of the Jewish Bible. That version, known as the Septuagint and usually abbreviated as LXX, is the source of the biblical quotations found in *Mark*. It is important to the mindset of the author that he found key words and names *in Greek* in that Bible. Where the Old Testament reads "Joshua" LXX reads "Jesus." Where the Old Testament reads "Messiah" or "anointed one" LXX reads "Christ." Where the Old Testament reads "glad tidings" LXX reads "gospel." There was thus in the Bible which Mark used a powerful impetus toward continuity between a Hellenized translation of scripture and a Hellenized version of Judaism as it was lived out in the lives of Jesus and his associates.

CHAPTER ONE
THE OFFER OF SONSHIP

The key to understanding *Mark* is its first sentence properly translated. For centuries the message of the Gospel has been obscured because the intent of the first sentence was improperly read. Rarely has biblical scholarship been so profoundly affected by a translator's decision. As printed in the Revised Standard Version, the sentence reads:

> The beginning of the gosepl of Jesus Christ, the son of God. As it is written in Isaish the prophet, "Behold, I send my messenger before thy face, who shall prepare thy way; the voice of one crying in the wilderness: Prepare the way of the Lord, make his paths straight."

The translators made four decisions in the R.S.V. text which make it difficult for readers to comprehend the original intent of the sentence and the book which follows from it. They are: the division of the sentence as if it were two sentences, the reference to Jesus Christ as if Christ were part of a name rather than a title, the capitalization of "Son" to make it appear that Mark began by affirming Jesus' divinity, and the use of a single set of quotation marks to give the impression that there is only one quotation in the passage. An English translation which would avoid all four difficulties is:

> The beginning of the gospel of Jesus, the messiah, the son of God, as it is written in Isaish the prophet:
> "Behold, I send my messenger before thy face, who shall prepare thy way;"
> "The voice of one crying in the wilderness: 'Prepare the way of the Lord, make his paths straight'."

The principal difference is the single sentence. When divided as two sentences, scholars have most often read the first sentence as a title for the whole book and the second sentence as the beginning of the text. My proposed translation connects the beginning of the good news (gospel) with the two quotations attributed by Mark to *Isaiah*. It is that connection which unlocks the door behind which the meanings of *Mark* have been unseen for centuries.

Before spelling out the implications of connecting the origin of gospel with *Isaiah*, brief attention needs to be given to the other three changes. It is well known that the Greek word "christos" is the counterpart of the Hebrew word "messiah." Technically both words mean "the anointed one" but in general parlance they refer to a leader or a type of leadership hoped for in the future. Among the Jews, both in scripture and apart from it, there were many alternative concepts of the identity and function of such a leader or leadership. To translate "christos" as a title helps keep open for the reader the possibility of distinguishing among the several concepts of messiahship which Mark presents.

Ancient Greek literary customs about capitalizing words differed from modern American ones. There is no hint in the early Greek manuscripts of *Mark* as to whether the author intended "son of God" to refer to divinity. The flow of thought in the book suggests that he did not. To write "son" in lower case letters keeps open to the reader a greater possibility for discovering that flow of thought.

The apparent quotation from *Isaiah.* is really two quotations, one from *Isaiah,* one from *Malachi.* They are blended by Mark into a single idea which differs from both originals and then attributed to *Isaiah* alone. This has raised serious questions about the author's intention, about his competence, about his sources, and about the preservation of the text. When the question of intention is adequately dealt with the other difficulties disappear. It is the author's intention which is clarified by recognizing the single sentence declaration of Mark that the gospel began in the time of *Isaiah*.

Questions Raised by the One Sentence Translation

Translating the opening words of *Mark* as one sentence, as suggested above, raises a number of questions. One is what there was in the original Greek manuscripts which occasioned the two-sentence punctuation. At the time *Mark* was written, the Greek language had no punctuation marks either as spaces between words or as marks between units of meaning. Thus in Greek the first sentence would have been written entirely in lower case or in upper case letters, and would appear as its English translation would if written as follows:

thebeginningofthegospelofjesuschristthesonofgodasitiswritten
inisaiahtheprophetbeholdisendmymessengerbeforethyface
whoshallpreparethywaythevoiceofonecryinginthewildernesspre-
paretHewayofthelordmakehispathsstraight.

It was up to the reader to excerpt from such a text a logical structure of meanings. The opening of *Mark* is clearly a case in which two entirely different logical structures have been discovered, the traditional two-sentence one and the proposed one-sentence one.

This raises a methodological question: when two logical possibilities are present, how is the reader to choose between them? The answer proposed by Composition Criticism is simple to state, difficult to apply.

It is always to be assumed in a well written document that the author intended to express meaning in a manner which is logically consistent with the whole document. That possibility is to be chosen which is most consistent with the total known context of the passage in the document within which the interpretative possibilities occur. The "intention of the author" cannot be an historical fact known in advance and imposed upon the book. The expression, the intent of the author, refers to the end product of the logical reconstruction of the book's meaning. When the most logical pattern of meaning is discovered, that pattern of meaning is assumed to have been the intention of the author. Note that this methodology applies only to writings with sufficient consistency of literary qualities to be designated as well written.

I myself am a Christian with certain emotional commitments to Jesus as Christ and Son of God and as the source of the gospel. Those beliefs are irrelevant, even though shared by millions, when it comes to determining the interpretation of *Mark*. As consistently as possible, evidence must be limited to that provided internally by *Mark*. Within that context, for reasons which can only become apparent as this book continues, I find the single sentence translation of Mark's opening words to be far more consistent with the flow of thought than the two-sentence translation.

A second question concerns the assertion that the good news began in *Isaiah*. In what senses could that possibly be true, and what might have led Mark to such a statement? The answer relates to the fact that the word "gospel" appears seven times, in five sentences, in the Greek version of the Bible (LXX) which Mark used. Four of the five sentences are in the poetic section of *Isaiah* (chapters 40-66), the other one in *Nahum*. The Nahum passage is virtually identical to *Isaiah* 52.7.

The use of the word "gospel" in the Jewish Bible has been obscured to Christians in English translations because the word has been translated differently in the Old and New Testaments. In R.S.V. the word appears as "gospel" in the New Testament, as "glad tidings" in the Old. Note how the *Isaiah* passages appeared to Mark when he read the word as "gospel."

"O Zion, herald of the gospel;...O Jerusalem, herald of the gospel." (*Is.* 40.9)
"...I will give to Jerusalem a herald of the gospel." (*Is.* 41.27)
"How beautiful upon the mountains are the feet of him who brings the gospel, who publishes peace, who brings the gospel of good..." (*Is.* 52.7)
"The spirit of the Lord is upon me, because the Lord has anointed me to bring the gospel to the afflicted." (Is. 61.1)

Mark knew that the gospel began in *Isaiah* for the simple literalistic reason that he found *Isaiah* using the word.

Why only in *Isaiah?* Why not also in *Nahun?* Mark was conscious of the fact that the gospel also began in *Nahum* but he found a different way of expressing it. He pictured the beginning of Jesus' proclamation of the gospel as occurring in the City of Nahum, a town whose name is transliterated as Capernaum in English translations. The subsequent flow of events in Capernaum is so closely related to the meaning of the biblical quotation that there can be little doubt about Mark's intention of having the gospel begin in Nahum City because *Nahum* used the word "gospel." Mark had a different reason for his opening explicit statement that the gospel began in *Isaiah*. He found in *Isaiah* in addition to the gospel references other themes which he used to enrich his presentation of Jesus.

If the gospel really began in *Isaiah,* why should Mark have attributed to *Isaiah* a quotation which in part was taken from *Malachi?* The internal evidence is that Mark knew scripture too well to be scored with a blunder. There seem to be two answers. The first is that Mark used the entire Jewish Bible as if it were a single set of source materials, freely choosing passages from many books and mixing them together to suit his own purposes. Inasmuch as the gospel began in *Isaiah* any section of any part of the Bible could be cited in conjunction with *Isaiah*. The second answer is an example of the first. Note the two quotations in their original form.

"A voice cries, 'In the wilderness prepare the way of the Lord, make straight in the desert a highway for our God'." (*Is.* 40.3)
"Behold, I send my messenger to prepare the way before me, and the Lord whom you seek will suddenly come to his temple; the messenger of the covenant in whom you delight, behold he is coming, says the Lord of hosts." (*Mal.* 3.1)

The *Isaiah* sentence implies the existence of a messenger; the *Malachi* sentence makes explicit and thus in a sense fulfills *Isaiah's* implication. Furthermore, "Malachi" is a word meaning "messenger" and was probably never intended as a name. Thus the book of *Malachi* would appropriately be titled in English "The Messenger." It was quite proper for Mark to quote from *The Messenger* to complete his interpretation of *Isaiah's* prediction of a coming wilderness voice.

What happened to the meaning of the quotations from *Isaiah* and *Malachi* when Mark combined them?

"Behold I send my messenger before thy face, who shall prepare thy way; the voice of one crying in the wilderness: 'Prepare the way of the Lord, make his paths straight'." (*Mark* 1.2-3)

Malachi's messenger was to come to the temple to deliver a message. *Isaiah's* voice was to tell people to construct a highway in a wilderness, without regard to the place in which the message was delivered. But Mark's messenger was to be in the wilderness to deliver his sermon, in a wilderness where presumably there would be no one to hear him.

If one assumes a wilderness to have been an uninhabited place, as seems reasonable, to whom was the message addressed? The answer lies in the use of wilderness as a symbol. In *Isaiah's* setting, the Jews were in exile in Babylon and were to return home across a desert wilderness. Their journey did not depend upon paving a road or even straightening one; camel caravans have no such needs. What the Jews needed to do, as *Isaiah* makes clear, was to straighten out their lives. Their lives were the wilderness within which a straight path needed to be built in order to prepare for the return of a people who would be God's people.

The setting was different for Mark. The Jews to whom his

messenger was to speak were already geographically at home; they were not on the other side of a desert, nor did they need to go into a desert. Nevertheless their lives were still a wilderness. They still needed to create a straight path for the coming of the Lord.

Mark added to that symbolism a second *Isaiah* insight, derived from two *Isaiah* quotations:

"Go and say to this people: 'Hear and hear, but do not understand; see and see, but do not perceive.' Make the heart of this people fat, and their ears heavy, and shut their eyes; lest they see with their eyes, and hear with their ears, and understand with their hearts, and turn and be healed." (*Is.* 6.8-10) "Bring forth the people who are blind, yet have eyes, who are deaf, yet have ears." (*Is.* 43.8)

With this addition, the wilderness became for Mark a symbol of men's unwillingness or inability to hear the message of God. It would make no difference whether the voice spoke to people in downtown Jerusalem or to the wind and sand on the last dune beyond the Dead Sea. No one would really be listening. Wilderness became Mark's symbol of forlornness. The messenger of good news, really exciting news, was to be a wilderness voice. He was to be the bearer of news which would be understandingly heard by no human ear. Only rocks and trees and sky and wind were to be his symbolic auditors. As the flow of thought developed in *Mark,* both John the Baptizer and Jesus were to be presented as such voices. Great crowds would gather for their speeches, but no one would truly hear them. They were thus to be voices crying in the wilderness of the deaf and the blind.

Careful interpretation of the first sentence of *Mark* provides several clues as to the kind of book which follows. It suggests that Mark took scripture seriously and leads the reader to expect that there will be much more in the way of biblical justification for the career of Jesus. Such references to Bible could vary all the way from simple literalism, as in the assertion that the gospel began in *Isaiah* because the word was found there, to sophisticated reinterpretation, as in Mark's transformation of the symbolic meaning of wilderness.

The first sentence also suggests that Mark can handle symbols unobtrusively. Millions have read the Markan accounts of the wilderness without raising any question other than the geographical location of the place referred to, e.g. was it a sandy desert or a river meadow? But likewise, Mark uses the symbol in such a way that the penetrating reader can break through to a second level of meaning: the wilderness of the lonely speaker in the midst of a crowd. Mark's ability to construct such a symbol leads one to anticipate that the technique will be used again in his book.

The obvious connection between the Hellenized name Jesus and the traditional Jewish title messiah alerts the reader from the beginning of the book to the possibility that at least part of the wilderness quality of the unhearing Jews would be related to their inability to hear the

13

truths of Hellenized Judaism as distinct from the more traditional Hebraic forms. What this might mean is not at all clear at the opening of *Mark,* but it will bear close attention throughout the study.

JOHN THE BAPTIZER AS THE NEW ELIJAH

The final paragraph of *Malachi* identified the messenger who was to come as Elijah. In *Malachi's* vision of the future, Elijah was to come to the temple and to demand that Jews purify their lives.

"Behold, I will send you Elijah the prophet before the great and terrible day of the Lord comes. And he will turn the hearts of fathers to their children, and the hearts of children to their fathers, lest I come and smite the land with a curse." (*Mal.* 4.5-6)

Either fathers and children would be reconciled to each other (bridging a generation gap??), or God's day of judgment would bring a great curse on the land. For reasons which appear later, those words were portrayed by Mark as having a great impact on Jesus. But that is to get ahead of the story.

Mark accepted *Malachi's* identification of the messenger as Elijah and added to the *Malachi* material all the other Elijah material from Jewish Bible. He pictured John the Baptizer as wearing those garments which *II Kings* 1.8 specified as the identifying garb of Elijah. John the Baptizer was the wilderness voice, and he was Elijah come again as *Malachi* had foretold.

Imagine the nervous excitement which must have pervaded Judea when John the Baptizer appeared in the uniform of Elijah, thus forecasting the possibility that God's day of judgment was near at hand. *Malachi's* prediction about that "great and terrible day" was that no one would be able to stand unless he had been purified by Elijah. But those who feared the Lord would be spared as a father spares his son.

No one would dare be absent from Elijah-John's audience. Insofar as the ritual of baptism provided a surface proof that one had been purified by Elijah-John, no one would dare pass up the opportunity to be baptized. No one would dare not confess his sins publicly so that Elijah-John knew that he had done so. Mark reported that all of the city of Jerusalem (every man, woman, and child; every priest, Pharisee, Sadducee, elder, scribe, Zealot; everyone) went to Elijah-John, as did people from every part of Judea. Everyone joined his movement by baptism and public confession of sin. No one would dare not do so.

For those who know the conclusion of *Mark,* that Jesus was executed in Jerusalem at the insistence of the religious establishment and with the support of the Jerusalem crowds, the irony of Elijah-John's success is already apparent. Those who were baptized by John were those who crucified Jesus.

Even without knowing about that event of the future, Elijah-John knew that he was a failure. He dressed in Elijah's clothing, but he was unable to complete Elijah's *Malachi* agenda. Elijah's coming was intended to reconcile fathers and children. It was supposed to create a

14

golden age, a time of good news as a consequence of the changed lives of people. That was the heart of the failure. Elijah-John asked people to repent: to change the direction of their lives, to transform their will and purpose toward the good. No one in the audience did so.

John intended the ritual of baptism only as a symbol of the desired change. He implied that God's forgiveness would come only to those who had actually changed life direction. No one changed. The crowds gave lip service to the symbols and went on living in the old ways. Baptism was little more than a wetting of the skin, quite apart from the cleansing of heart and mind and spirit.

In John's awareness that he had failed he was very much like the original Elijah. The prophet had begun his public career in a blaze of glory by besting the priests of the Baalim (false gods). In the flush of success he had all of them put to death. He stood alone as the victorious prophet of the living God. Jewish scripture declares this to have been a failure. Elijah fled into a wilderness in fear for his life, waiting for some new word from God. When it came, it was not as Elijah expected it in the turbulent voice of storm and wind. It came rather in the sound of silence as an unvoiced spirit. It told Elijah to recruit other faithful men for God's tasks. Result: Elijah called Elisha to follow him and ultimately to succeed him.

The imagery of the Elijah-Elisha cycle in *I-II Kings* served Mark's purposes better than that of *Malachi. Malachi* envisioned that the returned Elijah would succeed. Mark knew from his vantage point of hindsight that the ancient Elijah failure had been repeated. Public success had again soured into private gloom.

So it was that Elijah-John predicted an-as-yet-unnamed successor who would follow the ancient rhythm of replacing the externals of wind and storm with an internal quality of spirit. Specifically, John's prediction was that the mighty one to follow him would replace the external water baptism which John had used with an internal baptism of holy spirit. The successor would thus succeed in purifying the inside of men whereas John had failed by being able only to wash their outside.

The term "holy spirit" as used by Mark has become confusing to Christians because of the later development of the doctrine of the Trinity. There are three reasons internal to *Mark* which support a translation of "spirit of holiness" rather than "Holy Spirit". The first is that Elijah-John's prediction was inaccurate. Mark's Jesus was no more of a success than John in persuading the crowds to be spiritually baptized by transforming their lives. Both the crowds and the disciples consistently disappointed him and finally abandoned him altogether at the time of his death. They did not repent, if they ever did, until at least some time after Mark's narrative leaves off. Therefore, John's prophecy ought not to be treated as a revelation indicating his precise knowledge of the future and his specific acquaintance with Jesus as the successful third person of the Trinity.

The second reason is the simple fact that "spirit of holiness" fits the context of John's distinction between superficial water baptism and meaningful internal transformation. It fits in also with Mark's later designation of evil spirits as unclean. Thus a spirit of purification would be holy; an unclean spirit would be unholy.

The third reason concerns the relationship between the Elijah-Elisha cycle and *Mark*. Elijah's failure and John's failure follow similar rhythms: apparent opening success, followed by an awareness that externals are inadequate in comparison to spirit. This is the first instance of a literary style which Mark was to use many times in his Gospel: writing a Gospel story in the same rhythm as a story from Jewish Bible. It seems unlikely for all these reasons that Mark would intend his words to be translated as Holy Spirit rather than as holy spirit or spirit of holiness.

Elijah's instruction, given by the spirit voice, was to call others to follow him. He called only Elisha, and Elisha became his successor, endowed with a double portion of Elijah's spirit. It was in keeping with the Elijah-Elisha rhythm for Elijah-John to predict that his successor would be more successful than he in relation to spirit. In a way which Elijah-John did not imagine, his prediction was fulfilled when Jesus at his baptism heard the spirit voice communicating to him the love of God as father.

JESUS AS ELISHA

The relationship between Jesus and John is deeply involved in the meaning of names. Virtually every name mentioned in *Mark* has a generic meaning in addition to identifying a particular person. This was generally true in the Hebrew language, or at least in those Hebrew names used in the Bible. Among the names used in *Mark* which demand our immediate attention are Elijah, Elisha, Jesus, Joshua, Isaiah, John, Moses, and Jacob.

The most significant fact about these names is that Elisha, Joshua, and Jesus were names with virtually identical meanings: God Is Salvation. The only difference is that Joshua and Jesus were derived from the root of the proper name of God (Jahweh) whereas Elisha was derived from the root of the generic word for god (Elohim). Each of these three men is presented as the successor: Joshua succeeding Moses, Elisha succeeding Elijah, Jesus succeeding John. Moses and Elijah were much alike: they were the two great monotheists of Bible; they were the two great miracle workers of Bible; they were identified by Mark as belonging together by their appearance to Jesus on the Mount of Transfiguration. Elijah's name, "Jahweh Is God," brought together the roots of both Jahweh and Elohim, and probably was intended to mean that Jahweh is the only god, thus further securing his connection to the Mosaic monotheistic tradition. John also had a name rooted in Jahweh: "Jahweh Is Gracious."

In addition to the above, the name Isaiah meant "The Salvation of God," a name very similar to "God Is Salvation" which Jesus, Joshua,

16

and Elisha bore. Thus it was that the good news of God Is Salvation began in the book written by The Salvation of God.

The patterns in the above relationships of names are so unmistakable that there can be no doubt of Mark's awareness of them. The question still remains, however, about Mark's intention in using such patterns. The answer probably lies in a motif firmly established in *Genesis* and explicitly referred to in *Malachi*: the Jacob motif of brother supplanting brother. In its broad form in *Genesis*, God's people were quite often presented with a first opportunity (land, wife, child, etc.) which it would have been easy to accept. They were required to reject the first and go on to a more difficult choice.

The Jacob motif became the prime example of this rhythm. In the *Genesis* account, the birthright and blessing of Isaac belonged by right to the first son Esau, but both the birthright and blessing were given to Jacob instead. Esau's lineage became the Edomites; Jacob's, the Jews. Jacob's name took on a new meaning: He Who Supplants His Brother. *Malachi* begins by responding to a Jewish request for proof that God loves Israel. The proof offered is that God preferred Jacob to Esau; God loves whom He will and is not bound by the laws of inheritance.

Other examples might well have been chosen. Abel was preferred to Cain, Isaac to Ishmael, Rachel to Leah, the poor land of Abraham to the rich land of Lot, and Perez to Zerah. Joshua was permitted to enter the promised land and Moses excluded; Elisha fulfilled the prophecies of Elijah which Elijah himself could not do. And, in *Mark*, Jesus was the successor to John.

Mark was conscious of the Jacob motif. His use of the name Jacob is obscured from readers of English Bible because the name has been translated into English as James. To call attention to this, I shall henceforth refer to people named James in English Bibles as "Jacob (James)". Among Jesus' first four disciples was a set of brothers named John and Jacob (James). It is possible that their names symbolized the supplanting of John the Baptizer by Jesus. At the calling of the twelve, Jesus' fifth disciple, Levi the son of Alphaeus, was supplanted by his brother, Jacob (James) the son of Alphaeus. In the resurrection narrative Mary was identified in one sentence as the mother of Joses and in the next sentence as the mother of Jacob (James).

Mark's awareness of the Jacob motif makes it even more clear that he intended Elisha as the supplanter of Elijah, and Jesus as the supplanter of John. By their names they were both preferred to their predecessors.

According to Mark, Jesus was aware of these meanings of names. Imagine his state of mind when he heard Elijah-John's confession of failure and his prediction of a successor. He knew that the successor would have to be someone named God Is Salvation and that he was so named. He must have wondered, without evidence, if he was the one who would fulfill John's words. He must have explored the *Malachi* predictions about Elijah which would enable him to understand in what sense John had failed as Elijah and what success would mean. When he came to his baptism he must have been internally prepared for the spiritual experience he had there.

The Offer of Sonship

Mark portrayed Jesus' baptism as a dramatic situation. Elijah-John did not know that Jesus in particular was to be his successor. He did not perceive himself to be primarily the forerunner of someone else. His prediction of a spirit-baptizer to come stemmed from disappointment at his own failure in not attaining the *Malachi* Elijah goal, not as the fulfillment of his mission. When he baptized Jesus, he was totally unaware that his mantle and a double portion of his spirit had by that act been passed on to someone else. To him, Jesus was just one more Jew in the endless string who came to give lip service to Elijah as the price of escaping the curse of judgment.

Jesus, however, was actually different. Out of all the crowds which came to hear Elijah-John preach, Jesus alone was not from Judea. He alone asked the critical questions about the identity of the one to succeed Elijah-John. He alone sensed in his own name a calling of destiny. He alone must have asked what it would mean to be greater than Elijah-John.

Such greatness staggers the imagination. Perhaps alone among all the figures in Western literature Elijah-John had secured the consensus of an entire people. Most Judean Jews had formally joined his movement. They had given him their personal loyalty. What could be greater than that? How popular would a man have to be in Jerusalem to exceed securing the support of one hundred per cent of the population? What could one do beyond winning such a consensus?

That was the initial dilemma of Jesus as he listened. The vision of *Malachi* presented an answer. Elijah-John had succeeded in winning the people's loyalty to himself, but he had failed to reconcile fathers and children. Elijah-John misunderstood that failure by blaming it on the fact that people did not repent. Jesus understood, from *Malachi*, that God already loved his children and that all the children needed to do was to respond to that love. Elijah-John hoped for a more adeuqate Elijah, a better preacher, a more persuasive leader, a master psychologist who would somehow penetrate to the heart of men's wills.

Jesus came to his baptism with an intuition that John's version of the Elijah program was itself a failure, not because of the inadequacy of John, as John thought, but because the Johannine agenda was mistaken. It was as if Jesus, fully aware of the *Malachi* tradition, cut it neatly in two, separating out the judgmental Elijah with his impossible demands, leaving only the vision of father-son reconciliation. Elijah-John worked toward conversion; Jesus received love. Elijah-John thought of changes impinging on others; Jesus saw only a promise to himself. Thus it was at the baptism that the words which came to Jesus in a spiritual vision were:

"You are my beloved son. With you I am well pleased."

Such words were inconceivable either for Elijah or John, but totally consistent with anyone whose name was God Is Salvation. By this vision Jesus conceived of God as father. It completed half of the *Malachi* dream. What was left was for the son's heart to be turned to the father.

What was not spoken at the baptism is equally important. In no sense could the vision be interpreted as a calling to ministry or to any other specific task. In no sense did the vision inform Jesus that he was in fact John's successor as a new Elijah, a new Elisha, or in any other way. In no sense was Jesus empowered by this vision to baptize with spirit, to heal with miracle, to preach with power, to lead Israel to glory, or to turn the hearts of children to their fathers. The vision gave no direction whatsoever.

The directionlessness of the baptismal vision is a key fact in *Mark*. It established for Jesus the central problem which was to dominate the remainder of his career: how should he respond to the awareness that he was loved by God the way a father loves a son? What did it mean for him to be God's beloved son?

Behind that question was a more basic one which Mark never raised: how could Jesus be sure that he had not been deceived? The surface evidences were the opening sky, the descent of the spirit, and the spirit voice. In Mark's version, however, it is virtually certain that all three were symbolic events rather than physically visible ones. The story was told as if neither John nor the crowd were aware of any of the phenomena. The only interpretation totally consistent with all the evidence is that the experience was entirely inward to Jesus and therefore subject to misinterpretation. Perhaps the reason the question was not raised was that Mark and Jesus both accepted *Malachi's* offer of proof: the preference for Jacob over Esau automatically meant that all Jews were beloved by a father God. In any case the thrust of Mark's concern was not for the factuality of God's love, but for its meaning and content as Jesus sought to decide upon a proper response.

The Symbolic Temptation of Jesus

Jesus had now been confronted in turn by two experiences of great emotional power. First, he had applied to himself the prophecy of Elijah-John that there would arise a leader more powerful than Elijah-John who would combine spiritual leadership with public popularity. Afterward, he had applied to himself the Jacob motif from *Malachi* with a resultant vision which he interpreted as a personal offer of God's love to him as a son. From Elijah-John he had heard the call to continue the program of Elijah, to receive the mantle of Elijah in his identify as Elisha-Jesus. In one sense this would make him the new, new Elijah. At the same time, from God he had heard the invitation to think of himself as God's beloved son and thus to fulfill half the prediction of reconciliation between father and son which would accompany the success of Elijah at his coming.

Note carefully the distinction between those two *Malachi*-related callings. In one he would be the ancient hero returned to life. In the other he would be himself, a Jewish son reconciled to the father God. Both ideas are directly from *Malachi*, but they lead in opposite directions. Before the end of his career Jesus was to explore the meaning of both of them. Most of the time he focused his attention on the revivification of the models of great men of olden times. Only toward the end did he entirely discard that notion and identify himself solely as the son loved by the father.

The conflict between these two callings occurred "immediately". Markan scholars are generally convinced that Mark's use of the word immediately was an evidence of his poor writing style. This impression is heightened by comparing *Mark* with *Matthew* and *Luke*. Mark often used the word in a position in a sentence which appears nonsensical. In the corresponding sentence in the other Gospels the word is either eliminated entirely or moved to a seemingly more sensible grammatical position.

What the scholars have missed is that in *Mark* immediacy is related to temptation. Explicitly on this occasion, and implicitly in most temptative occasions in *Mark*, Jesus was driven into temptation by a high calling, by a spirit of holiness, by something good. Inherent in every high calling, that is immediately, was a corresponding low calling, an opposite side of the coin. This was true whether the temptation was symbolically identified by connection with Satan or an unclean spirit, or whether it emerged unobtrusively from an ordinary event. As Jesus explored good models for father-son reconciliation, he kept on discovering that inherent in each one of them was a temptative dimension which immediately, automatically surfaced when he adopted it for himself. Once this usage of immediacy is recognized Mark's positioning of the word in his sentences no longer seems nonsensical.

In the temptation episode which immediately followed Jesus' baptism it is said that the spirit of holiness drove Jesus out into a wilderness to be tempted by Satan. This statement requires both an understanding of spirit and of wilderness.

Mark personified both the spirit of holiness and unclean spirits. Both kinds of spirits spoke to Jesus. This phenomenon apparently was rooted in a popular belief that spirits were invisible supernatural creatures with separate existences who could inhabit and to some extent control the minds and bodies of those they inhabited. Mark used the common concept as the source of his symbol, but showed by his flow of thought that he held a view of spirit more akin to ordinary experience.

The definition of unclean spirits as separate supernatural beings has been a major stumbling block in Gospel studies. In Wrede's picture of

Jesus, both Jesus and the unclean spirits were supernatural and knew each other's identity from their contacts in a world apart from earth. This made sense out of Jesus' demand that the spirits keep quiet about revealing his identity, but it also made of Jesus a strange kind of man-in-disguise, a god who would not admit that he was a god. In face of being unable to make sense out of that reticence of Jesus, later scholars concluded that he was so unlike other human beings that it was impossible to read the stories of his life by methods of study which would be used for other historical people.

Such a difficulty is avoided by an understanding of spirits as symbols of the inner, spiritual struggle of a person. A holy spirit was the godly side of such a struggle; an unclean spirit was the temptative side. Both were equally spirit-like and equally non-existent as entities outside Jesus' own mental life. Wherever unclean spirits were reported as confronting Jesus, it means that temptation had become obvious to him and that he was resisting it by ordering the spirits of temptation to be silent. Temptations occurred on other occasions more subtly, with less immediate recognition, so that not all temptations involved reference to unclean spirits or Satan. But for those which did, Jesus recognized the unclean spirit as temptative even though the crowds, missing the point, still thought in terms of a demon-possessed individual apart from Jesus.

The imagery of the temptation story following Jesus' baptism makes it plain that Jesus was tempted in the form of Elijah. When the historic Elijah fled from fear of Queen Jezebel's wrath, he spent forty days being tempted in a wilderness. His temptation was to believe that he stood alone, that he and only he was holy in Israel. Angels helped him. Elijah's response, after the event, was to call Elisha who was plowing at the time with twelve oxen. In the Jesus story in *Mark*, the Elijah details of forty days, a wilderness, angelic help, and the aftermath of calling four fishermen who became the nucleus of the twelve disciples were all included. Later in *Mark* when the words of the unclean spirits were reported, they tempted Jesus to believe that he was the only Holy One, very comparable to the temptation of Elijah. All of this strongly suggests that Jesus' original temptation was of the same Elijah nature: to conceive of himself as the only one really true to God, the only son loved by the Father.

Note that the temptation was neither naughty nor evil for either Elijah or Jesus. Elijah was zealous to defend the reputation of the living God against the false claims of idolators. Jesus was responding to a spirit of holiness. Neither one was lured by personal gain, private pleasure, or dishonest achievement. Jesus would be untouched by such enticements. His concern, from the very beginning of his Markan career, was to be only the discovery of what it means to be God's son, and all temptation was to be limited to that. When the words of the unclean spirits were later reported it became obvious that they had zeroed in on temptations connected to sonship.

The concept "temptation" thus takes on a very limited and peculiar meaning in *Mark*. It always involves adopting or performing a good which is less than good enough, being satisfied with less than the best. Jesus' temptations were always *inadequate goods*, never alluring evils. All of the possibilities which Jesus explored to ascertain the meaning of being God's son were good, but only one was good enough. Each of the others involved some temptative aspect.

The occurrence of the first temptation *in a wilderness* raises a problem of interpretation. If one were to think of wilderness in geographical terms only, one would incongruously picture Jesus in the Jordan wilderness for baptism, and then being driven into some other wilderness for temptation. Or if one adopted the symbolic meaning of wilderness as the experience of being psychologically alone in the midst of an audience which failed to understand, it would still seem strange for Jesus to be driven from one such wilderness to a second one.

The example of Elijah's wilderness offers a probable solution. Elijah was alone in his wilderness not because he was rejected by the crowds, but because he was convinced that he stood alone when he really did not. He separated himself from others when he mistakenly considered himself to be rejected. It was apparently likewise with Jesus. His wilderness of temptation, unlike John's wilderness of preaching, was an imagined aloneness. When he overcame that initial temptation he sought out crowds to hear him preach and followers to assist him in the task of recruiting others.

From the perspective of an overview of Jesus' entire career the temptation had a deeper dimension. To be loved as a son is not an exclusive possession which shuts out others from being loved, nor is being loved as a son an indication of special power or might. If Jesus heard the offer of the Father's love in such a way as to conceive of himself as the Only Divine Son he would in fact have thought of sonship as something exclusive to himself. It would have justified the charge of blasphemy for which he was finally put to death by Jewish officialdom although they had to raise a different charge to secure the cooperation of the Romans. The "I-alone" nature of the temptation would be consistent with a claim of divinity. It would have been inviting for Jesus to think of himself in those terms because it could well require more than human powers to succeed where Elijah-John had failed.

The Problem for Jesus' Career

The implied continuity between Jesus' baptism-temptation and his opening sermon requires careful scrutiny. As the temptation episode suggested, Jesus set out at first to explore the adequacy of the Elijah-Elisha imagery for himself, rather than to explore the adequacy of a model of sonship.

The directionlessness of the baptismal calling left Jesus without any easily available guide other than scripture. To find out what it means to be God's beloved son and thus complete the reconciliation of father and son, as *Malachi* predicted, Jesus sought first to discover whether there were aspects of the Elijah-Elisha imagery which Elijah-John had not sufficiently used.

Later, after the Elijah-Elisha model had been tested and found wanting, Jesus turned to other messiah concepts and to a series of biblical meanings of being a son. According to Mark, all of them were to be found inadequate although some of them came remarkably close to gospel. The pattern which came closest was the description of The Suffering Servant from *Isaiah*, the book in which gospel began.

It may well be that *Mark* was intended historically by its author as a polemic against every non-Christian Judaism of his day. Mark argued that in virtually every significant religious pattern provided by Jewish scripture there was a temptative flaw which prevented one from achieving the proper Father-son relationship exemplified in the good news of Jesus, the messiah, the son of God. The weaknesses were not observable in the Bible; they became exposed only when Jesus sought to live by them in his quest for adequate sonship. Whether the author himself was conscious of such an intention, it is clear that such a literary intention is consistent with the structure of the Gospel.

The major issue between Jesus and his opponents was thus the interpretation of scripture. Those who disagreed with him most often were the official biblical scholars: the scribes. The crowds contrasted Jesus with the scribes. Jesus himself intuited that the scribes would disagree with him even before they openly manifested any opposition. Jesus knew himself to be functioning as an interpreter of scripture. He can best be thought of at the beginning of his career as an unofficial scribe, a scribe without the proper union card, interpreting scripture by testing out its adequacy for his own way of life.

In doing so, he moved through three distinct stages. These stages marked the development of his career. At first, he tested out the Jewish models which involved leadership of crowds. He devoted his full attention to Galilean Jewry. Late in that stage, opposition began to manifest itself, and Jesus himself began to be critical of Jewish beliefs which he had apparently taken for granted earlier.

In the second stage, highlighted by the calling of the twelve disciples, Jesus abandoned the crowds and devoted himself exclusively to the task of enabling this elite group to become fruit-bearers in a manner impossible for crowds. He expected great results from the twelve and was terribly disappointed. Not only did they fail to produce worthy lives and simple understanding, they also set in motion the chain of events which was to lead ultimately to Jesus' betrayal and desertion.

The final stage of Jesus' career, introduced by the conversation with a Gentile woman about her spirit-possessed daughter, can best be characterized as a solo stage. In contrast to the two previous periods, during which Jesus had depended upon positive responses from the crowds or the disciples, Jesus was now to test the adequacy of a series of religious ideals whose performance depended upon no one other than himself. It was in that spirit that he was led finally to the crucifixion, the most clearly solo act of all.

The sonship motif in the book went through a corresponding cyclical change. In the crowd section, Jesus explored the possibility of all the Jews being the sons of God and being reconciled to the Father. In the elite section, it was the Twelve who were to be the reconciled sons. And in the solo period of Jesus' career, it was he alone who was to be the son. As has often been noted, Jesus referred to himself as son of the Father almost exclusively in the Passion material. The underlying reason lies in the fact that only in the voluntary death model was there a pattern of life sufficiently appropriate for Marks' view of sonship.

CHAPTER TWO
SON MODELS FROM MALACHI: ELIJAH, JACOB

It is clear in *Mark* that the gospel which began in *Isaiah* took its early specifics from *Malachi*. During the first stage of Jesus' career, four sonship models from *Malachi* were explored by Jesus. We have already noted the first of them.

"Behold, I will send you Elijah the prophet before the great and terrible day of the Lord comes. And he will turn the hearts of fathers to their children and the hearts of children to their fathers, lest I come and smite the land with a curse." *Mal.* 4.5-6)

The thrust of that prediction was that Elijah's success would create an automatic reconciliation. If Jesus or John the Baptizer, or anyone else for that matter, could be a successful Elijah, Jesus' just-started quest to find out how a loving son should respond to a loving father would be ended. All sons and fathers would be reconciled.

The second *Malachi* model of sonship, which could conceivably have been influential in helping Jesus meet the wilderness temptation to think of himself as the only one, likewise assumed the universality of being God's son.

"Have we not all one father? Has not one God created us? Why then are we faithless to one another, profaning the covenant of our fathers?" (*Mal.* 2.10)

The issue as to whether Jesus was the only son or one son among all the children of God was to recur again and again in the early section of his career. The unclean spirits persistently pushed him toward thinking of himself as unique and different from others. It may well have been this passage from *Malachi* which inspired him to resist their invitations.

The third and fourth models of sonship in *Malachi* were more limited. The third distinguished the Jews as those loved by God from the Edomites as those hated by God.

"'I have loved you' says the Lord. But you say, 'How hast thou loved us?' 'Is not Esau Jacob's brother?' says the Lord. 'Yet I have loved Jacob but I have hated Esau. . .'." (*Mal.* 1.2-3) "For I the Lord do not change; therefore you, O sons of Jacob, are not consumed." (*Mal.* 3.6)

The love of God for Isaac's son, Jacob, rather than his first son, Esau, was sufficient evidence in *Malachi's* view to support the contention that God loved all the sons of Jacob, i.e. all the Jews, for all of them were bearers of Jacob's other name, Israel. In the setting of Hellenized Jewish Galilee, the model of the sons of Jacob raised a controversial issue for Jesus: was being the beloved son of God a state impossible for Gentiles? Was it limited only to the sons of Jacob? Or was it universal?

The final *Malachi* model of sonship took an even more restricted view. Among Jews it separated out the priests, the sons of Levi, for special attention.

"A son honors his father, and a servant his master. If then I am a father, where is my honor? And if I am a master, where is my fear? says the Lord of hosts to you, O priests who despise my name. You say, 'How have we despised thy name?" (*Mal.* 1.6)
"...The messenger of the covenant...will purify the sons of Levi and refine them like gold and silver, till they present right offerings to the Lord." (*Mal.* 3.1-3)

Note in particular here that the success of Elijah, the messenger of the covenant, would trigger the purification of the priests, the sons of Levi, with the result that the priests would honor their father God. According to *Malachi*, Levi and the priesthood which bore his name were faithful in olden days when other Jews were not. It was therefore expected in the day of Elijah that the sons of Levi would be especially faithful again.

These four references to sonship in *Malachi* provided the scriptural base for Jesus' initial series of experiments with what it meant for him personally to respond to the love of the Father. As the temptation story suggested that he might, he began his public career by seeking to determine if proper sonship could result from succeeding as Elijah where John had failed. He did so despite his name and baptismal experience, both of which it seemed would call him to be a new Elisha, to relate himself immediately to salvation rather than to judgment.

Jesus began his career when John was arrested. In a literal sense, that arrest was attributable to King Herod (*Mark* 6). In a more meaningful sense, John's career was arrested when he lost confidence in himself as Elijah and turned his hopes toward a successor. The real Elijah would not have permitted himself to be put at the mercy of a cruel monarch like Herod. Nor would Herod dared to have arrested John while the Judean population still unanimously supported him. John was arrested not so much by prison bars as by failure.

In that circumstance, Jesus began to preach a message much more akin to *Malachi's* Elijah than John's had been. It proclaimed the Day of Judgment (the time is fulfilled) when men would truly submit their lives to the sovereignty of God (the kingdom of God). In that day men would repent and believe that doing so was good news (gospel). Jesus reference to the kingdom of God, here as elsewhere in *Mark*, referred to people obeying God's will, not to God's act in establishing a government to replace all earthly governments. If the kingdom of God were to come it would mean that John's prophecy had been fulfilled: men would truly be baptized and purified in the spirt of holiness.

The opening sermon was in no way thematic for Jesus' entire career. It was not even close to the heart of gospel as understood by Mark even though the word "gospel" was used. To the contrary, the first sermon was thematic only for the first stage of Jesus' career. It said what people expected Elijah to say at his return. Jesus preached such a message only as long as he conceived of himself primarily as the new Elijah, and in fact not even that long because Jesus later discovered dimensions of the Elijah imagery which moved him toward interpretations of sonship higher than that of the repentance sermon.

Meanwhile, however, imagine the excitement in Galilee. Elijah-John had confined his mission to the Jordan wilderness, the scene of Elijah's ascent into heaven. Elijah-Jesus had returned to that portion of Israel, the North, which had been the scene of most of Elijah's career. Furthermore, Jesus' message was more like Elijah's than John's had been. Despite *Malachi's* predictions, John's preaching had been relatively bland with scarcely a hint of judgment. Elijah-Jesus implicitly threatened the unrepentant with all the doom accompanying the Day of Judgment. Jesus said that day was at hand. (Remember that the methodology of Composition Criticsm will not permit introduction of evidence from *Matthew* and *Luke* that John's message was also judgmental.)

It is appropriate to ask why either the Judeans or the Galileans should have been so excited about anyone appearing as Elijah. The answer seems to lie in an obscure sentence in *Daniel*.

"In the first year of Darius the son of Ahasuerus, by birth a Mede, who became king over the realm of the Chaldeans—in the first year of his reign, I, Daniel, perceived in the books the number of years which...must pass before the end of the desolations of Jerusalem, namely, seventy years." (*Dan.* 9.1-2) "Seventy weeks of years are decreed concerning your people and your holy city, to finish the transgression, to put an end to sin,...and to anoint a most holy place." (*Dan.* 9.24)

During that period, after sixty-nine weeks of years, "an anointed one shall be cut off". Mark would have read "anointed one" as Christ, thus a prediction of the coming of the messiah sometime between 483-490 years after the time of King Darius of Chaldea. Historians seem unable to authenticate the existence of such a king. However, there was a King Darius of Persia at about the same time to which Daniel refers. The seventy weeks of years since his time would have fallen roughly into the time period of John and Jesus, thus accounting for an increased expectancy of the coming of a messiah then.

THE CALLING OF FOUR FOLLOWERS

Who would dare refuse to do the bidding of Elijah? As he passed by the lake called the Sea of Galilee, Elijah-Jesus saw two pairs of brothers at work and demanded of them that they follow him without hesitation. Elijah had called Elisha the same way. Elisha had responded by slaughtering the twelve oxen with which he was plowing, to symbolize his willingness to shift from his old vocation to a new one. The four fishermen abandoned their nets and boats, armed only with the promise that their task would be to fish for men. They were

27

to be assistant recruiters for Jesus, not disciples. By the meaning of the word, a disciple is a student, a learner. The original calling of the four was to follow and to recruit others.

Why these particular four? Why two sets of brothers? Why is the name John introduced in *Mark* so soon after the first John's career was arrested? Historically the answers may be sheer happenstance. Logically there are some other possibilities consistent with Mark's flow of thought.

The first of them is Jacob motif. Jesus supplanted John as the new Elijah, and then called to his following another John whose brother's name meant He Who Supplants His Brother. The baptismal event in which Jesus had supplanted John was associated with a vision in which God's love was declared. *Malachi* used the theme of supplanting one's brother as proof of God's love. It would seem to be entirely too strong a coincidence for Mark not to have been conscous of these relationships in reporting this event.

What about the other pair of brothers? A different possibility seems to have been at work in the case of Simon and Andrew. Neither name was Hebraic. Simon was the Hellenized version of the Hebrew name Simeon. Andrew was a Greek name with no precise Hebrew counterpart. The root meaning of the name Simon is God Has Heard; of Andrew, the generic term for man with the connotation of Manly.

In Jewish Bible the most important Simeon was the second son of Jacob, one of the twelve sons whose names became attached to the twelve tribes of Israel. These names have amazing counterparts in *Mark*. Jesus has brothers named Jacob (James), Simon, and Judas. His fourth brother Joses may be a counterpart of Joseph as far as his name is concerned, but Jesus himself was more the counterpart of Joseph by being betrayed by Judas. In the list of the twelve there are two Simons, two Jacobs (James), and one Judas.

One possible interpretation of this repetition of names stems from the *Genesis* narratives of Jacob's family. His twelve sons came from four women, six from his first wife, Leah, whom he was trapped into marrying; two from Rachel, his favorite wife who in that sense supplanted Leah; and two each from two servants. Only the sons of the two wives became important in biblical history. Four of Jacob's sons, all from Leah, made trouble for him. They were Reuben, who opposed murdering Joseph but had him placed in the pit from which he was betrayed; Simeon and Levi, who murdered all the males of Shechem because a man of that city had seduced their sister; and Judah, who betrayed Joseph into slavery and who bore twins by a woman he thought to be a harlot. All of them were alike in a major respect: they did evil in the name of good.

Mark is highly likely to have chosen Simeon, Levi, and Judah as models from the list of the twelve sons of Jacob because they did evil while intending to do good. Judah became for Mark Judas the betrayer. Levi became for Mark a priest to be supplanted by a brother. Simeon became for Mark Simon who was to err many times.

28

A second possible interpretation of Mark's use of these names involves the fact that Andrew alone of the first four followers was not singled out for criticism in the Gospel. Andrew, by virtue of his name, was Manly in the universal human sense. The other three, Simon, John, and Jacob (James), each connected more directly to Judaism by a traditional Jewish name, were often portrayed as false to Jesus, climatically so when they went to sleep in Gethsemane when Jesus finally acknowledged the proper sonship relation to God. It is possible that the names of the first four followers introduced an idea which Mark never developed, that Simon, the Hellenized Jewish spokesman for the twelve, would be supplanted by manliness in general. This would make sense out of having two pairs of brothers, so that the supplanting motif would relate not only to the obvious supplanting of John by Jesus but also to the central concept of sonship in the book.

The calling of the four also introduced the first temptation in Jesus' public career. Jesus first called Simon and Andrew, and they immediately followed him. He then immediately called Jacob (James) and John. The immediacy was thus shifted from Simon and Andrew to Jesus. It was as if he called the first brothers without knowing what would occur. He learned that his authoritative command received an immediately positive response. Having been rewarded with success, he immediately adopted authoritative command as his style.

Acting with authority became the form of temptation which emanated from his proclamation of the Elijah message. It should not be concluded that Simon and Andrew also were tempted because they responded immediately. Immediacy of obedience was a correct response to a request by Elijah, particularly since his pronouncement had stressed that the time of obedience to God's sovereignty was at hand. To ask for immediate obedience to God and to be impressed that one's own authoritativeness was successful were the two sides of the coin of Jesus' attempt to reconcile fathers and children by adopting the strategies of Elijah. Only Jesus was so tempted, according to Mark. Only he had the upward call to be Elijah. Only he could be tempted by the immediate ambiguity in that calling.

The four fishermen were called to be fishers of men. Presumably this meant that they were to assist him by recruiting additional followers. This buttresses the impression that Jesus conceived of his career at that moment as an attempt to secure widespread support among both Hebraic and Hellenistic Jews since his fishermen represented both groups. He thought of himself as a Leader of the Jews, hence a messiah. He defined the success of the messiah at this point largely in terms of the number of followers he could secure, assuming that the followers did what he told them to do. The role definition of the four, the fishers of men, was specifically relevant to Jesus' leadership role at this time. When Jesus' role changed, so would theirs. They were not always to be fishers of men.

THE SYNAGOGUE UNCLEAN SPIRIT

Throughout that segment of his life in which Jesus identified himself with Elijah-Elisha, he also closely related himself to Jewish synagogues. Based only upon *Mark* we know very little about synagogues. Perhaps Mark intended that synagogues in Galilee would be for Elijah-Jesus what *Malachi* predicted the temple would be for Elijah. The synagogues in *Mark* seemed to be primarily places of instruction. Archaeological reconstructions of some synagogue buildings of the first century, including the one in Capernaum, indicate a strong worship component in their architectural features. For Mark, the synagogue was the symbol of Jewish concern for scripture; it was a Bible-oriented institution. In that respect the unclean spirit which accosted Jesus on the occastion of his first visit to Capernaum had a synagogue nature. It was not a coincidence that an unclean spirit spoke within Jesus on his first synagogue visit.

It was Jesus' success in authoritatively calling the four fishermen which led him immediately to the synagogue temptation. It reaffirmed in him the possibility which John the Baptizer's prediction and Jesus' own baptismal experience had generated: his unique holiness. Who else but Elijah, God's holy one, could command men to leave their means of monetary livelihood and have them obey instantaneously? The place to further explore that assumed fact was in the house of scripture, the synagogue.

In addition, the place for such exploration was Capernaum, the City of Nahum, the town in which the gospel must begin because *Nahum* in Jewish Bible had used the word "gospel". In *Nahum* the good news was that good people were saved and bad ones destroyed. When Elijah-Jesus came to Nahum City proclaiming the gospel of Judgment Day, the Capernaumites would have been false to their city's tradition in scripture had they not connected *Nahum's* concept of gospel to their own situation. Only in Nahum City were all the elements present which fed into this incident.

A resident of Nahum City who was reputed to be possessed of an unclean spirit interrupted Jesus' lesson in the synagogue to connect the biblical traditions of *Nahum* and Elijah.

"What have you to do with us, Jesus of Nazareth? Have you come to destroy us? I know who you are: the Holy One of God!"

The exact content of Jesus' speech on this occasion is not given in *Mark* but it may be presumed to be similar to the proclamation of good news prior to his calling of the four fishermen.

In the four sentence description of Jesus' response to the demon-possessed man, Mark incorporated the possibility of three completely different understandings of the situation. First, the demon-possessed man himself reacted in fear. Mark did not ever clarify what he or the Galileans considered demon possession to mean. However, he did distinguish it from three other kinds of ailments: disease, leprosy, and paralysis. By eliminating those kinds of possibilities and by noting Mark's description of the behavior of the demon possessed, it seems logical to assume that people who were in that day engaged in behavior which today would be labeled as neurotic or psychotic were then thought to have an unclean spirit. On this particular occasion, the man's offense was to interrupt a distinguished guest during his talk. A psychologically mature person would have waited until afterward to raise the question about the speaker's identity and intention. The irrational fear of the psychotic-neurotic mind did not permit such self-restraint. The man rudely interrupted in an accusatory manner.

If the assumption about neurosis or psychosis is correct, the man's terror was understandable. Already insecure in life, he was now confronted with two traditions of destruction. Both the Day of Judgment associated with Elijah and the wrath of God associated with *Nahum* were embodied in the gospel of this Elijah-Jesus who had come to Nahum City. This was too much for the insecure personality to bear. When Elijah-Jesus obviously rejected him by ordering him to be silent, the terror climaxed in convulsions.

The second interpretation of the total event was interior to Jesus. He recognized the accusation spoken in the words of the rude man to be saying the same thing that the unclean spirit of temptation was saying within himself. The incident confronted him once again with the temptation of Elijah: to think of himself as the only holy one of God and to announce it publicly as the man requested. Jesus commanded the temptation to be silent. In doing so he spoke simultaneously to the spirit of temptation within himself and to the words of the demon-possessed man in the synagogue. He refused to take advantage of this opportunity to announce that his identity as Elijah also meant that he was the only one holy before God.

In this incident Jesus recognized that the new Elijah imagery was clothed with the same temptative quality he had found in the old wilderness model of Elijah. It would be good to be holy and to belong to God, but it would be temptative to think of himself as the only holy one of God. The rebuke of the unclean spirit, although spoken aloud to the man, was aimed at the unclean spirit within himself.

In order to calculate the meaning of this rebuke of temptation one must note its relative place in the sequence of Jesus' confrontations with Satan and his unclean spirits. Mark told seven stories which explicitly referred to such spirits, from which stories the following are the key lines.

1. Jesus in the wilderness, tempted by Satan. (1.13)
2. "Be silent, and come out of him!" (1.25)
3. "He would not permit the demons to speak, because they knew him." (1.34)
4. "He strictly ordered them not to make him known." (3.12)

5. "Legion begged Jesus eagerly not to send them out of the country. 'Send us to the swine, let us enter them.' So he gave them leave." (5.10-13)
6. "Get thee behind me, Satan! For you are not on the side of God, but of man." (8.33)
7. "You dumb and deaf spirit, I command you, come out of him, and never enter him again." (9.25)

As described by Mark, the first of the seven incidents, the symbolic temptation in the wilderness, was a tie. In each of the succeeding ones Jesus outscored the tempter, but only in the final incident was the victory decisive. In each of the intervening narratives, Jesus resisted temptation but left it free to return, which it did. This was made explicit in the story of Legion: Jesus did what the tempting spirits asked even while he was opposing them.

In the context of that series, Jesus' confrontation with the synagogue spirit was rather mild. All he did was to order temporary silence. He did not resist the temptation to act authoritatively. In fact, the temptation to announce his identity as God's only son was so authoritatively opposed that Jesus thoroughly substantiated in the public mind their belief that he must indeed be the holy one. Later the same day Jesus had to prevent many people from praising him in such terms.

The third interpretation of the event centered in the reaction of the synagogue audience. They appreciated little of the drama they had observed. They heard only the surface expressions on both sides and comprehended neither Jesus' struggle against temptation nor the man's collapse into radical insecurity. What the audience saw was a miracle. They knew their fellow townsmen as one demon-possessed. They had presumably seen earlier evidences of his abnormal behavior, and had credited it to the causation of an unclean spirit. And now, before their very own eyes, they saw evidence that the unclean spirit had been exorcised from him in such a dramatic manner that the man went into convulsions. Hallelujah! Wow! Never before had they seen unclean spirits obey authoritative teaching. They knew they were in the presence of something radically new, something which they could define as miraculous power.

JESUS FIRST MIRACLE

Jesus himself knew that the act of casting out the synagogue spirit had not been a miracle. He knew that it had been an unexpected consequence of blending his own resistance to temptation and the man's terror at the destruction he associated with Elijah's return. He knew also, however, that the synagogue Jews now viewed his authority as having miraculous consequences. He struggled against the temptation to accede to the spirit beckoning him to announce himself as the Holy One, and did not recognize that the audience response was pulling him toward a different temptation.

After the synagogue service, Jesus went to the home of Simon and

Andrew, where Simon's mother-in-law lay in bed with fever. Immediately upon entering the house the men told Jesus about the fevered woman. The fact that they did so immediately presumably indicated that they agreed with the synagogue logic: if Jesus could cast out an unclean spirit he could also miraculously take away a fever. Without speaking, Jesus lifted the woman to her feet. According to the evidence in *Mark*, that was not only all that he did, but also all that he intended to do.

Then came the miracle. The fever disappeared. The authoritative act of compelling her to rise from bed had been transformed into the miraculously healing act. Jesus who had been trying to be successful as the preacher Elijah had suddenly taken on the curative powers of Elijah and Elisha instead. Elijah might come to destroy, as the synagogue spirit expected, but Elisha would come to save.

The incident occurred in a private home and did not call upon Jesus to make any public decision in regard to a change in role. It was the first evidence directly persuasive to Jesus himself that he possessed the power to perform miracle, a power associated in Bible with both Elijah and Elisha. Note the acceleration of authoritative acts which had brought Jesus to this recognition.

1. Authoritative preaching to the crowds: "Repent!"
2. Authoritative command to the fishermen: "Leave your nets and follow me."
3. Authoritative exorcism of the synagogue spirit: "Be silent and come out of him."
4. Authoritative act: "He took her by the hand and lifted her up."

By the logic of that series of events, miraculousness is the culmination of authoritativeness, and Jesus could be expected to continue to perform miracles as long as he continued to act authoratively.

MASS HEALING IN CAPERNAUM

By sundown, the official end of the sabbath, the word had spread. The whole town of Capernaum brought to Jesus everyone who was sick or possessed by demons. Later healing stories in *Mark* make clear that the author distinguished carefully between demon-possession and disease, and between both of them and other ailments such as paralysis, leprosy, deafness, and blindness. None of the latter, by Mark's definition, was disease. Thus it is necessary to assume that the good news of the healing incidents in both the synagogue and Simon's house had traveled through the town. The townspeople bore witness to the strength of their conviction about sabbath observance by waiting until the sabbath was over before asking the miraculous Elijah-Elisha-Jesus to heal their sick. Jesus responded to them as a doctor and exorcist rather than as a preacher and teacher. In a long-to-be-remembered night he cured every sick or demon-possessed inhabitant of Capernaum. Imagine the excitement which must have risen there and elsewhere in Galilee when the news of that night spread.

Imagine too Jesus' own emotional state. He had arisen from bed that morning as a man who thought of himself as fairly ordinary except for his charismatic ability to induce others to follow him, coupled with an unusually strong sense of personal destiny. But by bedtime that night his authoritativeness had progressed rapidly toward the miraculous. By logical extension he must have known that it now lay within his power to eradicate disease from the entire world. His counterpart in our day would be for a master physician to empty all the hospitals and convalescent homes in a major city in a single day and put the entire medical profession out of business. At the end of such a day Jesus must have been both exhilarated and puzzled in regard to the powers he had discovered within himself and about their meaning for his quest of appropriate sonship.

Jesus must also have been crushingly disappointed at the end of the evening when he realized that Capernaum wanted only something for nothing. Capernaum did not want to repent. It did not want to be ruled by God. It did not want to hear preaching or teaching. It wanted free medical care, guaranteed to cure; it wanted miracle. Jesus had given Capernaum what it wanted. He had permitted Capernaum to define his role, to impose upon him the role of physician, to convert him from preacher Elijah to healer Elijah-Elisha.

In the synagogue there had been only one man who was convinced that Jesus was the holy one of God. That is, there had been only one possessed by an unclean spirit. By evening the number had swollen to "many" and Jesus still refused to permit them to speak their opinion aloud. The many were different from the one. They had been brought to Jesus by acquaintances who were convinced that Jesus could help them. In that respect they were consistent with the name of their town, for Nahum means compassion. The City of Compassion was now seeking out a master physician so that the diseased and the possessed could be healed by his miraculous art. The one man in the synagogue had been motivated by fear of destruction. Not so the crowds. Again and again during the evening they expressed their opinion that only the Holy One of God could perform such medical feats. Again and again Jesus had to resist the temptation to adopt their point of view.

Note that there is no hint of a motive in Mark's accounts of these early miracles. Even though the events occurred in the City of Compassion, there was no hint of compassion. Jesus seemed not to have been concerned about the terror of the convulsed man in the synagogue nor about the added burden which would have been imposed on Simon's mother-in-law by his insistence that she get out of bed with a fever. He exorcised the demons, but resisted the words spoken by them. It is clear, at this stage of *Mark's* flow of thought, that Jesus' miraculousness was simply and only the consequence of authoritativeness.

There is a difficulty in the interpretation as given above. Mark's report of the incident concludes with the statement that Jesus would not permit the demons to speak "because they knew him." That clause has been the root of the Wrede tradition that both Jesus and the unclean spirits were supernatural figures, that the spirits actually did know Jesus from their contacts in another world, and that Jesus was ordering them to keep his real identity a secret. If that interpretation is incorrect, what then is the meaning of "because they knew him?" The answer probably lies in a comparison of the earlier setting in the synagogue and the present one. In the synagogue Jesus had been acting out only the preaching tradition of the Elijah cycle, a type of activity which seemed closely connected with the hoped for result of father-son reconciliation. At evening Jesus shifted to the miracle tradition of the Elijah-Elisha cycle, a type of activity which seemed to bear no connection to father-son reconciliation. What had earlier been only a remote possibility had become by evening a course of action to which he at least temporarily committed himself: to actually be the miraculous One, the Holy One. It was in that sense that the unclean spirits that evening were correct: They did know who he was, i.e. they knew what identity he was trying on for size at that moment.

What they did not know was the intensity of the struggle going on within Jesus himself in this regard. Even while adopting the external deeds of the miraculous Holy One he was struggling inwardly against such identification. He was confronted with two distinctly different career objectives. He could be the new Elijah who preached repentance and announced the nearness of God's sovereignty over men's lives, as the synagogue spirit had seen him. Or he could be the new Elijah-Elisha who eliminated physical and mental illness, and who satiated the desires of the crowds for physical comfort and compassion.

Jesus clearly had to choose. During the evening he commanded the spirits not to speak because they knew him only in one of the two career identities, and Jesus was not sure that he would adopt it. After the crowd had gone home, Jesus went alone early in the morning before daybreak to the hills to resolve the conflict in prayer. Mark did not report the content of the prayer, but only its result. Jesus decided to renew his original intention to be the new Elijah, preacher of repentance, "for that is why I came out." Consequently, he left Nahum City to visit "throughout all Galilee, preaching in their synagogues and casting out demons." As long as he was to be able to limit his activity to preaching he hoped to be able to resist the twin temptations of adopting for himself the Holy One role suggested by the unclean spirits and the medical role desired by the crowds.

The tour of Galilee was to be a synagogue preaching tour. During this stage of Jesus' career there was no hint of a break with Judaism, either with its institutions or its regulations. Jesus himself observed the sabbath and sought to find answers for himself which were consistent with scripture. His present choice was limited to Elijah and Elisha, both biblical models.

As one might expect, the preaching mission of Elijah-Jesus to the synagogues of Galilee was apparently a colossal failure. The crowds wanted miracles rather than sermons. They lost interest in him to such an extent that he was finally alone. Neither crowds nor fishermen stayed with him. When he refused to use the miraculous healing powers which he was known to possess, the Galilean Jews rejected him. It was obvious that the Elijah model had proved itself inadequate again and that some new approach to father-son reconciliation was needed.

CHAPTER THREE
JESUS-ELISHA-LEVI: THE GIFT OF FORGIVENESS

The original Elisha had achieved an international reputation by healing the leprosy of a Syrian general named Naaman. The word from Capernaum that Jesus had the healing powers of Elisha reached the ears of at least one leper in Galilee. When the crowds abandoned Jesus and he was alone, the leper dared to violate the law which required a safe distance between the leprous and the non-leprous. He approached Elisha-Jesus with what sounds like an accusation of prejudice: "You could make me clean if you really wanted to do so." He had heard of Jesus' medical miracles in Capernaum; he knew of Elisha's power over leprosy. His only question was whether Elisha-Jesus would be Elisha for him as he had been for the Capernaumites. Jesus had healed socially acceptable Jews in Capernaum; would he also heal a social outcast?

Jesus was thus trapped by the conflict of two goods. On the one hand he wanted to assure the leper that he held no bias against him because of his disease. On the other hand he had decided in prayer that the son of God was to be Elijah rather than Elisha, a preacher rather than a physician. He did not want to start down the path which would lead him again to become the community doctor.

Jesus sought to avoid the trap by a compromise. He proposed to heal the leper in secret and then to go on with his Elijah-type preaching as if the exception had not occurred. The healing was unquestionably a good act, worthy of praise. It was a compassionate act, consistent with the meanings of Nahum, Elisha, and Jesus. There were sound reasons for the compromise. All of them must have occurred to Jesus as temptation worked through the leper's accusation to persuade Jesus to make just one exception to his decision not to be a medical healer. The temptation did not come through a medium symbolically identifiable as satanic, as in the case of the synagogue unclean spirit. It came in the guise of a human being clearly in need of compassion.

The compromise itself had scriptural justification. When Naaman had been healed by Elisha he promised to worship Elisha's God. The healing occurred by bathing in the Jordan River, much as Jesus was later baptized there. *Leviticus,* one of the five books of Jewish Law, gave detailed instructions about religious rituals for cleansed lepers. Naaman in his day had agreed to follow them to the letter, and Jesus instructed his leper to do so likewise.

It was probably the intrusion of *Leviticus* into the decision of Jesus which clinched the point in favor of the compromise. In *Malachi,* much of the author's concern was the distinction between the original

Levi (for whom *Leviticus* was named) and the false priests (Levites) who bore his name. *Malachi* said of Levi:

"He stood in awe of my name. True instruction was in his mouth, and no wrong was on his lips. He walked with me tin peace and uprightness, and he turned away many from iniquity." (Mal. 2.6)

Malachi went on to label Levi as a messenger of the Lord, thus suggesting a second identity for the messiah. Jesus could well have reasoned that if Jews acted in the tradition of Levi, as described by *Malachi* and *Leviticus,* fathers and children would be reconciled. To send the healed leper to the Levites for the purpose of having them perform all the proper rituals would be an act consistent with *Malachi's* concern for Levi.

The compromise failed. Instead of going privately to the priests and keeping quiet about Jesus' identity as his healer, the cured ex-leper broadcast to everyone the news that Jesus had resumed his identity as physician Elijah-Elisha and was back in the medical business again. The word spread like wildfire. Crowds descended upon Jesus in such numbers out in the countryside that it was no longer possible for him to enter a town.

THE RETURN TO CAPERNAUM

What becomes certain now to the reader of *Mark* is the failure of the Elijah-Elisha model. John's failure to become the new Elijah could have been blamed on John's inability to explicate the entire Elijah motif. Not so with Jesus. He had pushed the Elijah possibility to the extreme which now showed that Elijah would always have to become the miraculous one. The crowds would never repent, no matter which century. Public opinion would always value charismatic authority, superhuman power, and physical health above righteous living, and at the same time be more fascinated with destruction than with saving.

The leper, without intending to do so, insured Jesus' return to Capernaum, City of Compassion, by eliciting from him a compassionate act, and then by frustrating the intended result of the compassion. The multitudes which descended upon Jesus in the countryside took away Jesus' reason for having left Capernaum. Jesus had once thought that he could escape the temptation of turning authority into miracle by leaving the Capernaumites who demanded such a conversion. He discovered that there was no escape in Galilee. There was therefore no reason to stay away from Capernaum in particular unless he chose to leave Galilee altogether. He was not yet ready for that decision.

In the leper incident, Jesus identified himself with both Elisha and Levi. Upon his return to Capernaum he sought to abondon the Elisha identity again and to explore only the meaning of Levi for his quest. In doing so, he talked about forgiveness (a priestly function), called a follower named Levi, disputed with Jews about the significance of priestly rituals, and claimed the authority of David as precedent for violating priestly rules about food. Missing from the entire series of stories is any concern for such Elijah themes as repentance, judgment, and the sovereignty of God.

Recall that in the message of John the Baptizer that forgiveness had stood out as an un-Elijah-like theme. When Jesus had first adopted the goal of becoming an Elijah greater than Elijah-John he had cut forgiveness out of his sermons. But now that the repentance message was to be abandoned the forgiveness theme of John was to be brought to the fore.

On the occasion of Jesus' return to Capernaum, Mark reported that Jesus was "at home". Having earlier specified that Jesus came from Nazareth to be baptized, Mark's reference to Capernaum as home for Jesus represents a shift. Mark later called Jesus a Nazarene (15.67) and labeled his home town as his "fatherland" (6.1). The apparent confusion of these references is likely to have been caused by the fact that Mark was using place designations thematically rather than as items of geographical data.

The gospel began in Capernaum in at least four senses. A composite of all four could justify labeling Capernaum as Jesus' home even if his familial home was in Nazareth. First, the gospel began in *Nahum* as well as in *Isaiah* because *Nahum* used the word gospel. Second, Jesus' earliest recorded public acts occurred in Capernaum. Third, it was in Capernaum that the plots which led ultimately to Jesus' death were originally instituted. Inasmuch as the gospel culminated in Jesus' acceptance of death, it is appropriate to think of Capernaum as the place in which that part of gospel began. Finally, the name God Is Salvation would be most at home in Capernaum, City of Compassion.

Forgiveness as an Inadequate Good

Upon the occasion of Jesus' return to Capernaum, the narrative of the first incident implied that he came to offer forgiveness rather than to preach repentance. The crowds had again eagerly gathered around him. Nothing about being offered forgiveness was offensive to the something-for-nothing-minded Capernaumites. Like miraculous healing, forgiveness could well have seemed to be a highly valued gift bestowed upon the recipient without cost or obligation. The people jammed the house and yard where Jesus was preaching, hoping to be beneficiaries of his largesse.

This context trapped Jesus in a new conflict of goods. There was a tradition, taken for granted by both Jesus and the crowds, that paralysis is caused by sin. The presumed fact set paralysis apart from other types of disease. The common logic held that, because the source of paralysis was sin, the cure of paralysis was forgiveness of sin. Or, in reverse, anyone who was medically an uncured paralytic was religiously an unforgiven sinner.

Acting on the basis of such a belief, four men brought a friend, a paralytic, to Jesus to be forgiven-healed. Their act can be read in at least two ways. They may have thought that the man's sin was such that in their eyes it was forgivable, or they may have had such confidence in Jesus' miraculous power that he could overcome the unforgivableness of the sin and heal the paralysis in spite of it. Whichever it was, they went to great trouble to call Jesus' attention to their friend's plight—by cutting a hole through the roof and lowering the man into Jesus' presence.

Jesus' initial response centered on the faith of the four stretcher bearers. "Seeing their faith," he announced that the man's sins were forgiven. In doing so he called the man, "My son." Several interpretations are possible. The first and most likely is, "Your friends, by their faith, have forgiven you. I recognize that fact, approve of it, and publicly announce it." There are two reasons why this reading of Jesus' intent is preferable to the alternatives discussed below: 1) because it introduces in a subtle way the possibility, which was to be realized soon afterward in *Mark*, that Jesus' miraculousness depends at least in part on the faith of the other person, and 2) because it gives credit to the extreme efforts expended by the four on behalf of the paralytic.

A second interpretative possibility is that Jesus meant: "I by my own authority have forgiven you." This would fit the developing theme of authoritativeness and its conversion into miracle. A third interpretation is: "I by the authority of God the Father have forgiven you as a son." The advantage of this choice is that it picks up the sonship theme and fits the interpretation which Jesus somehow knew that the scribes would adopt. Thus, all the possible interpretations have points in their favor. It is possible that Mark intended the ambiguity because it shows that Jesus was trapped by more possibilities than he originally conceived of when he uttered the words.

This incident brought Jesus formally to the attention of Jewish religious officials for the first time in his career. Those present to hear his statement about forgiveness were scribes, experts in writing and interpreting Jewish scripture. Jesus intuited that in at least one sense, if not more, his words were inconsistent with Jewish Law, and that the listening scribes would be silently criticizing him for having committed the offense of blasphemy. Their teaching, as Jesus understood it, was that no one can forgive sins other than God Himself. The scribes did not say a word. Nevertheless, Jesus felt that he had to respond to the criticism which he imagined to be in their minds. In so doing he was led from forgiveness to medical miracle exactly as the Capernaum crowds and the four friends hoped.

Jesus' surface problem was that there is no external evidence of forgiveness. Neither the man, nor his friends, nor the scribes, nor the crowd believed that the paralytic was really forgiven. To prove the point to everyone, Jesus had to provide external evidence by the miraculous healing of paralysis. The crowd seduced the good news of forgiveness into what seemed to them to be the better news of authority and healing. They persuaded Jesus to announce his power to heal.

> "That you may know that the Son of man has authority on earth to forgive sins, I say to you, 'Rise, take up your pallet and go home'." (2.10-11)

A new form of miracle! They had previously seen Jesus heal disease and cast out demons; they had probably heard about his healing of leprosy; now they had witnessed the healing of paralysis. They had never seen such a thing. Little the crowds cared about the charge of blasphemy. The paralytic apparently did not care whether or not he was forgiven; his joy was that his legs had been restored to health. He picked up his bed and went home.

In *Mark's* context the incident was clearly temptative. The text reads that Jesus "perceived in his spirit" that the scribes were raising the question of blasphemy. It was that spirit perception which led him to shift his emphasis from forgiveness to miraculous restoration of the paralytic's legs. This serves to reinforce Mark's view that unclean spirits of temptation need not be housed in the body of some other person. The exact charge intuited by Jesus' spirit is significant because Jesus was ultimately to be condemned to death by Jewish officials for the religious offense of blasphemy. Blasphemy is an offense dealing generally with an improper relationship to divinity, and specifically in Jesus' case to his claim of being God's son. In Jesus' trial before the chief priests he pled guilty to that charge, but in Capernaum he defended himself against it. His method of defense was to resort to miracle and to claim for himself the identity of the son of man.

Jewish Bible often uses the title "son of man", primarily in *Ezekiel* where it properly appears in lower case letters, and in *Daniel* where it properly appears in capitalized form. This was the first of many times in which Jesus appropriated the title for himself. The consensus of recent Markan scholarship has been that Jesus always intended the title in its Danielic sense, in a manner consistent with the sentence from *Daniel* loosely quoted in *Mark* 13, "the Son of man coming on the clouds of heaven." That Son of man was a supernatural figure, a messiah, who would appear at Judgment Day. That Son of man was thus closely related to *Malachi's* vision of Elijah whose coming would precede Judgment Day.

Mark's use of the sonship motif is too complicated to be limited to any one interpretation. It involved both a complex of internal developments within Jesus' career quest and the ambiguity of the *Ezekiel-Daniel* son of man references. The details of the incident depended more upon the former than the latter.

It was when Jesus came "home" to Capernaum and sought to discover a model for father-son reconciliation more adequate than that of Elijah the preacher that he first explicitly referred to sonship. He did so in two ways. First he called the paralytic "my son" although there was no justification for him doing so in the context of the event.

Then he called himself "son of man". Assuming that Mark was conscious of using both terms in that order, an interesting possibility develops.

The Jacob motif from *Malachi* declared God's love for His children, the Jews. The Elijah motif assumed that the children of Israel would earn that love by living repentant lives. The experience of both John-Elijah and Jesus-Elijah had demonstrated that such was not the case. Therefore, God's love had to be predicated upon the assumption that God forgave the unrepentant. In the sense that Israel was a sinner, an unforgiven sinner, Israel was also a paralytic, inasmuch as unforgiven sin causes paralysis. The paralytic let down through the roof was all Jews. If the act of forgiveness were to be fulfilled symbolically in his case and realistically in the case of all Jews then Jesus would find the answer to his quest: fathers and children would be reconciled.

I do not know the origin of the Sin-paralysis relationship, but I assume that it is related to the common biblical prophetic practice of symbolizing sinful people as being stiff-necked, a symbol for their pride and stubbornness. My assumption is that in the original religious interpretation of the sin-paralysis syndrome the paralysis was never intended to be physical. It was only in the public's irreligious rejection of the prophetic insight that spiritual paralysis was transformed into bodily paralysis. Whether or not that was true in general, it certainly seems to have the case in this incident. Neither the paralytic himself nor the observing crowd were interested in spiritual forgiveness, but only in medical healing.

Jesus' exploration of the possibility that father-son reconciliation would result from forgiveness of "my son" was complicated by an ambiguity built into the nature of forgiveness. It is well known in the twentieth century that forgiveness is a type of activity which one human being can perform for another. The implication of the charge which Jesus imagined that the scribes were making against him is that such was not the case then. The scribes believed that forgiveness was an action which could be undertaken only by God.

Jesus apparently recognized that forgiveness is of such a nature that it cannot be bound by rules or limitations as to who can be compassionate or whose compassion will be effective. It was appropriate that such an insight should find its first public expression in the City of Compassion. The name of the town was itself a symbolic protest against the rigidity of the scripture scholars who dominated the town's religious life.

One of the consequences of direct human forgiveness is that the priests are by-passed. The function of the priesthood was to meditate between man and God in matters of sin and forgiveness. In this particular Markan context the elimination of priesthood was especially significant because the preceding story stressed the leper doing all that the priests commanded, and the succeeding story centered on calling a new Levi to Jesus' following. It is scarcely possible then that Mark would not have been conscious of the relationship of this story to the Levitic tradition. A far-out possibility is that the paralytic was intended as Levi or the sons of Levi, and that the four stretcher bearers were the counterparts of the four brothers already recruited to Jesus' entourage. In the absence of actual priests in Capernaum, the scribes represented the priestly position, rejected the forgiveness offered the symbolic Levi-paralytic, and thus needed to be offered forgiveness again in the succeeding account of the calling of Levi.

What is more clear is that Jesus' recognition of the significance of direct human forgiveness justified him in adopting the *Ezekiel* title of son of man. It is the son of man, any son of man, all sons of men, who can forgive and whose forgiveness will heal the spiritual paralysis of the one forgiven. Jesus had lightly touched upon such an emphasis on humanness by the calling of Andrew, Manly, among the first four. Alone among the first four, Andrew's name was non-Jewish. Now with Jesus' awareness of the human qualities of forgiveness he had arrived at a position which he knew to be at odds with that of the official Jewish interpreters of scripture. By calling himself son of man in such a setting he took full responsibility for the act of forgiveness. To the extent that "son of man" would be recognized by the scribes as a traditional biblical title, he set his authority as an interpreter of scripture against theirs and claimed for himself the justification of the biblical tradition.

Ezekiel 20 contains a remarkable parallel to *Mark* which may well have been the specific model which Jesus had in mind in making the son of man claim at that moment. In that chapter, God reminded Ezekiel, the son of man, that the Israelites in the wilderness between Egypt and the promised land were sinners and did not deserve anything other than wrath. But God in his mercy forgave them. Their response was blasphemy; they rejected God in favor of idols. In the act of doing so, they also rejected God's forgiveness.

In *Mark*, Elijah-Jesus had been rejected by the crowds in the symbolic wilderness of lip service. The crowds deserved only wrath according to the predictions of *Malachi* and *Daniel*. In place of destruction, however, Jesus offered forgiveness, compassion, salvation. Still the response was negative. The crowds desired miraculous healing in lieu of forgiveness. Jesus intuited that the scribes would receive his offer of forgiveness as blasphemous.

The parallelism between *Ezekiel* and *Mark* continues in the aftermath of this event. In the ensuing pericopes, Jesus was described as coming to an open break with Judaism over the issue of sabbath observance and ritual rules. In *Ezekiel* 20, the sabbath was given to man as a special sign of God's salvation. In *Mark* 2-3, the sabbath had become a regulatory device working against human needs.

Despite the fact that there are too many parallels between *Ezekiel* 20 and *Mark* 2-3 to regard them as coincidental, there is one major problem. *Ezekiel* 20 supported the scribes rather than Jesus in the argument as to whether God alone can forgive sins. Forgiveness, as there described, was clearly an act of God and God alone. The son of man was in no sense a forgiver; he was only a voice to speak to the elders of Israel, a voice to condemn them for following the idolatrous traditions of their fathers. It was God who was to forgive, to show mercy, to save.

By appropriating for himself the *Ezekiel* title son of man, Jesus seemed to put himself in the position of disagreeing with *Ezekiel*. Why would he have done so? The most simple and legalistic answer is that he did not. What he did do was to declare that the scribes were wrong. *Ezekiel* said that God forgave; it did not say that *only* God forgave, as the scribes alleged. Thus the argument was not between Jesus and scripture; it was between Jesus and the scribes, between Jesus and Galilean Judaism of his day.

The argument over forgiveness was complicated, however, by the Danielic Son of man tradition and Jesus' own predilection toward authoritativeness. Note his exact words: "But that you may know that the Son of man has authority on earth to forgive sins, I say to you, 'Rise, take up your pallet, and go home.'" In that sentence the issue is not the nature of forgiveness; it is Jesus' authority. The intent of the sentence is that the miraculous healing of paralysis will confirm such authority rather than confirming the forgiveness. The meaning of the sentence would have been quite different had it read, "But that you may know that you are forgiven, the son of man says to you, 'Rise, take up your pallet, and go home.'" In that version, the emphasis would have been upon forgiveness. The intrusion of the issue of authority into the relationship between Jesus and the scribes led him once again into temptation and thus indicated that forgiveness in itself was not an adequate answer to his quest for sonship. Forgiveness was a coin with one opposite side for Jesus, the augmentation of his own authority, and a different opposite side for the crowds, the demand for the healing of paralysis as a new type of medical mircale.

Whether son of man or Son of man, whether forgiveness was an adequate or an inadequate answer to Jesus' quest, one further simple observation needs to be made about Jesus' sonship. At his baptism, he was called to be God's son. In this incident, he claimed to be man's son. Even in the supernatural version of Son of man in *Daniel* there was no hint that the Son of man was also the son of God. In a very literal sense, the fact that Jesus did not use the title "son of God" was a clear clue that no matter what the accompanying incident was about he had not yet arrived at the answer to his question about being reconciled to God as his father. Jesus was not to arrive consistently at such a terminology until Gethsemane. Between the healing of the paralytic and Gethsemane, Jesus was to explore many concepts of sonship, but never consistently to think of himself as God's son or of God as his father.

It is important to note that Jesus' intuition of the scribal charge of blasphemy was the first evidence of irreconcilibility between Judaism and Jesus' ultimate interpretation of the meaning of sonship. According to the passage, Jesus' conflict was with Judaism, not with the scribes. His problem was with what he understood to be the classical position of Judaism that God alone can forgive sins. The scribes were only the representatives of that tradition, those who by their physical presence reminded Jesus of it.

The scribes *at this stage of Jesus' career* were neither enemies nor even opponents of Jesus. They were soon afterward to fit into both of those categories. As for now, they were interpreters of Judaism, and Jesus was seeking to reconcile all Jews to their Father God. They thus fell within the general category of sons of God for whom reconciliation was predicted by Malachi and sought by Elijah-Jesus. As part of the general population they had rejected the earlier command to repent. Now, as official custodians of biblical interpretation, they were the spokesmen for the tradition which gave Jews a reason for rejecting forgiveness when offered.

It cannot be too strongly emphasized that Jesus took the initiative in turning the scribes into opponents. This was to be true in later relationships with other sub-groupings in Judaism. Mark did not primarily present the scribes, Pharisees, priests, et.al. as recalcitrant bad guys maliciously intent on somehow destroying the good man Jesus. Rather they were authentic representatives of a religious tradition which, as it became gradually obvious to Jesus, was imcapable of reconciling Father and sons. It was not scribes and Pharisees at their worst who resisted Jesus. It was they at their best who did so. And in most of the initial instances they did so because Jesus himself recognized the contradiction between his point of view and theirs before they did so themselves.

The chasm opened between Jesus and the scribes on this occasion was never closed. From this moment on Jesus was led increasingly to discover in Judaism differences of opinion between himself and the scribes and all their allies in Jewish religious leadership. It was not too many days afterward before they began to express their animosity by plotting how best to kill him.

THE CALLING OF *MALACHI'S* LEVI

Disappointed with the reaction of the Capernaum audience, Jesus left the town once again, this time in the direction of the lakeshore from which he had originally called the two sets of brothers. His only action there was to call Levi to be his follower. He apparently called him as authoritatively as he had the four, and apparently received the same instantaneous response.

The full name, Levi son of Alphaeus, contains within its language roots the same bridge between Jewish and Greek which characterized the names of the fishermen. Levi is one of the most traditional of all Hebrew names; Alphaeus is a Greek name, possibly without a Hebrew counterpart. Thus, again on the lakeshore, Jesus repeated the symbolic act of closing the gap between Jew and Gentile.

Mark consistently used the shore of Lake Galilee as a theological dividing line between Jew and non-Jew. In general the lake marked the eastern boundary of that portion of Galilee in which Capernaum was located. Whenever Jesus approached the shore from the West or crossed the lake going East, there was something in his activity which was anti-Jewish or at least opposed to some aspect of Judaism. Whenever he returned to Galilee from the lake there was a pro-Judaism aspect to his movement. This Markan usage is loosely consistent with *Isaiah* 40-66 in which Gentile lands are designated as coastlands, but the parallelism may not have been consciously intended by Mark. Inasmuch as other place names such as Galilee and Capernaum are highly ideological in *Mark*, it is possible that all of Mark's geographical references were of such a nature, however, much they may also have been rooted in the actual career of an historical Jesus.

The calling of Levi on the seashore was the culmination of motifs which have already been discussed. His name symbolized the Jewish priesthood. All those who carried the name of Levi, and who were thus members of the tribe of Levi, were supposed to be priests. But this particular Levi had defected in favor of what was apparently a notoriously evil occupation of collecting taxes for the Romans. For Jesus to have called such a man was in itself an act of forgiveness. Thus were the roles reversed. The priests were entrusted with the rituals through which other people were to be forgiven. But this priest was himself forgiven by a non-priest, by one who claimed for himself only the title of a son of man.

In an overall sense the calling of Levi was Jesus' act of calling Judaism to a non-priestly religion, to a religion in which forgiveness was the task of every person. The envisioned religion was to be very much the same as what Martin Luther was later to call the priesthood of all believers. To symbolize that new Judaism, Jesus and Levi sat at table with other tax collectors and persons with infamous reputations. The Markan narrative implies that there were rules against such behavior roughly comparable to the latter-day American racial bias against Whites and Blacks eating at the same table. In Jesus' new vision of a religion-of-compassion there was no room for such a regulatory device. He called all priests to join with him in humanly compassionate acts such as eating with sinners.

The use of eating as a symbol for human relationship introduced in *Mark* at this point a motif which the author was later to build upon. Perhaps it is not correct to say that it was introduced in this pericope, because the story of John the Baptizer had contained a reference to his consumption of locusts and wild honey. I have not been able to discover either a biblical reason or a developmental theme within *Mark* which could account for those specific foods. They may have been intended only to embellish the wilderness motif.

Moses As Son of Levi

One of the most puzzling aspects of Mark's surface flow of thought is the introduction of Moses in the account of the transfiguration and references to disputes about Mosaic law in the pericopes immediately following the Levi pericope. The difficulties are eliminated by recognizing that Moses was a Levite, a descendant of Levi on both his paternal and maternal side, thus symbolically a son of Levi. By such a genealogy, Law is the child of Priestliness. Mark's introduction of issues concerning law came appropriately in the section which began with the exploration of priestly religion and the forgiving of Levi.

The contradictions between law and forgiveness, which the ensuing pericopes were to describe, already foreshadowed the disappearance of Levi from the list of followers of Jesus, and the disappearance of Moses from the company of Jesus on the Mount of Transfiguration. Neither Levi nor his "son" Moses could be part of the New Israel 'which Jesus was to seek to institute with the calling of the twelve disciples or part of the crucifixion answer which ultimately was to displace all the Jewish alternatives.

JEWISH OUTRAGE AND JESUS' RESPONSE

The Jewish response to Jesus' public act of eating with sinners was one of outrage. The scribes who belonged to the sect of Pharisees raised the issue. Historically, the Pharisees are known to have been the leaders of moral reform in Israel. In *Mark* and other New Testament books they are caricatured as those whose concern for moral law led them to legalistic extremes which violated the ethical goals they sought to attain.

Jesus reacted initially to their charge by proclaiming himself a physician for sinners in contrast to a physician for diseased bodies. This claim may have sounded as blasphemous as his earlier offer of forgiveness. Occasionally in Jewish Bible, God was referred to as the healer of Israel or of the nations. It was assumed that the prerogative of being a physician to sinners was reserved for God. Jesus' response made two facts clear: 1. he did not intend to let the healing of the paralytic's leg be a precedent whcih would lead him back into mass healings as a medical doctor; and 2. he was not afraid of the charge of blasphemy.

A series of controversies followed. In each, Jesus adopted for himself positions which may well have supported the charge of blasphemy. He referred to himself as the bridegroom in whose presence men should feast rather than fast, whereas in Jewish scripture God was often the bridegroom and Israel the bride, and whereas in Jewish tradition fasting was a virtually mandatory activity for those who took their religion seriously. Both by preempting the place of honor from God and by claiming superiority to tradition, Jesus indicated to his Pharisaic opponents that he was a dangerous radical.

He then generalized this claim into a principle: that he represented only "the new". He was the new wine for new wineskins, the new unpatched garment. By implication Judaism was the old, hardened wineskin and the old worn-out garment no longer worthy of being patched. Such sayings were virtually declarations of defection from Jewish religion, but it turned out in the course of the development of Jesus' career that they were only temporary positions adopted in response to the legalism of the Pharisees rather than permanent opposition to Judaism.

The series continued with the Pharisees accusing Jesus of permitting his disciples to eat grain which they had plucked from a field through which they walked on a sabbath day. Technically this was a violation of the law against working on the sabbath, however nit-picking it may seem to us. In any event, Jesus used the occasion to announce a principle which struck at the heart of Pharisaic Judaism: "The sabbath was made for man, not man for the sabbath." This broad humanitarian stand was comparable to his earlier support of forgiveness: it could not be bound by rules or laws. It was a stand in favor of compassion, concern for human need; it was a stand against the narrowness of rituals and observance of days.

The sharpness of the issue between Jesus and the Pharisees was blurred by the temptation of authoritativeness which accompanied Jesus' declaration of his newness. It had begun in his identification of himself with the bridegroom. It was completed when the needs of mankind as a whole were transformed in his mind into the Danielic Son of man in particular.

"The sabbath was made for man, not man for the sabbath; so the
Son of man is lord even of the sabbath." (2.27-28)

The second statement does not follow the first, either as a logical conclusion or as a poetic restatement. It is in fact opposed to the first. It gave the Pharisees solid gound for accusing Jesus of blasphemy even though they had been bested on the humanitarian issue.

This was the second time Jesus had referred to himself as son of man. On the first occasion he had toyed with the adoption of the Danielic title; on this second occasion he firmly grasped it for himself. In his anger at the continuously negative responses of Pharisaic Jewry he permitted himself to be drawn into an affirmation which he had earlier resisted. Mark probably meant to suggest that Jesus did not recognize the temptation which confronted him. Earlier, when urged to affirm himself as God's holy one, he knew that the urgers were unclean spirits. Now, when up against opposition from the moral leaders of Galilee, he was pushed unwittingly into the affirmation of himself as God's son of man whose functions and authority were the same as those of God's holy one.

There were powerful strengths on the side of good leading him to such an affirmation. Prophets such as Amos and Hosea had stood against the legalistic leadership of their day.

"And I will betroth you to me in righteousness and in justice, in steadfast love, and in mercy." (*Hosea* 2.19)

48

"For I desire steadfast love and not sacrifice, the knowledge of God rather than burnt offerings." (*Hosea* 6.6)

"I hate, I despise your feasts, and I take no part in your solemn assemblies. Even though you offer me your burnt offerings and cereal offerings, I will not accept them. . . . Take away from me the noise of your songs; to the melody of your harps I will not listen. But let justice roll down like waters, and righteousness like an overflowing stream." (*Amos* 5.21-24)

Surely such precedents justified Jesus in standing authoritatively against the legalists of Galilee, against the legalistic synagogue, against the legalistic Pharisees. Surely such precedents justified a human son of man for whom the sabbath had been established, as *Ezekiel* 20 had argued.

It took a satanic influence to turn the son of man of steadfast love and mercy into the Son of man of authority and power reacting in anger. The concluding event of the series of controversies makes that obvious. At a sabbath service, his synagogue opponents set up a trap to force Jesus into a public commitment. They made sure that Jesus was aware of a paralytic in the synagogue audience. If he persisted in the twin blasphemies that he could forgive sins and that he was lord of the sabbath, he would heal the paralysis and thus violate the scriptural rule against working on the sabbath. It would be a highly volatile public act comparable to a twentieth century American refusing to salute the flag or treating the president with disrespect. Furthermore his opponents knew that paralysis of the hand could not in any way constitute an emergency and that the scriptural exception about emergencies (getting one's ox out of the ditch on the sabbath) would not apply.

Jesus responded in anger. He by-passed the intermediate step of offering forgiveness, and healed the paralysis by a direct medical miracle. He did so in the name of a higher religious law, that it is legitimate on the sabbath to do anything good to save life regardless of emergencies.

The battle lines were drawn. The Pharisees sought the support of the Herodians (followers of Herod?) in plotting Jesus' death. Jesus became an opponent of all forms of Jewish legalism. The scribes, the Pharisees, and presumably the disciples of John the Baptizer dropped out of the consensus which had previously supported Jesus.

The healing of the paralytic in the synagogue had the same effect on Jesus which the healing of the leper had earlier. It was a qualitative breach in his determination not to be a medical doctor. By analogy Mark seems to have been describing Jesus' temptation problem very much as alcoholics describe their own problem today. The temptation is permanent; the most dangerous act is the first drink. It is the first drink for the alcoholic, the first healing for Jesus, which in each case opens the floodgates for a return to the dreaded condition.

For many readers of this book, the implication that Jesus was addicted in the sense that an alcoholic is will seem so outrageous that it seems necessary to interrupt the narrative development of *Mark* and comment on the long range significance of such a charge. When Jesus' career is viewed from its end, looking backward, as Mark inevitably had to see it, everything has to be related to the crucifixion-resurrection. Crucifixion, by Mark's definition, was the voluntary surrender of all human powers. The opposite of crucifixion, for Mark, was the act of clinging to human powers. Of those powers, the power to do good by use of miraculous power created for Jesus the greatest difficulty. It was so very good, and so very popular, that it was hardest to abandon. From the beginning to the end, the crowds and Jewish leadership and disciples all were agreed that the Jesus they liked best was the miracle man. It was in that sense that he was addicted to the use of such power, and in that sense that his willingness to give it up was an almost unbelievable triumph of the human spirit. It was that triumph which resulted in the resurrection.

After the healing of the paralytic, Jesus became Elisha-Jesus again. After healing the paralyzed hand without forgiving the man, Jesus "healed many, so that all who had diseases pressed upon him to touch him." Mark does not indicate that they were successful in securing health merely by touching Jesus, but it is likely that some of those who were ill thought that they could. They raised for Jesus the possibility which was to become a problem for him at later stages of his healing career.

As Elisha-Jesus the old temptations returned in recognizable form. Unclean spirits knelt before him in token of his divinity and thus implored him to admit that he was the divine Son of God. Jesus realized the nature of the dilemma into which he had been driven and firmly resisted their urging. "He strictly ordered them not to make him known."

In retrospect the calling of Levi functioned in *Mark* as if Levi had been a symbol rather than a person. In the preaching-repentance stage, Jesus had dealt directly with the crowds, with the total Jewish population of Galilee. In the offering-forgiveness stage, he had dealt primarily with the leaders of the Galilean Jewish crowds, the priests, the scribes, and the Pharisees, all of whom were agreed with each other against Jesus' emerging position. Without being specific, Mark implied that the crowds went along with their leaders. The calling of Levi was the symbolic effort by Jesus to call to his following the priestly-oriented Galilean Jewish leadership. Levi himself, as an individual, played no role whatever in Jesus' career development and disappeared from the story immediately upon being introduced into it. It seems most logical to conclude that Jesus' act of calling Levi was a symbol of his effort to enlist the support of the priestly leadership, and that their failure to accept the invitation was tantamount to Levi's inability to be a disciple of Jesus after having been called. When Jesus named his followers soon afterward, Levi's name was not on the list.

As stated above, the issue seems to have been a conflict between

Jesus as the good guy and the priests-scribes-Pharisees as the bad guys. That impression needs to be corrected. The issue was rather a dispute between two goods. One was a religion centered on God as the sovereign of law; the other was a religion centered on the importance of forgiveness and compassion in human relationships. Both were of great value then and remain so today; Christians still divide from each other in their relative emphasis upon one or the other.

The conflict between the two good religions was made fuzzy by the common meeting ground of personal authority. The scribes-Pharisees-priests strongly urged the exclusive authority of God and holy scripture. Jesus asserted the authority of mankind. The two came together when Jesus interpreted human authority as his own personal authority, and when the Jewish leadership heard such an assertion by Jesus as a blasphemous declaration of divine power. The dividing line between the human authority in general and Jesus' authority in particular was thin. It did in fact require on Jesus' part a considerable sense of personal authority for him to stand publicly in opposition to what he recognized as the position of the official scholars of his religion and thus to risk the charge of blasphemy.

There was an important sense in which Jesus' willingness to take a stance in opposition to the scribal scriptural tradition fulfilled the substance of John's prediction of a leader greater than John himself. The crowds had never heard anything like it.

CHAPTER FOUR
JESUS AND THE ELITE TWELVE: NEW ISRAEL

The open break between Jesus and the Capernaum Pharisees marked the end of the first stage of his career. Its primary characteristic had been his intention to be a leader, a messiah, in the tradition of Elijah and Elijah's successors. Had Jesus been successful, his victory would have been determined exclusively by the reaction of crowds and their leaders, as had also been the case with John the Baptizer. For each, his failure was the result of improper popular response to the good news of repentance and forgiveness.

Never again after this departure from Capernaum did Jesus function as the leader of Jewish crowds, even though he sometimes spoke to them or healed them. Never again did he pin his hopes on persuading all Galilee to repent or to accept forgiveness. Never again did he expect from the official leaders of Judaism anything but opposition. Never again did he conceive his identity as son of God to include acceptance by Judaism as a whole.

Jesus' separation from Judaism was first described symbolically by Mark.

"Jesus withdrew with his disciples to the sea.... He told his disciples to have a boat ready for him because of the crowd, lest they should crush him...." (*Mark* 3.9)

Why should Jesus have been afraid of the crowd? Armed with powers such as he now knew himself to possess, he could have thrown up around himself a shield of protection against any physical harm. Furthermore, he knew that the crowd had no desire to hurt him. They revered him because of his powers and would have done everything possible to preserve his life so that his medical career could continue for their benefit.

Jesus' fear had a different source. The crowds had grown. In addition to Galileans there were now in his admiring audiences people from Judea, Idumea, Transjordan, Tyre, and Sidon. Jesus had achieved an international reputation as a healer. The option open to him when he rejected Capernaum the first time was no longer available. There was no nearby place to which he could retire where he would not be expected to function as a master physician.

If he accepted the crowd's view of what his career should be he would be crushed. He had sought to be a preacher of repentance, and the crowds had subverted his attention into medical miracle. He had sought to be the forgiver of sinners, and the crowds had subverted his intention into medical miracle. He had sought to fulfill the imagery of Elijah, of Elisha, of Levi, of the son of man, of John the Baptizer, and of the spiritual religion of *Hosea* and *Amos*; and the crowds had subverted all his intentions into medical miracle. If he accepted the vocational choice advocated by popular adulation he would be crushed. No longer would he be free to respond to God. He would become the slave of the populace, a puppet dangling on the strings of men's legitimate desire for physical well-being. He would be crushed.

Lest the crowds should crush him in that manner, he separated himself from them. Symbolically he did so by boarding a boat on that lake which itself symbolized the dividing line between Israel and the Gentiles.

THE SECOND STAGE: LEADING TWELVE DISCIPLES

In *Mark*, the section from 3.7—7.23 portrays an intermediate stage in Jesus' effort to find an adequate content for his vision of being the beloved son of God. In it, Jesus was the leader of twelve men and only twelve. This stage was like the first in that it depended upon leadership and upon an adequate response from those who were led. It was different from the first in that it rejected any expectation of a response from the crowds and relied solely on the twelve disciples as a spiritually elite group. Taken as a whole the section raises two major problems, neither of which admits of completely satisfactory answers: why exactly twelve men? and why these particular men?

Why exactly twelve? *Mark* makes clear that twelve was not an incidental number. In this stage of Jesus' career, not only were there twelve disciples of Jesus, but there was also a twelve year old daughter of a ruler of the synagogue; there was a woman who had hemorrhaged for twelve years; there were twelve baskets of crumbs gathered after feeding the 5,000; and there were definite overlaps between the lists of twelve disciples and the twelve sons of Jacob. Furthermore, as *Mark's* flow of thought developed, these references became mutually interdependent.

In retrospect the obvious significance attached here to the number of disciples compels us to look back at the earlier numbers of disciples: the original four and Levi as the fifth. It was noted that the relationship of the four to the fifth probably accounted for the four stretcher bearers and the paralytic let down through the roof. This seemed to have been the only act of recruiting accomplished by the four after they were called to be fishers of men.

Another possibility is that Mark intended the incident in Simon's home to be a recruiting event. Upon the occasion of Jesus' first visit to the synagogue, the four took Jesus to Simon's home and immediately informed him that Simon's mother-in-law was abed with fever. What this demonstrated was that the four understood their task as followers of Elijah to be the gathering of sinners who would repent. Then, when in the forgiveness episode they did bring Jesus a sinner to be forgiven, they brought a paralytic for whom forgiveness would also mean medical cure.

Assuming the above to be consistent with *Mark* it would still have to be said that there was no apparent reason for having *four* disciples rather than five or eight or some other number except as the incidental total arrived at by having two pairs of brothers. It seemed to be their status as brothers rather than their total number which symbolized their significance for Jesus' career. It was not to be so with the number twelve.

The dominant meaning of the number twelve in Jewish scripture was the number of tribes of Israel, named basically for the twelve sons of Jacob. To speak of the twelve tribes was to speak of Israel. It seems inconceivable that Mark could have used the number twelve to mean anything other than Israel unless he put forward an obvious reason for doing so. He did not do so.

The names of the twelve disciples provide several clues that Mark intended parallels with Israel. Jesus had previously called five followers, the two pairs of brothers and Levi. The most glaring fact in the list of the twelve disciples is that Levi was not included. He was supplanted by his brother Jacob (James) the son of Alphaeus. By that symbolic act, Jesus excluded the priesthood (Levi) from his new career objective and broadened the supplanting theme. Priestly Judaism was to be replaced by some different form of Judaism as yet not made explicit. Priesthood was a significant part of traditional Judaism. It would seem then that the supplanting of Levi by Jacob would symbolize the creation of a new twelve sons of Jacob, a new twelve tribes, a new Judaism, a new Israel.

The logic of that conclusion fits well with other relationships between names in the two lists. The names Simon and Judas are Hellenized versions of the *Genesis* names Simeon and Judas, both sons of Jacob. Judah (Judas) was specified as a betrayer in both lists. Mark included Jacob (James) as the name of two disciples whereas in *Genesis* Jacob was the name of the father of the twelve.

Mark had no apparent interest in any of the twelve disciples other than the four fishermen, Judas, and an extra Simon and Jacob (James). No disciple other than Judas and the four fishermen is referred to by name other than in the original list in *Mark* 13. This removes from the reader any necessity of analyzing the other names for the purpose of finding biblical parallels or meanings based on linguistic roots. It also supports the conclusion that, however much the disciples were historically followers of Jesus, their primary role in *Mark* was their twelveness. It was their twelveness which symbolized for Jesus his intention of establishing a new Israel in place of the old one named for Jacob's sons.

The most interesting name to be omitted from the list of Jacob's sons was that of Joseph. There is a sense in which the name was not needed: Jesus himself was the counterpart of Joseph in that he was to be the one betrayed by the new Judah. But Mark later used the name Joseph in two other contexts. The most obvious was Joseph of Arimathea who provided Jesus' burial tomb. In that usage, Joseph was a Hebrew name; Arimathea was the Greek name of a town. While Joseph himself was not necessarily Hellenized, he came from a town which was. The other reference to Joseph in *Mark* is more hypothetical, a brother of Jesus (6.3) and a son of Mary (14.40,47) named Joses. It is clear that Joses is a Greek name and it is clear that it was intended to be a Hellenized version of Joseph. But in the LXX it did not appear. The name Joseph there was written as "Ioseph", not as "Ioses". Nevertheless, since the names of all of Jesus' other brothers were from the Jacob cycle and since the reference to Joses in *Mark* 14 fitted into the Jacob motif, it is likely that Mark intended Joses to be a Hellenized Joseph.

It should be noted in passing that Mark did not ever refer to Jesus' biological father, either by the name of Joseph or by any other name. This seems unusual to modern readers because of the strong Mathew-Luke traditions associating Jesus with a father Joseph. It is difficult to resist the impulse to assume as fact that Jesus' mother had a husband named Joseph and that Mark must have known about him. That assumption does injustice to all three synoptic authors. In *Mark*, the central question of the book concerned Jesus' relationship to a heavenly Father; there was no room for an earthly father. It would only have confused the imagery.

One of the most striking features of the list of the twelve is the exceptional treatment given to Simon, John, and Jacob (James). There are two different explanatory possibilities which need attention. One concerns the number three; the other the imagery of a special designation given followers of Elijah and Elisha: sons of the prophets. Both are drawn largely from the Elijah-Elisha cycle.

There is, however, a preliminary observation which may make sense out of reducing the four original followers to three by giving special attention to all but Andrew. The number three had many historic memories for Jews. Perhaps chief among them was the number of the three patriarchs: Abraham, Isaac, and Jacob, the father of Judaism and the sons. The exclusion of Andrew, the symbol of universality, tended to emphasize the Jewishness of the three whose names were stressed among the twelve, and might thereby point to the three patriarchs. If so, Mark did not seem to build on the idea.

Elijah-Elisha Explanation for the Twelve and the Big Three

The second stage of Jesus' career is covered by the material in *Mark* 3.7—7.23. In that section there are many Elijah-Elisha parallels, indicating that Jesus had elected to return to an exploration of additional themes from that cycle after having abandoned it for the Levi material from Malachi in the preceding stage. Among them are the feeding of the 5,000, the charge that Jesus was possessed by Beelzebub, and the resurrection of Jairus' daughter.

Although the feeding of the 5,000 comes toward the end of the section and its main significance will not be discussed until we reach its proper position in Mark's narrative sequence, the numbers which are in the story need attention now in order to understand the Elijah-Elisha motif of the entire section. An otherwise puzzling detail of the feeding incident was that Jesus ordered the crowd to be seated in groups of fifty and a hundred. The numbers fifty and one hundred were intimately associated with the followers of Elijah and Elisha in Jewish Bible.

Several stories from *I* and *II Kings* illustrate the point. In *I Kings* 17, Obadiah hid and fed 100 sons of the prophets, as disciples of the prophets were called, in two groups of fifty to prevent their murder by Jezebel. Elijah knew they were alive when he was tempted to think of himself as the only one left who was true to God, thus putting the lie to his temptation. In *II Kings* 1, a king sent three bands of soldiers to seek Elijah, each in a group of fifty. The first two fifties were consumed by fire from heaven; the third group was saved at the price of the king's life.

In *II Kings* 2, Elijah's ascension into heaven was misunderstood by the sons of the prophets who asked Elisha to send fifty strong men to look for Elijah on earth. Elisha was tempted to cooperate with their request even though he knew the search would be fruitless. Thereafter the sons of the prophets were mentioned many times but never by number.

In *II Kings* 4.42-44, Elisha fed one hundred men with twenty loaves of bread and some ears of grain despite the protest of his servant that it could not be done. Elisha knew that there would be food left over, and there was.

There can be no question but that the feeding of the 5,000 was built on the Elijah-Elisha tradition. The details were rearranged, but the point was the same. Many were fed with little food; the crowd sat by fifties and hundreds; there was food left over.

For our present purpose it was the fact that there were twelve baskets of food left over which is most important. After the fifties and hundreds were fed, twelve baskets remained. Noting how Mark's mind seems to have worked, it is highly likely that he intended the leftovers to symbolize Jesus' willingness to feed an additional twelve (the new Israel disciples) after the fifties and hundreds of old Israel were cared for. Thus again, in a roundabout way, a new Israel replaced an old one.

The parallelism between the disciples and the sons of the prophets may explain why the list of the names of the disciples placed such strong emphasis on sons. Jacob (James) and John were named as sons of Zebedee and surnamed as sons of thunder. Jacob (James) was named as son of Alphaeus; and the prefix "bar" in Bartholomew should be translated as "son of," hence son of Tholomew.

To the extent that Jesus considered the disciples to be the new sons of the prophets, the major theme of *Mark* is affected. Jesus was searching for the meaning of being son of God. His earlier exploration of son of men was a sidetrack. It turns out that his exploration of sons of the prophets would be also.

The number three had a near-magical meaning in the Elijah-Elisha cycle. Elijah lay three times on the corpse of the son of the widow of Zarephath to restore him to life. Elijah sought three times to die alone before being raised to heaven. Elisha's sons of the prophets sought the corpse of Elijah for three days before giving up the search and admitting that it had been taken away from earth. Elisha once performed a resurrection by having his staff laid once on a child's face and then by stretching himself twice on the corpse for a total of three contacts. Elisha himself died immediately after King Joash struck the ground with magical arrows only three times. Such threeness in Elijah-Elisha also has obvious implications for Mark's strong emphasis that resurrection was an event which occurred on the third day. It may also be, however, that in the mind of Jesus or Mark there was a numerical reason such as this traditional emphasis on the sacredness of the number three for singling out three disciples for special attention. Whether it is true or not, it is a peculiar phenomenon in *Mark* that the twelve were often represented by the Big Three disciples to the exclusion of the rest.

Surnames provide an interesting phenomenon in the list of names of the Big Three disciples. Simon was surnamed Peter; Jacob (James) and John, Boanerges or sons of thunder. Mark probably borrowed the idea of surnaming from *Isaiah* 45.1-4, in which King Cyrus was surnamed as messiah, as the Christ, as the anointed leader of Israel even though he had no knowledge of the Jewish God. Remember that Mark, reading his Jewish Bible in the Greek language, would have read the word leader as "christ" and is not likely to have been able to ignore it.

Mark expanded the idea of surnaming for his own purposes. He used names to contrast the success for which the twelve were called with the failures in which their careers ended. On the surface the twelve were called for success. Jesus gave them a three-part task: "to be with him, and to be sent out to preach and to have authority to cast out demons." It seems that they could have succeeded at those tasks. The surnames substantiate the impression given by including Judas the betrayer in the list: they were doomed to failure.

In English, the surname Peter should be translated as Rock or Rocky (as in Rock Hudson or Rocky Marciano). To do so would call attention to Mark's interpretation of rockiness. In the parable of the soils, rocky ground represents people who

> "when they hear the word immediately receive it with joy; and they have no root in themselves, but endure for a while; then, when tribulation or persecution arises on account of the word, immediately they fall away." (*Mark* 4.16-17)

An apt description of Rocky (Peter)! Note that the word "immediately" appears twice in the description. It indicates the two sides of the temptation of the twelve, the immediacy with which they originally followed Jesus and the immediacy with which they abandoned him when danger arose.

The surname "Sons of Thunder" is less easy to identify. First there is a linguistic problem, as is true of many Markan names. Mark himself gave the surname as Boanerges and then translated the name into Greek as Sons of Thunder. Linguists have been unable to justify his translation. Perhaps if we knew for sure what Mark intended in writing the name Boanerges we would have the clue for finding its specific meaning in *Mark*'s context. Jacob (James) and John, the sons of thunder, were separated out for special mention in *Mark* only once. After Jesus' third prediction of his suffering, death, and resurrection (10.33-34), the two asked for reserved seats next to Jesus in glory. His response was that he could only promise them the route of suffering, not the reward at the end. This would fit their surnames if they were called to be sons of the storm of persecution. There is no linguistic justification for such an identification. The possibility is supported only by its logical consistency with *Mark* and the absence of evidence to the contrary.

Linguistic problems also frustrate efforts to discover exactly what Mark meant by calling a second Simon "the Canaanean" and by calling Judas "Iscariot." The derivation of neither word is certain. Many possibilities have been suggested, none of them wholly satisfactory, and none of them particularly helpful in understanding *Mark*. One linguistic fact which is helpful is that Philip, like Andrew, is a Greek name, thus supporting the already established conclusion that in calling followers Jesus bridged the gap between a racially separate Judaism and a racially mixed, international or universal Judaism.

THE ELIJAH ROLE OF THE TWELVE IN THE NEW ISRAEL

The most amazing fact about the calling of the twelve disciples was that it represented a reversal in Jesus' career. He called them to the type of task which he himself had already essentially rejected, that of preaching. Jesus himself would never again preach to the crowds with the expectation that they would follow him or obey him. The twelve, however, would be expected not only to preach but to be able to overcome the temptations associated with preaching. Jesus had not been able to do so.

The calling of the twelve in that particular context reopens a question which appeared earlier to have been closed. Was the failure of the Elijah vision inherent in the nature of preaching or was it only related to the identity of the preacher? Jesus had first thought that the failure was to be blamed on the inadequacy of John, and that he, Jesus, could do better. He had discovered that great temptations emerged from authoritative preaching, from authoritativeness associated with preaching. In the calling of the twelve to preach, Jesus apparently reasoned that the twelve would not be blessed (and cursed) with that authority and that they would therefore not be seduced into miraculousness. *Malachi*'s Elijah hope could thus be fulfilled; men would be able to respond to the preaching itself and reconciliation between fathers and children would follow.

There is a tendency to gloss over the first of the three tasks to which the twelve were called. "To be sent out to preach, and to have authority to cast out demons" are tasks whose meaning is obvious to us by now in the book. Preaching and resisting the temptations associated with it was the substance of the introduction to Jesus' public career. But what kind of a task was it simply for Jesus to ask the twelve "to be with him"? Assuming that the twelve were sons of the prophets in Jesus' mind, and assuming that four of them had in fact failed him both during his own preaching career and when he was offering forgiveness, there is an important sense in which they had not been with him. Superficially, they had not been with him during the decision night he spent in prayer outside Capernaum or when the crowds abandoned him in Galilee when he would only preach but not heal. At a deeper level, they had not been with him when they played instrumental roles in converting both his preaching and his forgiving into medical practice.

Quite apart from the long range sense of father-son reconciliation in *Malachi* and its importance for Jesus' quest, there was an immediate sense in which Jesus needed disciples who would be really with him. He needed their faithfulness, their loyalty, their concerns for his concerns, their understanding. Of the three tasks, this was by far the most important.

In that context the word "disciples" suffers from translation. If translated into ordinary English it would be read as "students" or "pupils"; as it stands it is merely the transliteration of the Greek term. How were Jesus' pupils to learn from him, by his words or by his example? He hoped it would be by his words, for he told them to avoid temptation. *Mark* makes it clear that they learned by his example, for they were tempted in their preaching exactly as he had been in his. Thus was the Elijah style to fail again.

The disciples' first failure occurred almost immediately. When Jesus returned home after calling the twelve, an enormous crowd gathered. Mark implied that Jesus ventured out into the multitude and that the twelve were worried about his physical safety. At least some of them remembered how Jesus had recently sought refuge from the danger of being crushed by getting onto a boat. They had not understood that his danger was psychological. Having misconceived his dilemma the first time, they now thought him to be out of his mind for venturing into danger again. This began their chain of consistent failures to respond properly to Jesus' situations.

The crowd pericope is illustrative of a facet of *Mark*'s literary style which has often intrigued scholars. Mark often told part of a story, interrupted it with a second story, and then returned to complete the first one. This has often been referred to as Mark's sandwich style. Typically, as in this instance, Mark used the sandwich to demonstrate how the original direction of an event was modified by the intervention of a second event. Originally Jesus had separated himself from the crowds out of fear of their influence. But after having firmly decided to commit himself to twelve followers only, the crowd seduction was no longer attractive to him. He could therefore walk into any crowd without danger. The twelve did not comprehend.

Jesus' new confidence had consequences both for himself and for the twelve. On Jesus' part, it led to a new insight about the relationship of forgiveness to sin. Scribes came from Jerusalem to accuse Jesus of having an unclean spirit. Jesus replied that the kinds of blasphemy with which he and other sons of men had been charged were all forgivable. What was not forgivable was to reject the invitation which the spirit of holiness had extended to him at his baptism, the invitation to be the beloved son of God. The only unforgivable sin would be to reject love when it is offered. In a broad sense all Capernaum had been pronounced guilty of that sin by rejecting forgiveness when Jesus offered it. In a more long range sense, all Israel was guilty of rejecting the love of God who preferred Jacob to Esau. In a narrow sense Jesus alone could be guilty of that sin, for in *Mark* it was to Jesus along that the holy spirit gift was presented. It was Jesus alone who knew that God's love had been given to him and who therefore had to accept it or reject it.

The scribes perceived that Jesus' pronouncement about unforgivable sin was directed against them. Based on the narrow logic above, one would have to conclude that they were in error. But they were not. In the narrow sense, as described above, God's fatherly love was given to "Jesus alone". It is inviting for us as readers to agree with that because we know the end of the story. It would be incorrect at this juncture because Jesus was still wrestling with the problem of how to reconcile sons to the Father, not just himself, not even primarily himself. In the *Malachi* imagery, God loved all Israel, all the sons of Jacob. The scribes were in fact guilty of rejecting that love. They were thus separated out from the sons of God for whom Jesus had hope of reconciliation. He had now focussed his attention exclusively on the twelve, the New Israel, the new sons of Jacob.

The consequence for the twelve was that Jesus expected them to become his new family. In a dramatic confrontation before the crowd, Jesus formally renounced his biological family and adopted as family anyone who would do the will of God. In that act his separation from old Israel became theoretically complete. But also in that act the demand upon the twelve to let God become truly sovereign over their lives was made explicit. The coming of God's sovereignty, the Elijah theme which Jesus had announced at the beginning of his public preaching career, was now to be fulfilled in the lives of the elite group, the twelve. By their success, Jesus would have a new family, and the vision of *Malachi* would be fulfilled in a peculiar way. Instead of fathers and children being reconciled to each other, a mother and brothers and sisters would be reconciled. The possibility was good enough and sufficiently similar to *Malachi* to be inviting, and yet enough different from what *Malachi* really predicted that it would be doomed to failure as an inadequate good.

Speaking in Parables

For the fourth time in his career, Jesus left Capernaum to go to the seashore. As always before, the separation motif was strongly in evidence. Physically, Jesus sat in a boat, apart from the audience. Psychologically, he took refuge in riddles, which Mark called parables, so that he could speak to the crowd without any chance of being understood.

The irony of the situation was that the twelve were supposed to be automatically able to solve the riddles, but they could not. When the audience departed, Jesus' students made known their frustration. He replied by applying to the twelve an amended version of *Isaiah's* famous saying about ears and eyes.

"To you has been given the secret of the kingdom of God (God's sovereignty), but for those outside everything is in parables; so that they may indeed see but not perceive, and may indeed hear but not understand; lest they should turn again and be forgiven." (*Mark* 4.11-12).

He then interpreted the parable of the soils to them so as to make it mean that the prerequisite for understanding Jesus' teaching was to live rightly, to yield to God's sovereignty, that is, to bear fruit 30 or 60 or 100 times as much as the seed planted. Anyone who lived that way could understand; anyone who did not live that way could not understand. It was obvious that the twelve did not so live.

Parables, as defined by *Mark's* Jesus, were not puzzles to be solved by logic. They were ordinary statements which were made puzzling by the fact that the hearer did not live the kind of life necessary for making sense out of the statement. In that respect, Jesus had uttered many parables prior to this occasion. When he had told the synagogue spirit to be quiet, and the man heard an Elijah order of destruction; when Jesus announced that a son of man can forgive sin, and the crowds heard him call himself Daniel's Son of man; when Jesus had separated himself psychologically from crowd adulation, and the twelve thought he was in physical danger—all such statements by Jesus were parabolic. The puzzle lay in listener, not in the speaker except insofar as the speaker knew in advance that it would be that way. What was new when Jesus announced that he would always henceforth speak to the crowds in parables was a formalization of an existing fact: the crowds had never understood him; once he had hoped that they would but now he saw no reason to expect that they ever would.

The problem in *Mark* at this juncture is: what should Jesus do about the twelve? He had staked his career on their capacity to bear living fruit and to understand. but according to *Mark* 4.34 he had to explain everything to them—which was to say that they understood nothing and therefore did not ever bear fruit. Jesus must have been greatly disappointed.

Jesus refused to accept the disciples' failure as final. He set himself to work with them toward overcoming it. He told them that teachings which were secrets now would later be brought to light, that the hidden would become manifest. He told them, in parables which they could not understand, that the process of growth toward yielding to God's sovereignty would be virtually unobservable, like the growth of a crop toward harvest. All that would be required of the disciples was the tiniest seed of right living; that seed would be planted and grow into a mighty shrub, as the mustard seed does. So the question for Jesus was: could he find a mustard seed of accomplishment in the lives of the twelve? He set himself to do so.

This series of sayings by Jesus seem to have no direct Jewish biblical counterpart. They appear to be new in the sense that they are not patterned after some biblical model. In that regard they are like the earlier sayings (physician for sinners, bridegroom, new wineskins, new garments) which were also largely without biblical precedent. The earlier series had as its content the claim to newness; the later series is related to Jesus' intention to create of the twelve a New Israel. Jesus' gradual break with Judaism thus seemed to be freeing him to enunciate new teachings even though his activities were still modeled largely after biblical events.

JESUS' SYMBOLIC ATTEMPT TO ENABLE THE TWELVE TO BEAR FRUIT

During the intermediate stage of Jesus' career there was only a single item on his agenda. He had to enable the twelve to succeed. Somehow they had to become fruit-bearers.

His first attempt in that direction was symbolic. The five pericopes from *Mark* 4.35—6.5 function in the book as a unit, a symbolic interlude in the flow of events. In this unit Jesus assigned the twelve a task at which they failed, with the result that his old Elijah-Elisha problems were brought back to life in multiplied intensity. At the end of the unit, it was as if Jesus did not know about this process of failure; he started over again to entrust the twelve with a task.

The task assigned in the symbolic unit was to ask the twelve to sail (or row) a boat across the lake. Whether any of the twelve other than the four original ones had boating experience is not known, but four experienced sailors should have been sufficient for the task at hand. It was their lake; they had made their livelihood fishing from its waters. Because of their experience, Jesus was confident that he could trust them to succeed; he went to sleep and left them with their assignment.

Jesus was awakened by the twelve when they became afraid that a storm on the lake would result in their death. This was the mark of their failure. Had they succeeded they would have demonstrated that they possessed the mustard seed of faith in their own ability which could have grown into a fruit-bearing tree. They did not succeed, and Jesus knew it.

A new and unrecognized temptation now confronted Jesus. He had already set the stage for it in Capernaum. Recall how in the synagogue he had responded to the Pharisaic entrapment by arguing that it was always legitimate to save life. He had intended the maxim to apply to their lack of charity in the legalism of sabbath observance. But the twelve now confronted him with a direct request to save their lives in a very different context. It was a legitimate request, except—

Except that it undercut everything Jesus now intended. He needed fruitbearing from the twelve. Symbolically he needed them to get the boat to the designated shore. By intervening miraculously to save their lives he also calmed the storm and eliminated all obstacles to bringing the boat to shore. By so doing, he symbolically assured that the twelve would never become fruitbearers. Whenever any challenge confronted them, such as tribulation or persecution (the storms on the lake of life), the twelve would turn to the miracle man for rescue. Even when Jesus upbraided them for their lack of faith on this occasion they were not listening. Their attention was overwhelmed by the fact that Jesus' miraculousness had now been extended to control over nature: he had commanded wind and wave, and the elements had obeyed.

There was a second dimension to the failure. The intended goal was the Gentile shore of the lake. Had the twelve succeeded in bringing the boat to that shore, Jesus' break with old Israel would have been symbolically completed. The Hellenized twelve would have established a link between Jew and Greek. The twelve would have been well on their way to becoming the new Israel. Their failure was to thrust Jesus back toward old Israel.

JESUS' MASSIVE TEMPTATION

Jesus alone brought the boat to shore. He alone stepped foot on land. He alone was confronted by Legion, the military term comparable to the word crowd. He alone was tempted by an unclean spirit which Mark described as

"a man with an unclean spirit who lived among the tombs; and no one could bind him any more, even with a chain; for he had often been bound with fetters and chains, but the chains he had wrenched apart, and the fetters he broke in pieces; and no one had the strength to subdue him. Night and day among the tombs and on the mountains he was always crying out, and bruising himself with stones." (*Mark* 5.2-5)

The words spoken by the man with the unclean spirit were virtually identical to those of the man possessed with the synagogue unclean spirit earlier:

"What have you to do with me, Jesus, Son of the Most High God? I adjure you by God, do not torment me." (*Mark* 5.7)

In the context of *Mark*, such words could only have been addressed to an Elijah, one who carried in his identity the temptations both to be God's son in an exclusive sense and to destroy those who are evil. Elijah-Jesus had faced such temptations previously. The description of the unclean spirit as one who lived among tombs but could neither be fettered nor chained promised that Jesus' temptations on this occasion were to be far more disruptive and disturbing to him than had any previous allurement. Even after struggling with the temptations at length he would have to compromise.

Our recognition of the symbolic compromise makes sense out of an otherwise puzzling detail. At the request of the unclean spirit, Jesus sent Legion into a herd of swine with the result that the swine rushed into the sea and were drowned. In a Jewish context, pork had the reputation of being most forbidden of all foods, the symbol of Jewish ritual food laws. In the Markan context, the slaughter of swine in Gentile territory was most likely to have meant that Jesus was now forced by the failure of his New Israel to return to the ritual regulations of Old Israel, or at least to the kosher food regulation which he had previously rejected in principle by condemning ritual religion. The fact that in the following pericope Jesus was depicted returning to Israel to heal the daughter of a ruler of the synagogue virtually guarantees that Mark's intention in the symbol of the swine was to point to Jesus' reconciliation with Jewish ritualism.

This temptation was so difficult to bind and fetter because it came so unexpectedly to Jesus. He had thought that by calling the twelve he could both fulfill the Elijah dream and bypass the temptations associated with it. He had expected the twelve to be able to bear symbolic fruit, to sail a boat. Their failure had led Jesus to rescue them with miracle. The miracle placed the mantle of Elijah again on his own shoulders, not theirs, and with it all the Elijah temptations. Both Elijah and Elisha performed miracles of nature, including such feats as bringing fire from the sky to burn water, floating an axehead, and producing virtually non-ending food supplies.

The location of this event in the country of the Gerasenes is another of *Mark*'s unexplained details. The derivation of the name is unclear. A town called Gerasa is forty miles from the lake and would therefore not fit the story. It is not known whether there was a thematic reason for Mark locating the story at this precise place.

The conclusion of the story was similar to that in the cleansing of the leper. Jesus ordered the man to give credit to God. Instead, the man spread thought the Decapolis (land of Ten Cities) the news that Jesus had healed him of demon possession. Thus Jesus' reputation as a healer spread in Gentile territory.

The Return to Israel

When Jesus returned to Galilee, a great crowd gathered on the seashore. In the crowd was Jairus, a synagogue ruler whose daughter was at the point of death. He sought Jesus' aid as a physician, and Jesus agreed to serve in that capacity.

En route to the ruler's house, a woman in the crowd touched Jesus' clothing and extracted from him a miracle which healed a hemorrhage from which she had been suffering for twelve years. Jesus had no control over this miracle. He did not know who had been healed or of what ailment until he asked and the woman volunteered the information. That was exactly what Jesus had feared when he had earlier recognized that the crowd could crush him. On that earlier occasion, people had sought healing by touching him. Jesus had resisted such a loss of control over his powers. Now his resistance was symbolically crushed. He was no longer the healer who decided when and where and whom. He was now the puppet of the masses, programmed to heal when they said so. To the woman he spoke the words of healing, but they were spoken after the fact. The woman's faith in his miraculousness had already made her well.

When Jesus arrived at Jairus' house he was told that the girl had died. Without being requested to do so, he restored her to life; he resurrected her. After having done so he tried to treat the event as he had each of the preceding temptation events, strictly charging the girl's family and his own Big Three disciples to keep it secret.

The pair of incidents formed a Markan sandwich, the two halves of the Jairus story interrupted by the healing of the hemorrhage. In the first half, Jesus set out to perform an ordinary healing of a sick child, a type of event in which he had often participated. The success of the hemorrhaging woman in wresting control of Jesus' powers from him sent him into the last half of the Jairus' event prepared to participate in an entirely new type of curative event: bodily resurrection. This was the first time, according to Mark's account, that the possibility of resurrection occurred to Jesus. It provided a simple definition of resurrection: being brought back to life without the deceased having had to make any contribution whatsoever. On each subsequent occasion when Mark returned to resurrection imagery he was to modify this definition until finally he had virtually discarded it altogether.

Several details help make sense out of this Markan sandwich. The name Jairus means either "he will enlighten" or "he will awaken." The linguistic evidence favors the former alternative, but the Markan context demands the latter. Jesus interpreted the girl's death as sleep: "the child is not dead but sleeping." Everyone laughed at what they thought was an error by Jesus, but he fulfilled the meaning of her father's name by awakening her. The father and the child were reconciled to each other, after having been parted by death, by the miracle of resurrection. This was the type of reconciliation desired by the synagogue Jews, whom Jairus symbolized. They wanted the Father, He Will Awaken, to do it all by resurrecting the child to a condition of reconciliation.

The number twelve figured in both parts of the sandwich. Both the hemorrhage and the girl were twelve years old. The latter fact is stated by Mark in the language of immediacy, the clue pointing to temptation.

> "And immediately the girl got up and walked; for she was twelve years old. And immediately they were overcome with amazement." (*Mark* 5.42)

The two miracles in the sandwich, both oriented toward the number twelve, have peculiar significance because they point to failure of the twelve disciples on the lake. It was the new twelve, the New Israel, who had failed. The resulting temptation threw Jesus back toward Old Israel, toward the old twelve, toward kosher food laws, toward the synagogue. He returned to the Galilean crowds to do what they desired, to heal disease. He yielded himself to their faith in his ability to be their physician.

Note that when Jesus resurrected the daughter of the synagogue ruler, only the Big Three were present. He consciously excluded all others who had been his followers. This heightens the impression that the Big Three of Jesus' disciples were symbols of the biblical Big Three who were virtually synonymous with Judaism: Abraham, Isaac, and Jacob. Even of the original four, Andrew was excluded. Andrew's name pointed to manliness whereas the surnames of the three pointed to failure. The dissolution of the new twelve and the symbolic restoration of the old twelve was a distinctively Jewish failure-oriented agenda; Jesus knew it to be a temptation and sought to hush the news of it almost as soon as he had performed the deed.

A different way to assess the failure involved in this incident is to focus on the fact that it was Jesus himself who excluded nine of the twelve disciples from his presence during the healing of the girl. His specific and most important instruction to the twelve at the time of their calling had been "to be with him." The massiveness of his own temptation experience with Legion resulting from his miraculous rescue of the twelve had made it impossible for them to do so. Fruitbearers, men assigned the task of producing their own results, could not do so in the presence of the miracle man who had lost control of his power to the synagogue crowd.

Both Elijah and Elisha had performed miracles of resurrection. Elijah had raised the son of a widow of Zarephath, a Gentile town near Sidon, after having previously provided her with an unending food supply from a single jar of meal. He performed the resurrection miracle by stretching himself on the child three times. Elisha resurrected the son of a woman of Shunem, a son who had been born after Elisha miraculously enabled the woman to become pregnant in her husband's old age. There is little question but that the resurrection of Jairus' daughter placed Jesus more firmly than ever in the Elijah-Elisha tradition and thus compounded the temptations which went with it. Perhaps Mark intended to model the hemorrhaging woman after the mothers of the two resurrected sons, but that is not clear in *Mark*. For Mark's literary purpose, the parent would have to be a father.

Completion of the Symbolic Temptation in the Fatherless Fatherland

After having performed the two miracles on the shore of Lake Galilee, Jesus returned to a place which Mark designated as Jesus' "fatherland". The Greek word for fatherland has usually been translated idiomatically as "his own country" or as his home town, but *Mark* makes the most sense if the word is translated literally. The single question in *Mark* was Jesus' relation to his father. On this occasion he returned to his fatherland and found people there remembering his relationship to his biological mother and brothers and sisters, the family which he had previously rejected in favor of the twelve as his new family because they yielded themselves to the sovereignty of God. The irony was that in his fatherland he had no father. He openly declared himself to be a miracle-worker, asked for public acceptance on that basis, and was disappointed that his old acquaintances diminished his miraculous power by their memories of him prior to the beginning of his career as Elijah.

Thus, symbolically, Jesus had come full circle. The simple failure of the fishermen to get a boat across a lake had led Jesus to recreate all the bridges he had earlier burned behind himself. He had reunited with synagogue Judaism, with the Galilean crowds, with the vocation of medical healing, with the image of the miraculous Elijah-Elisha, and with his biological family. And he had left no place for a Father God or a son who could identify with Andrew the manly one. All of that happened in symbol only.

AN ACTUAL TASK FOR THE TWELVE

The symbolic events described above had no apparent effect on Jesus. He functioned thereafter as if the entire series of incidents had never occurred. The reader of *Mark* knows that it has occurred and that it forebodes failure in the series of actual events which is to follow. That, however, was an element of Mark's literary style, comparable to prophecy in Jewish Bible, and not a factor in Jesus' own decision-making process.

Likewise, the distinction between symbolic events and actual events is a literary distinction and not an historical one. It distinguishes only within the limits of *The Gospel of Mark*. To designate an event as an actual one is to point to the fact that within the book the event functioned so as to be remembered, to influence other events, and to be known both to Jesus and other people. Whether it ever occurred in the life of the Jesus of history is entirely another question. To designate an event as symbolic is to point to the fact that within *Mark* neither Jesus not others acted as if the event had actually occurred. It only pointed to the meaning of actual events.

The first actual event in which Jesus sought to enable the twelve to become fruit-bearers for him was to send them out by pairs on a mission. As contrasted with the simple symbolic task of fishermen rowing a boat, the actual task was a demanding one. The twelve were to resist temptation and to live in poverty.

"He charged them to take nothing for their journey except a staff; no bread, no bag, no money in their belts; but to wear sandals and not put on two tunics." (*Mark* 6.8)

Their instructions further implied that they were to speak to people and to depart from those who would not hear. They were to depend upon the generosity of those whom they talked to for their sustenance.

Given the flow of thought in *Mark* it seems highly likely that such a set of instructions would eventuate from Elijah material. The speaking and departing motif was certainly comparable to preaching repentance and bringing judgment, although neither was specified. The living in poverty and depending upon others for daily food was comparable to the two accounts of Elijah being fed day by day in the wilderness (*I Kings* 17.6; 19.4-8). Both Elijah stories and Mark's story are more like the *Exodus* 16 account of the children of Israel being fed manna and quail in the wilderness than they are like each other. That possibility would fit the theme of the twelve being sent out to become a new Israel by their faithfulness in the face of adversity just as the Hebrew slaves from Egypt had been sent out to become the original Israel by trust in the desert. It would not explain the particular details of *Mark*'s instructions or indicate why the twelve were sent in pairs. It might suggest that Mark considered the original Elijah as a new Moses (Elijah's wilderness the same as the wilderness between Egypt and the promised land, etc.), and thus help provide a reason why it was Moses who appeared with Elijah later at Jesus' transfiguration.

The important conclusion of the mission of the twelve was that they failed. Instead of following their instructions exactly, they followed the previous example of Jesus as the miraculous Elijah-Elisha. They preached repentance; they cast out demons as an act of medical healing; and they functioned as physicians for disease. Furthermore, when they returned from their mission they brought bread with them, not much, but enough to indicate that they had not trusted themselves solely to the generosity of their hosts. In short, they had repeated the mistakes of Jesus. They had imitated what he had done rather than doing what he said to do. They were not to be blamed; it was natural for them to have done so. What was important was that they shattered Jesus' dream that they could fulfill the Elijah imagery in a way he had been unable to do. It must have been instructive to him that they also had miraculous power, although Mark did not develop that possibility.

THE DEATH OF JOHN THE BAPTIZER

The first stage of Jesus' career had begun when John's work was arrested. The second stage included the death of John. If, as was surmised, the arrest was more psychological than physical, the question must be raised as to whether there was also a psychological death of John which fits in well with the development of Jesus' public career.

The pericope about John's death contains several peculiar phenomena. First, the Roman governor Herod whom Mark titled as king believed in bodily resurrection. He thought that John the Baptizer, whom he had killed, had returned to life in the person of Jesus. This was the same Herod whose followers had been requested by the Pharisees to join them in plotting Jesus' death. One can imagine that Herod would be somewhat reluctant to plot the murder of a man whom he was convinced had already been dead once and who presumably could come back to life again. Other people thought that Jesus was Elijah come back to life.

Second, to the extent that John the Baptizer was Elijah, Herod and his wife Herodias were the counterparts of the biblical King Ahab and Queen Jezebel. It was Jezebel who hated Elijah most and who most earnestly sought his death. Herodias more than Herod was responsible for seeking the death of John. The Elijah theme was thus reinforced.

Third, the pericope has strong connections with *Malachi* material. The issue between John and the royal couple concerned an inversion of the brother supplanting brother motif: Herod had supplanted his brother Philip as the husband of Herodias. The Jacob tradition was that the legal bad brother was replaced by the illegal good brother. Not so in the case of Herod; he was both illegal and bad. And if Mark was conscious of the fact that brother Philip had the same purely Greek name as one of the twelve disciples, he was both legal and good.

Also from *Malachi* came a connection between Herod and Judah (Judas). *Malachi* named as a major fault of Judah's that he married the daughter of a foreign god. In *Mark*, Herod married the wife of a brother with a foreign name. Herod was betrayer to John, as Judah was to Joseph, as Judas was to Jesus.

"Herod feared John, knowing that he was a righteous and holy man, and kept him safe." (*Mark* 6.20)

Judas Iscariot at the betrayal of Jesus requested that he be led away safely. Judah had said at the betrayal of Joseph, "Let not our hand be upon him." (*Genesis* 37.27) Herod's betrayal was evil despite his intention to be a man of his promised word. He believed in John's holiness in the same sense that the unclean spirits believed in Jesus' holiness. Herod betrayed more than a particular man. He betrayed the entire process by which God's love to Israel was made known: by reversing the brother supplanting brother theme and by killing the new Elijah in whom he believed.

The insights into the meaning of the account of John's death as depicted above are sufficient to demonstrate Mark's intention to weave John's death into his Elijah theme. In *Mark's* flow of thought, the failure of the twelve was symbolized by the death of the John the Baptizer aspect of Elijah, the preacher of repentance. Jesus now knew that neither he nor anyone representing him could preach in the John-Elijah tradition and also avoid the temptations which were associated with it. The death of John was not merely the end of an era in the sense that John the giant had fallen; it symbolized the end of an era in Jesus' expectations about himself and his search for an adequate answer to his Elijah-as-preacher problem of finding reconciliation between himself and the Father.

It should be noted, however that the death of John was already complicated by Herod's belief in resurrection. Resurrection was also an Elijah motif. The end of Elijah-as-preacher did not mean the end of Elijah-as-resurrected. That theme was still to be dealt with, and the death of John was thus transitional between a vision of Elijah as preacher and a vision of Elijah as the resurrected one. In that respect, the resurrection of Jairus' daughter was in a different idiom another forerunner of Jesus' treatment of the Elijah-resurrection theme. Herod's belief in resurrection combined two concepts, each more miraculous than the Jairus' daughter event. First, the original Elijah had never really died, and thus his resurrection was from a non-death. Second, John had been dead for some time, and Herod's belief that Jesus was the revivified John would be more astounding than the possibility that Jairus' daughter had indeed merely been in a coma and had been revived by Jesus after a few minutes.

It should also be noted that the death of John was the consequence of the relationship between a child and a mother. It was mother Herodias who persuaded the child to use the father's good intention to create evil. This is another subtle Markan hint that the answer to parent-child reconciliation would not ultimately be found in any of the motifs present in the pericope concerning events in the court of father Herod.

AN ELISHA TASK: FEEDING THE HUNGRY

The story of the mission of the twelve was made into a sandwich by the intervention of the account of the death of John the Baptizer. Prior to the death of John, Jesus assumed that the twelve could succeed on their mission. His instructions had been that the preachers, when people would not receive them and listen to them, should "leave, shake off the dust that is on your feet for a testimony against them." In their reported success, the disciples did not indicate whether they had ever used such a strategy. After the death of John, it was clear that they would no longer be able to do so. The crowds which had once attached themselves to Jesus because of his miracles now were equally insistent upon following all of the twelve. So many people were coming and going that none of the disciples nor Jesus had any leisure, even to eat.

Eating was the symbolic act which held the entire sandwich together. In their original charge, the twelve had been told "to take nothing for their journey, except a staff: no bread...." They were to depend upon the generosity of whatever host they happened upon. The death of John occurred, by contrast, at a banquet. It was in the midst of the excesses of the banquet that a distorted sense of values led Herod to order the death of the very man whom he held to be holy. Upon the disciples' return, they had no leisure to eat and were taken by Jesus alone to a place of rest—with the result that 5,000 people were fed.

When the twelve returned Jesus intended to go off alone with them. Given the context in *Mark* I assume that means that he intended to take the twelve away from the crowds to which they were becoming as much subject as he had once feared himself to be. He might have succeeded had it not been for the fame which the twelve had earned in their own right as preachers and healers. The crowd followed them, not Jesus, even to the point of anticipating where they were going and arriving there ahead of them. That was probably a subtle Markan touch, indicating that the twelve had become subject to the crowd every bit as much as Jesus had, and that the crowd was setting their agenda.

At that juncture in *Mark's* narrative, Jesus made exactly the same shift which he had earlier made at mid-point in his visits to Capernaum. He changed from preaching repentance to offering compassion. In this more recent instance it was the disciples who were to change from preaching repentance to offering compassion. Just as the preaching technique had failed when Jesus had used it, so it had failed for the twelve, a failure symbolized by the death of John the Baptizer who had been Elijah but not Elisha. Just as Jesus had consequently adopted the identify of the compassionate Elisha in place of Elijah, so now he was to ask the twelve to be compassionate in the Elisha tradition.

When the crowds gathered, Jesus had compassion on them and evidenced it by teaching them. The disciples were compassionate in their concern for people who would be hungry at the end of a long day of listening. Jesus took the clue from their expression of concern to ask the twelve to give everything they possessed as food for the crowd. Said he, "You give them something to eat." Superficially, he was asking them to share their picnic lunch, give away their groceries. At the deeper level of symbolic meaning, he was asking them to do far more than that. In either case, the disciples were not supposed to have any bread of their own. To do so was a violation of the explicit instructions they had been given for their mission. They had five loaves, two fish. And they were unwilling to give it away, excusing themselves on the grounds that it would not be enough for everyone.

The unwillingness of the twelve to share whatever they had was the final failure of their mission. They did not have within themselves the compassion necessary for sharing despite their lip service to the needs of the hungry crowd. Their failure forced back upon Jesus' shoulders the mantle of Elisha in its temptative form. Whereas shortly before he had been concerned for the people as sheep without a shepherd and had taught them, now he devoted himself to the miraculous multiplication of bread to assuage stomach hunger. As in the symbolic task unit of *Mark* when Jesus responded to the failure of the twelve by miraculously bringing the boat to shore, now he again responded to their failure by miraculously performing their assigned task for them. He had asked them to feed many with little, just as Elisha had done in ancient times. They could not do it, so he did it for them. It would always be difficult for them to accomplish what he assigned as long as they were assured that he would come to their rescue.

The details of the account of the feeding of the 5,000 were drawn, as noted earlier, from the Elijah-Elisha cycle. The main thrust of the event, however, had little connection to those details. It firmly established the connection between eating and giving oneself. As Jesus' career moved toward its peak, the references to eating (and to a lesser extent, drinking) were to increase in frequency. Why this is so never becomes certain in *Mark*, but it may well be because there were many "eating" themes in Judaism, such as kosher food laws, fasting, and the paschal supper at Passover time.

SYMBOLIC DISMISSAL OF THE TWELVE DISCIPLES

After feeding the 5,000, Jesus sent the twelve home in a boat while he went into the hills to pray. This event was every bit as much symbolic as the previous boat experiences had been. The symbolism, however, was reversed because the boat was headed toward Galilee, not away from it.

In the symbol, Jesus sent the twelve home. This was not a "good night, I'll see you tomorrow" dismissal. It was a cessation of the teacher-disciple relationship. Elijah was dead; the sons of the prophets were no longer needed. Home for them was Bethsaida, literally "House of Fishermen" or perhaps idiomatically "City of Fishermen". How many of them lived there historically is not known. What is important is that it fits *Mark*'s logical development for Jesus to have sent them to a town whose name represented the home of the fishermen.

Mark reported that Jesus "immediately" sent them home. That word, calling attention to temptation in *Mark*, alerts the reader to the strange events which followed. The twelve rowed against a headwind from late in the evening when they separated from Jesus until early in the morning between 3:00 and 6:00 a.m., probably a time span of 5-10 hours. Without Jesus in the boat to rescue them from their plight, they stayed at their oars, "distressed" in rowing. Whether the distress was from weariness or danger or both, Mark did not say. Whichever it was, they did not give up. They were about to create in themselves that symbolic grain of mustard seed which could grow into a full-sized fruit-bearing shrub for Jesus' service. Their own miraculousness apparently did not extend to control of wind and wave. They had to depend upon their own raw courage.

But Jesus had been tempted to believe that he no longer needed them. Like Elijah of old, he felt again that he could stand alone without assistance. In that setting, Jesus undercut the efforts of the twelve men by using his miraculous power for his own personal comfort. Rather than walking home the long way around the lake, he took a short cut over the waves, walking on top of the water. When he saw the twelve men struggling against the headwind he ignored them.

He intended to pass them by because they were no longer part of his program.

When they saw him their courage collapsed. They were terrified at the sight of a ghost walking on the water. In an act of compassion which dealt sentimentally with their immediate terror but permanently destroyed their ability to attain difficult goals by their own effort. Jesus joined them in the boat, stopped the storm, and brought the boat to shore.

The boat did not reach Bethsaida. It touched land at Gennesaret. The interpretative problem involved in the relationship between those two names is made more complex by a subsequent boating incident reported in *Mark* 8.10-22 in which a boat destined for Dalmanutha arrived at Bethsaida. Both Gennesaret and Dalmanutha are words of uncertain deriviation, although there is a loose connection in Greek between Gennesaret and genesis (words such as birth, origin, beginning). All three locations are uncertain. Gennesaret may have been the Plain of Gennesaret, a broad area at the northwest corner of Lake Galilee. Cullman states in Kittel's *Theological Dictionary of the New Testament,* VI,.101, that Bethsaida was "a small Jewish town on the east bank of the Jordan which was under Greek influence." That would fit all of *Mark*'s requirements for Bethsaida. It would be somewhere other than on the Plain of Gennesaret and it would be an appropriate "home" for Hellenized Jews such as Simon Peter and Andrew and Philip.

Mark probably intended the two boat trips to symbolize the relationship between Jesus and the twelve. On the first trip, Jesus intended to dismiss the twelve from his service by sending them home. They did not arrive at their home; instead they arrived with Jesus at the scene of a mass healing. On the latter trip, Jesus intended by miracle to heal the deafness and blindness which prevented the twelve from understanding, but his plan miscalculated. When it did, the new Israel really ceased to exist, and the twelve had gone home sybolically.

All of that was internal Markan symbolism. The disciples did not subsequently understand any of it. Jesus did not subsequently act as if it had occurred.

One detail of the story must, however, be read as an actual event. Jesus went to the hills to pray. As was true in the earlier prayer incident in the hills outside Capernaum, the content of the prayer can be known only by careful observation of the flow of events. In this instance, the prayer occurred just before Jesus was to make a significant change in the direction of his career. We have noted its temptative form in Jesus' act of sending the disciples home, thinking that he could stand alone without them. The temptation was a parody of the truth. Jesus was eventually to discover the meaning of the father-son relationship by exploring types of religious living which did not depend upon the responses of others. The prayer decision undoubtedly was a choice of that direction even though it took a unique combination of events to actually set Jesus on that path.

TOTAL LOSS OF CONTROL OVER MIRACULOUS HEALING

Recall that in the *Mark* 4.35—6.5 unit the sandwiched miracle of the woman with a hemorrhage symbolically predicted that Jesus would in fact lose control over his miraculour power, and that the loss would result from the failure of the twelve to bear fruit. Upon arriving at the Gennesaret shore all of the elements of that prediction were fulfilled. The twelve had failed on their mission and had been unable to feed the crowds on their little bread. Jesus had been unable to recognize in them even what courage they did have for rowing a boat against a headwind and had resolved in prayer to rely on his own powers alone. In that setting, the masses descended upon him with their sick.

"Wherever he came, in villages, cities, or country, they laid the sick in the market places, and besought him that they might touch even the fringe of his garment; and as many as touched it were made well." (*Mark* 6.56)

Thus was the compassion of Elisha-Jesus finally made captive to the will of the crowds, and the independence of Elisha-Jesus crushed by them. What a change from the proud Elijah in whose presence men feared for their lives even to the point of undergoing convulsions when he spoke, to the docile Elisha subject to the demanding touch of every diseased person, powerless to resist anyone. Thus had Jesus descended from the pinnacle to the pit of his career.

THE ACTUAL BREAK WITH THE TWELVE DISCIPLES

Recall that in Capernaum when Jesus had first publicly evidenced his compassion by forgiving sin and healing paralysis, the result was a battle with the Pharisees about ritual observances. So it was again in this phase of Jesus' career. After yielding himself to the will of the populace by becoming their automatic source of physical health, Jesus was attacked by the Pharisees, in concert with Jerusalem scribes, for violating ritual laws of Judaism, this time laws associated with preparation for eating.

Mark had been developing a major theme connected with food. When the daughter of Jairus was resurrected, Jesus "told them to give her something to eat." The twelve were sent out with instructions to take no bread. John was killed while Herod was at a banquet. The 5,000 were fed on five loaves and two fish. The disciples were reported not to have understood the incident on the lake because they "did not understand about the loaves." And now the dispute with the Pharisees concerning rituals of eating. It is not yet clear to the reader what Mark intended by such a sequence. Later on food and drink were to become major symbols of Jesus' voluntary suffering and death. Perhaps these earlier references are in preparation for that meaning.

Jesus' condemnation of the Pharisees on this occasion gathered up some of the most important themes developed by Mark. His initial words were to quote *Isaiah:*

"This people honors me with their lips, but their heart is far from me; in vain do they worship me, teaching as doctrines the precepts of men."(*Mark* 7.6-7)

The extended quotation in *Isaiah* 29 attributed the reason for such lip service as symbolic blindness and symbolic drunkenness of the prophets. Isaiah also predicted that a day would come when the deaf would be able to hear and the blind to see. Until then, prophetic vision for the religious leaders would be a sealed book.

In the next poem, Isaiah referred to the Jews as "rebel sons", a phrase appropriate to the continuation of Jesus' blast at the Pharisees. He told them that they prevented any possible reconciliation of parents and children by invoking the law of Corban, a non-biblical tradition by which children could avoid taking care of their parents by dedicating their possessions to God. In Mark's context, this charge was the most extreme one possible for Jesus. It indicated that there could be nothing in Pharisaic Judaism which would be valuable for Jesus in discovering the path to Father-son reconciliation.

Jesus then called the crowds to him and announced a principle which would have destroyed all Jewish ritualism:

"There is nothing outside a man which by going into him can defile him; but the things which come out of a man are what defile him." (*Mark* 7.15)

Despite Jesus' long experience that it would be otherwise, he apparently expected the crowds and the twelve to understand that principle. They did not.

The failure of the twelve to understand was, for Jesus, the crowning blow. He stated in the form of a rhetorical question the answer which he should have known all along but had refused to recognize: "Then are you also without understanding?" They were, and it seemed that nothing could be done about it.

The difference between the *Isaiah* passages quoted at the beginning and the end of the second stage of Jesus' career is very instructive. The earlier passage, connected with the call of Isaiah himself, argued that the prophet understood his message but that the crowds would not. Translated into the context of the twelve disciples they were supposed to be the ones to comprehend, whereas again the crowds would not be able to. The crowds were to be blind and deaf; the twelve were to be internally sighted and hearing. In the *Isaiah* passage at the end of the second stage, Isaiah had recognized that blindness and deafness to the meaning of God's message was not merely a phenomenon of the crowds; they also were afflictions of other prophets. It was the prophets who gave lip service only. In *Mark* this had its counterpart in Jesus' ultimate recognition that his own twelve were equally as blind and deaf as the crowds.

On the basis of the story of John the Baptizer, one might have predicted that this would come to pass. The entire population of Jerusalem had gone out to John and had given him lip service. The entire population included both the crowds and their religious leaders, the modern representatives of the prophets (scribes, priests, elders, etc.). The first two stages of Jesus' career explored in detail the probability which had already been inherently present in John's preaching wilderness, namely that use of biblical patterns relying either on Jewish crowds in Old Israel or Jewish leadership in New Israel would prove to be inadequate for discovering the route to Father-son reconciliation.

ABANDONMENT OF JESUS' CAREER

One of the most overlooked sentences in previous interpretations of *The Gospel of Mark* is Mark 7.24.

"And from there he arose and went away to the region of Tyre and Sidon, and he entered a house and would not have anyone know it."

Tyre and Sidon, north from Galilee, were far out of Jewish territory. It was near Sidon that Elijah had provided a miraculous food supply and had resurrected the son of a Gentile woman. Now Jesus emigrated to that area and dealt there with a Gentile woman.

The logic of *Mark* has been crystal clear to this point. Jesus, in seeking an answer to his root question about what it means to be God's beloved son, had explored two major implications of biblical imagery. The first had been that Elijah-Elisha (supplemented by Levi and the son of man) would return as a leader of all Israel, a charismatic figure calling the masses to repentance or a compassionate figure offering forgiveness to the masses. In either case, the leader would be accepted by Israel and his message would receive a positive response. When the first plan failed, a second was tried. Elijah-Elisha would return as the teacher-leader of the sons of the prophets, an elite group of fruit-bearers numbered twelve to point to their identity as the new Israel. Both schemes failed. Jesus saw no hope remaining in Israel. He may well have been persuaded that his baptismal vision had been illusory, a mistake on his part. He intended to retire from the Jewish arena in which lip service audiences constantly subverted his high religious intentions into acts of physical miracle. He abandoned his career in Israel and went into hibernation in a foreign land.

In the third year of Elijah's exile near Tyre and Sidon, God commanded him to return to Israel. By re-introducing the Elijah imagery at this spot in the narrative, Mark virtually promised that Elijah-Jesus would be recalled to a career in Israel, and that a new chapter in his quest for father-son reconciliation would begin.

CHAPTER FIVE
EASY VICTORY: MIRACULOUS RESTORATION OF THE TWELVE

Jesus' hiding place near Tyre and Sidon was quickly discovered by a woman in need. The event which followed was dramatic in several respects. At the surface level it concerned a woman who was discontented with her young daughter. She felt that the girl had an unclean spirit. She came to Jesus asking him to exorcise the demon. Jesus, without compassion, replied symbolically that since he had decided no longer to feed the children of Israel with the bread of his service he certainly was not going to feed a Gentile child (whom the Jews would call a dog) with it. In different idiom, this was very nearly the same reply he had made to the leper who asked him for healing when Jesus had just abandoned his medical career in Capernaum. The woman, like the leper, had a clever reply which cut through Jesus' resistance. She told him that she did not need bread for her daughter; she would be satisfied with table scraps, with crumbs such as the Jewish children fed their pet dogs under the table. Jesus recognized that if the woman would be truly contented with crumbs, she would no longer be discontented with her daughter. In the act of the mother becoming contented, the unclean spirit left the daughter. There was no necessity of a miracle although the mother probably understood the event in terms of one.

At a deeper level, the story was about Jesus' discontent. After this incident, the Gentile woman disappeared from Mark's book but Jesus returned to the Sea of Galilee. The occasion functioned as a way for God to call Jesus back to his baptismal task, the discovery of what there was in the biblical imagery which would fulfill *Malachi*'s hope of reconciliation between fathers and children. The nature of the incident, the reconciliation of a mother to her daughter, must have reminded Jesus of his unfinished quest.

Elijah had experienced a similar call. Early in his career he had gone to the area of Tyre for three years and had lived there in the home of a Gentile woman. He had restored the woman's son to her by resurrecting him from the dead. After that event, God ordered Elijah to return to his prophetic career in Israel.

In Jesus' case, he was called to be satisfied with crumbs, not bread, with little, not much. The experience symbolically informed him that he had been expecting too much from the crowds and the twelve, from Israel old and new. Subsequent events were to make it clear that the "too much" was his expectation of fulfilling the Elijah imagery by being a leader of others. His new calling was to perform acts for which he and he alone was responsible, to be satisfied with his own success as the criterion for being God's son rather than depending upon the responses of other people. Elijah and Elisha provided the pattern for such a career, their miraculousness which did not depend upon anyone other than themselves. In Mark's context this incident now made sense out of the twelve baskets of broken pieces (crumbs?) left over after feeding of the 5,000. The conversation now said to Jesus that the significant aspect of the feeding of the 5,000 was not the food which the crowds ate, but the crumbs which were left over. Had he been satisfied with them, he would not have abandoned the twelve. The symbol was open on the question as to whether the twelve referred to Old Israel or to New. But in either case, the effect of the incident in Syria was to send Jesus back to Israel.

It was a Gentile woman who called Jesus back to a task in Israel. There were powerful pro-Gentile motifs in both the Elijah and Elisha tales, and Mark's account of Jesus was increasingly from this time geared to increase the roles of foreigners and foreignness in Jesus' restored career.

At this juncture, however, the emphasis was still on Israel. Recall that in the resurrection of Jairus' daughter her twelve-year-oldness made her symbolize Israel. Mark often later depicted Jesus as dealing with individual young persons, the Syrophoenician daughter, the young man who fled naked from Jesus' arrest, and the boy with the unclean spirit at the base of the mountain of transfiguration. In each case the context was to make clear that the young person was symbolically Israel, not specified as a twelve-year-old but having the youth which characterizes a twelve-year-old. Prior to the healing of the Syrophoenician daughter Jesus apparently believed that an unclean spirit was so inexorably in Israel as a whole that it could never be permanently exorcised. The mother's example of contentment with crumbs led Jesus to cast the demon out of Israel once more and to return home with far less demanding standards than he had advocated earlier.

MIRACULOUS HEALING OF SPIRITUAL DEAFNESS

Jesus took the long way home in order to cross the Sea of Galilee from East to West. It would have been shorter to come straight South from Tyre to Galilee. Jesus went far out of his way to the East, probably to perpetuate the consistent Markan symbolism that a return to Galilee from the lake meant a reconciliation with Judaism.

Recall that in the beginning of Jesus' experiences with the twelve he had informed them that the difference between the masses and the elite was in *Isaiah*'s concept of psychological deafness and blindness. The masses heard only with their physical ears and saw only with their physical eyes; they did not understand what they heard and saw. The twelve, the elite, were expected to hear and see both physically and psychologically, but they consistently failed in the latter, spiritual dimension.

Thus it was that Jesus' reconciliation with Israel took the form of an attempt to create by miracle a following which would truly see and hear. The event itself was obviously symbolic of the healing of the prophet-disciples in the *Isaiah* tradition. A deaf-mute was healed by Jesus in the manner of popular magic.

> "Jesus put his fingers into his ears, and he spat and touched his tongue; and looking up to heaven he sighed and said to him, "Ephphatha," that is, "Be opened." (*Mark* 7.34)

It was the imitative quality of the procedure which designated it as an act of magic, fingers in ears to heal hearing, touching tongue to heal muteness. Elisha had closed his career with a similar event, instructing a king to strike arrows on the floor to symbolize striking a foe with defeats. Both Elisha and Elijah had performed resurrections from the dead magically, imitating the death and rising by stretching themselves out at full length on the corpse.

Jesus intended the healing to be spiritual in nature. He knew that the physical restoration of speech and hearing would renew a public clamor for medical service. He knew that was temptation for him and asked that the event be kept secret. No one paid any attention to such a request.

The miracle was intended to symbolize two consequences. Israel would be made able to hear, and Jesus would become able to speak plainly. He would no longer have to address his audiences in parables. The hearing impediment in their understanding would have been removed. Thus the miracle was intended in an important respect for Jesus himself as well as for others.

A NON-TASK: FEEDING THE 4,000

The pericope of feeding the 4,000 has long been recognized as a retelling of the story of feeding the 5,000, a phenomenon which biblical scholars have referred to as a doublet. It calls attention to other less obvious doublet features of this section of *Mark* as related to the preceding one.

Mark 6.30—7.30	Mark 7.31—9.29
Feeding of 5,000	Feeding of 4,000
Jesus at prayer	A sign from heaven
Crossing the lake in a boat	Crossing the lake in a boat
Medical healing	Healing deaf-mute and blind man
Failure of the twelve to understand	Failure of key disciples to understand
Encounter with unclean spirit	Encounter with unclean spirit

No pericope is left out. The pericopes of the deaf-mute and blind man are joined together in the outline because they are two parts of a Markan sandwich and thus belong together. The symmetry of the sequence of doublets is too consistent to be accidental and must thus point to the interpretation of *Mark*. Symbolically, the point of the sequence was to demonstrate the difference between a career in which

Jesus was satisfied with crumbs and his previous high demands upon Israel for bearing fruit.

The changed details of the feeding stories made that clear. In the earlier event, Jesus had asked the twelve to feed the crowd; now, he intended from the beginning to do it himself. In the earlier event, the audience was seated in fifties and hundreds to represent the sons of the prophets; now, they were not. In the earlier event, the leftover crumbs filled twelve baskets to represent Israel; now, they numbered seven. There is a long established tradition that seven was a special number representing the Gentiles. Despite the consistency of that tradition with the fact that in *Acts* 6 seven Hellenists chosen as men to feed others on broken bread, there is nothing in *Mark* to support such a tradition.

After the 4,000 were dismissed, Jesus and the twelve talked about the two feeding stories while returning by boat from the feeding site. Jesus assumed that the twelve would automatically know the meanings of both twelve and seven in relationship to the baskets of leftover crumbs. If seven was supposed to have a meaning which any biblically informed reader in Mark's day would have known about, that meaning must have referred to the number of days in the week, specifically to the seventh day, the sabbath. Sabbath observance had earlier served as the divisive issue between Jesus and the Capernaum Jews, particularly the Pharisees. It is likely that the seven baskets were to represent Jesus' reconciliation with ritualistic Israel. It would mean that Jesus had dropped his objections to Pharisiac ritualism even though he was to warn the twelve about the leaven of the Pharisees and Herod, namely their belief in miraculous proofs. Note the distinction. Jesus' opposition was not to the Pharisees as a party. His opposition was to particular positions promulgated by the Pharisees and not to others. In this case, he was probably indicating a willingness to be reconciled to Judaism which included ritualism, but not miraculousness as proof of holiness.

In the feeding of the 5,000, Jesus had viewed the twelve as the sons of the prophets through whose faithful service he was to succeed. They were to feed the crowds. Even when they failed, they were still to be the New Israel. In the feeding of the 4,000, Jesus now viewed the twelve as part of Old Israel. He expected nothing special from them. He intended by miracle to restore to Israel, even to ritualistic, Pharisaic Israel the capacity to hear and see truth. Nothing was expected of the twelve. They were not to be feeders; they along with other Jews were the crumbs with which Jesus was to be satisfied. Mark might well have appreciated the modern idiom: what a crumby group of followers.

NEW TEMPTATION FROM THE PHARISEES

The logic of Jesus' new approach to his aspirations was becoming obvious even to his opponents. As Elijah-Jesus he was relying exclusively upon miracle with no concern either for the judgmental preaching of repentance or the compassionate offer of forgiveness.

The Pharisees approached him accordingly, seeking from him an Elijah-type proof that the source of his miraculousness was godly rather than satanic. They asked him for a proof of his divinity, a sign from heaven which would thoroughly substantiate his identity as Elijah, the Holy One from God. When the unclean spirits had tempted Jesus in that manner, their emphasis was on Jesus' holiness and righteousness in contrast with the recalcitrance of the masses. Not so with the Pharisees. They bluntly stated the issue in terms of power. That is how it had been with Elijah in the contest with the priests of the Baalim. Elijah had called down fire from the sky, a sign which proved that Jahweh, not Baal, was the true god.

The motivation of the Pharisees is not clear to us. On one hand, they were like the church which has largely sided with them against Jesus on this issue. It is the church which has argued thousands of times that the divinity of Jesus was documented by his miracles and especially by the miracle of resurrection. The Pharisees may well have been like the church, the sincere, conscientious religious majority throughout the centuries who have been more impressed with Jesus' miraculous power than with the criterion which Mark was ultimately to propose as the key to Jesus' sonship.

On the other hand, the Pharisees may have intended a trap based on a law from Jewish Bible.

"If a prophet arises among you, or a dreamer of dreams, and gives you a sign or wonder, and the sign or wonder comes to pass, and if he says, 'Let us go after other gods,' which you have not known, 'and let us serve them,' you shall not listen to the words of that prophet or to that dreamer of dreams; for the Lord your God is testing you, to know whether you love the Lord your God with all your heart and with all your soul." (Deut. 13. 1-5)

The Pharisees had once accused Jesus of blasphemy, a charge very similar to "going after other gods". If this thought was still in their minds they would not have been impressed by a sign even if Jesus had offered one.

Jesus' response was clear. He refused to give any sign, any miraculous proof of his identity, to his entire generation. But by doing so, he was also resisting or denying his Elijah identity. Other than the encounter with the Pharisees he had no reason to do so. Since his return from Tyre and Sidon he himself had not failed in any respect, nor had he been disappointed in any audience response. He thus had no reason to conclude that his newly adopted Elijah-Elisha miraculous model was inadequate. In each of the following events, however, the failure motif was to be dominant. The Pharisaic challenge may have alerted Jesus to the hertofore hidden conflict between the Deuteronomic law and the example of Elijah.

The doublet for this pericope is so short that it is difficult for us to draw any sharp comparisons from it. In the earlier story, Jesus had sent his disciples on ahead in a boat and he had gone to the hills to pray, apparently seeking guidance from God. On the latter occasion, the argument with the Pharisees had occurred while he was on board a boat with his disciples, and he had refused to provide a sign from God.

THE FINAL BOAT TRIP

Jesus and the twelve prepared to sail to Dalmanutha. This time there was no mention of a task assigned to the sailors, whereas in the doublet they had been left on their own to row against a headwind. There was only a discussion of the danger in the leaven of the Pharisees and Herod. The twelve thought that Jesus was talking about bakery bread which had been multiplied for the 5,000 and 4,000 and thus missed the entire point. Jesus expected them to understand, thus indicating that the healing of the deaf-mute ought to have been symbolically sufficient to have cured their failure to understand.

When the twelve indicated that they had no idea what Jesus was talking about, he learned that they were still both deaf and blind, and that he himself was consequently mute. The symbolic cure of the deaf-mute had not succeeded in its intended spiritual purpose. The attentive reader of *Mark* would now expect an attempt to heal a blind person, and would expect it to fail also.

In the doublet, the boat bound for Bethsaida had landed at Gennesaret. Now, the intended destination was Dalmanutha, but the boat arrived at Bethsaida. Earlier, when Jesus had dismissed the fishermen from his service and had sent them to their symbolic home in Bethsaida a storm of temptation had driven them instead to Gennesaret and had kept them in his retinue. Now, when Jesus was trying miraculously to heal their spiritual blindness and deafness, their comprehension, their continued failure to understand sent them home despite Jesus' intentions. The entire story functioned for Mark as a symbol, as did the other boat incidents, and had no influence on subsequent events or relationships between Jesus and the twelve. In event fact, they did not go home; they physically stayed with him. In meaning, however, they remained as those who did not comprehend; they had not reached the spiritual designation at which he hoped they would arrive.

THE TWICE-HEALED BLIND MAN

In his encounter with the blind man, Jesus experienced for the first time a significant failure of his miraculous power. It took two acts of magic to heal the man. In the surface story, the man responded to the first effort by seeing people who looked like trees walking. Only after a second attempt by Jesus was the man able to see clearly. As in the healing of the deaf-mute the imitative techniques of popular magic were employed: spitting on the man's eyes and laying hands on him.

Even at the surface level, the incident points to the likelihood of failure. Instead of a command, such as Jesus had authoritatively used many earlier times in his career, he asked a question, "Do you see anything?" The uncertainty grew out of the sandwich nature of the event. The confidence in miraculous restoration of spiritual sight and hearing had been eroded in Jesus by the aftermath of the feeding of the 4,000. The twelve could not yet understand even such simple truths as the meanings of the numbers twelve and seven. The question, "Do you see anything?", was comparable to the question he had asked the twelve: "Having eyes do you not see?" All Jesus could do was try harder the second time, with little hope of success.

ACTUAL FAILURE BY THE TWELVE

As a literary device, Mark's use of the story of the twice-healed blind man to introduce the account of the conversation on the road to Caesarea Philippi was one of his most masterful strokes. Each pericope illuminates the other, and the combination makes exceptionally clear the point of the actual event which might otherwise be missed.

When Jesus asked the twelve what popular opinion was in regard to Jesus' identity, they gave him the answer of Herod and the Herodians: Jesus was John the Baptizer or Elijah or another of the prophets resurrected. Jesus had just recently warned them against such an answer: the leaven of Herod.

When Jesus asked the twelve for their own opinion as to his identity, Peter (Rocky) apparently answered for all of them: "You are the messiah," that is, you are the leader for whom we Jews have been waiting. The words were different, but the meaning was the same as in the popular answer. Elijah was the messiah whom Israel had been expecting. To be the messiah would be to recognize oneself as the holy one of God, God's anointed (the literal root meaning of messiah). This was the very temptation which Jesus had been carefully seeking to avoid even while he had been conceiving himself as the new Elijah.

As in all the temptations of Jesus, according to *Mark*, the wrong was a subversion of the right. The temptation was related to a genuine truth. As *Mark's* opening sentence had indicated, Jesus was indeed the messiah, the son of God. How could it be that Peter's words were at once unvarnished truth and at the same time temptation for Jesus? The answer was that Peter was the half-healed blind man of the acted parable, he who saw people who looked like trees walking. Peter saw the truth, but he saw it as error. He saw the messiah, but the messiah whom he saw was not the messiah of the crucifixion which Jesus was to become. It is more likely that Peter saw the messiah of the mount of transfiguration: the heavenly figure clothed in unearthly whiteness, perhaps *Daniel's* Son of man on the clouds of heaven.

Jesus' initial reply was to define the word messiah for the first time in such a way that it included the forthcoming death of the son of man. Peter rebuked Jesus for such an answer; and Jesus recognized that Peter's half-blind answer was satanic. Jesus thus learned that Satan could wear the disguise of one of Jesus' own followers. Something in Peter's vision of the messiah was tempting to Jesus in this new setting, so much so that he sought to put it behind him.

Jesus spoke plainly in response to Peter's identification of Jesus as messiah. The reader of *Mark* knows that such could not previously have been the case. Speaking plainly, i.e. not in parables, depended upon having an audience which saw and heard with comprehension. Where the latter did not occur the former was impossible. The conversation in the boat after feeding of the 4,000, and the acted parable of the twice-healed blind man had implied that the twelve had not yet learned to see or to hear with understanding. The satanic quality of Peter's intention proved his half blindness. The necessary conclusion is that it was impossible for Jesus to speak plainly.

Jesus intended to speak plainly, just as he had intended to heal the sight and hearing of the twelve and had intended to do for them what he had previously asked them to do for themselves. He failed in the restoration of their sight and hearing. He failed to change them by doing their tasks for them. The logical pattern would suggest some failure in his present attempt to speak plainly. Thus the reader is alerted that Mark was developing some new theme by reference to Jesus' plainly spoken words.

CHAPTER SIX
EASY VICTORY: MIRACULOUS RESURRECTION

Jesus' reply to Peter's affirmation of messiahship opens up for the reader one of the most complex and intriguing interpretative problems in *The Gospel of Mark*. The overall problem consists of four separate sub-problems, each stemming from Jesus' single sentence answer.

> "And he began to teach them that the son of man must suffer many things, and be rejected by the elders and the chief priests and the scribes, and be killed, and after three days rise again." (*Mark* 8.31)

In that sentence Jesus reidentified himself with the Son of man, predicted accurately both his death and resurrection, specified that the resurrection would occur on the third day, and placed the blame for his suffering and death upon the chief priests, scribes, and elders, i.e. upon the top Jewish leadership in Jerusalem. That sentence, with modifications, was to be repeated twice more in *Mark*.

> "The son of man will be delivered into the hands of men, and they will kill him; and when he is killed, after three days he will rise." (*Mark* 9.31)
> "Behold, we are going up to Jerusalem; and the son of man will be delivered to the chief priests and the scribes, and they will condemn him to death, and deliver him to the Gentiles; and they will mock him, and spit upon him, and scourge him, and kill him; and after three days he will rise." (*Mark* 10.33-34)

The three predictions, together with their intervening material, constitute what is known as the passion prediction unit. It has two significant consequences. First, it marked an immediately important shift in Jesus' career plans. Second, it pointed with great accuracy to the events of passion week at the end of Jesus' life and thus introduced for the first time in *Mark* the elements of Mark's final answer to Jesus' basic dilemma about Father and son.

Who Was Predicted to Kill Jesus?

The interpretative problem was complicated because in each of the three predictions Jesus changed the identity of the culprits. Mark's penchant for theological geography contributes to the complexity of the problem. The first passion prediction blamed only the Jerusalem Jewish leadership. It was spoken in foreign territory among the villages of Caesarea Philippi. The second prediction blamed men in general and was spoken in Galilee, but Jesus would not let anyone other than the twelve know that he was in Galilee. This was the only time in his career that he was successful in hiding his whereabouts. The final prediction blamed foreigners, and was spoken in Judea on the road going up to Jerusalem. Note the pattern.

Spoken in foreign territory   Blamed Jewish leadership

Spoken in Galilee, secretly   Blamed men in general

Spoken in Jewish territory   Blamed foreign leadership

The pattern is so symmetrically balanced that it must have been intentional on the author's part.

One explanatory clue comes from the Elijah-Elisha stories in Jewish Bible. The villages of Caesarea Philippi are in the same general area as Damascus, Syria, a city with which both Elijah and Elisha were associated. Both Jesus and Elijah made two trips northward into Gentile territory, the first to the Tyre-Sidon region, the second to the Damascus region. On the first, Elijah was recalled to Israel with good news of rain to end a drought and with a miraculous sign sent by God in Elijah's contest with the priests of the Baalim. So it was with Jesus on his return from Tyre and Sidon. He showed the miraculous signs of healing the deaf-mute and the blind man, and fed the 4,000. On Elijah's second northern journey, to Damascus, he was called back to prepare for his death. He was to anoint a new king of Syria, a new king of Israel, and a new prophet to replace himself. The parallel is striking, because Jesus' first awareness of his own impending death stemmed from his visit to the Damascus area.

I suspect that Mark intentionally referred to the Syrian area by the name of Caesarea Philippi rather than as Syria or Damascus because of his interest in the name Philip. Philip was a purely Greek name. One of the twelve was named Philip. Herod's brother, the one whose wife he took, was named Philip and was a ruler. For Mark now to refer to an area named jointly for the great foreign ruler, Caesar, and for Philip seems too much for simple coincidence. However, Mark's specific reason for doing so seems not to be obvious unless he was merely underscoring the foreignness motif.

Assuming that Mark was conscious of the parallelism between the visits of Elijah and Jesus to Syrian territory, other geographical parallels between the two become important. Most of Elijah's career was spent in Samaria, the capital city of the northern kingdom of Israel. When it came time for Elijah to die, however, he went from Gilgal to Bethel to Jericho to the Jordan, all locations within Judea. So with Jesus. Most of his career was based on Galilee, but all of the events of his passion occurred in Judea.

The major conclusion to be drawn from such parallelism is that Jesus was again consciously modeling his career on an Elijah pattern. Specifically, he was exploring for himself what it would mean to know in advance that he was to die and that he was to choose and prepare his successors. His foreboding of death thus came not so much from a sense of failure as it did from a continuation of his already well established procedure of probing the Elijah imagery to its depth to discover if it contained the clue which would enable him to fulfill *Malachi's* prediction of reconciliation between fathers and children. The sense of failure, however, should not be entirely eliminated. Jesus had already discovered several Elijah patterns to be inadequate for the *Malachi* dream; when he picked up the death motif from Elijah he was scraping the bottom of the Elijah barrel.

The same Elijah story which introduced the death motif also provided a pattern for the shift of blame in Jesus' passion predictions. When Elijah was to prepare for his death, he was also to anoint new kings for Syria and Israel, tasks which were actually performed posthumously for him by Elisha. Both Jehu who replaced the dynasty of Ahab in Israel, and Hazael who replaced Benhadad in Syria were murderers many times over. One was as evil as the other. It was this fact in the Elijah tradition which may have triggered in Jesus the awareness that he would fare no better at the hands of the Hellenized men of Galilee or the totally foreign political rulers of Jerusalem that he would at the hands of Jewish officialdom.

PREDICTION OF RESURRECTION

The death of Elijah provided a major clue for the predictions of resurrection because it was a non-death in two respects. Instead of dying in the ordinary sense, Elijah was carried to heaven by a chariot of fire and horses of fire. His mantle fell immediately upon Elisha who took up Elijah's tasks and in significant ways relived Elijah's life: the first new Elijah. The combination of the disappearance of Elijah's body and the reappearance of Elijah's leadership in Elisha was the source of the widespread Jewish conviction that Elijah would be resurrected or reincarnated at the Day of Judgment.

For Jesus to investigate the applicability of Elijah's death motif for himself brought with it the requirement that he also investigate the resurrection motif. Specifically, Jesus had to explore what it would mean for him to have a death which would be a nondeath. As described in *Mark*, it would mean for him to be dead on three consecutive days and to awaken automatically on the third day. There would be no risk of staying dead, or at least no more of a risk than all men have of not waking up when they go to sleep each day.

Resurrection on the Third Day

Why on the third day? Why not on the second or the fourth or the seventh? In the Elijah-Elisha material there was a mysterious connection between the number three and the concept of resurrection. Elijah lay three times on the corpse of the son of the widow of Zarephath to restore him to life. Elijah sought three times to die alone before being raised to heaven. Elisha's sons of the prophets sought the corpse of Elijah for three days before giving up the search and admitting that it had been taken away from earth. Elisha once performed a resurrection by having his staff laid once on a child's face and then by stretching himself twice on the corpse for a total of three contacts. Elisha himself died immediately after King Joash struck the ground with magical arrows only three times. When another man's corpse was placed in a grave with Elisha the man was resurrected as soon as his corpse touched Elisha's bones.

It has often been argued that a scientific proof of the historical accuracy of the New Testament resurrection narratives is the fact that there was no specific justification in Jewish Bible for the resurrection occurring on the third day. The argument says, in effect, that there must have been some kind of an experience among the disciples *on the third day* to account for the resurrection narratives, since they are so insistent upon that particular detail. It would not be proper to argue that nothing did happen on the third day. But it is equally improper to argue that the New Testament narratives can be accounted for only by an historical event on the third day. The consistency of those narratives with the Elijah-Elisha material linking resurrection and the number three is much too persuasive to be ignored. In particular the parallel between the experience of the disciples and that of the sons of the prophets is instructive. Neither the sons of the prophets nor the twelve were actually present at the death of their respective master. Both were persuaded on the third day that something significant had occurred.

Jesus as the Son of Man

If Jesus was investigating only the relevance of Elijah's death and resurrection for himself, why did he further complicate the issue by referring to himself as the son of man? He did so in each of three predictions. The answer to that question lies in the other principal resurrection tradition in Jewish scripture. Recall that Jesus had earlier recognized the connection between Elijah-Jesus as prophet of doom and the son of man as prophet of doom. Now Mark provides implicit evidence that Jesus recognized a similar connection between Elijah-Jesus as dead and resurrected, and the son of man in relationship to death and resurrection.

The primary material in that tradition comes from *Ezekiel.* The man Ezekiel was addressed throughout his book as son of man. As son of man, he was commanded to speak but was made dumb, unable to speak, because of the rebelliousness of Israel. As son of man, he argued with the elders of Israel who were untrue to God. As son of man, he spoke in riddles. As son of man, he had also been associated with Tyre and Sidon and had preached against those cities. Each of those activities of the son of man were closely comparable to activities of Jesus in the Markan material immediately preceding the passion predictions or in them.

The most important *Ezekiel* passage, for Mark's present purpose, was the son of man's vision of the resurrection of the bodies of all dead Jews whose dry bones were strewn throughout a particular valley. The resurrected Jews were to symbolize all Israel, and they were to become the New Israel. All of old, living Israel would be destroyed; the only surviving Israel would be the new resurrectred Israel. This concept was consistent with *Mark's* flow of thought. Early in Jesus' career, Mark had defined Israel in terms of all Galilee, later in terms of only the twelve disciples, and now as Jesus alone, the resurrected Israel. Mark's rhythm: from the crowds to the elite to the one.

An additional confirming fact from *Ezekiel* which helps substantiate Mark's reliance on it is that the next stage in Jesus' career after resurrection-as-easy-victory was to be exploration of Davidic political messiahship. In *Ezekiel,* the son of man proclaimed that David was to be the king over two resurrected Jewish kingdoms associated with the names of Judah and Joseph, and that he would unite the two as one. Thus Mark's interest in the son of David flowed naturally from his references to son of man.

Mark 8.38 makes clear that the *Ezekiel* imagery of the son of man had been transformed in Jesus' mind into *Daniel* imagery of the Son of man. The shift was subtle but important. When the son of man was resurrected, he would be glorified. He would appear in glory as the Son of man. His victory over death would be publicly visible. In fact, many of those in the multitude to whom he was speaking, he predicted, would see that victory during their own lifetimes. By his resurrection, Jesus would receive the power to do what *Daniel* said the Son of man would do and what *Malachi* said Elijah would do, to judge between the sinful and the righteous.

The emphasis on the biblical parallels for the son of man title should not be permitted to obscure the natural meanings of the term in Jesus' own setting. The prediction of the suffering and death of the son of man was consistent with earlier humanistic uses of the title: the sons of men for whom the sabbath was made, the sons of men who could forgive sins on earth, the sons of men who were to do good rather than obey rules. Likewise, the ambiguity of the earlier uses was also present again in the glorification of the resurrected Son of man who would appear in the glory of his Father: the Son of man who was Lord of the sabbath, the Son of man who exercised his miraculous authority in healing.

In the *Ezekiel* sense of the humanistic son of man, Jesus had functioned as the prophet who could not speak other than in riddles (parables). He had been limited throughout his career in that regard.

But now, having made the attempt by miracle to restore sight and hearing to his audiences, he had thus also sought to escape the limitations of *Ezekiel's* son of man and to become *Daniel's* glorified Son of man.

The Guarantee of Easy Victory

The transition from son of man to Son of man, from suffering to glory, was to occur without risk according to this entire section of Jesus' career. It would be true for himself; it would be true for others. *Malachi,* as Jesus knew, assumed that Elijah would be resurrected. *Malachi* further promised that if the Jews would faithfully bring their tithes and offerings to God's temple, God would guarantee rewards. Jesus apparently picked up that idea and made it his dominant concern in the resurrection-as-easy-victory stage. He predicted of himself that he would suffer death and be automatically rewarded. He promised others that similar rhythms would work for them.

"For whoever would save his life will lose it; and whoever loses his life for my sake and the gospel's will save it." (*Mark* 8.35)
He gave the twelve a formula for success.
"If anyone would be first, he must be last of all and servant of all. Whoever receives one such child in my name receives me; and whoever receives me, receives not me but him who sent me." (*Mark* 9.35-37)

The guarantee would be equally as certain for small deeds as for large ones.

"For he that is not against us is for us. For truly, I say to you, whoever gives you a cup of water to drink because you bear the name of Christ, will by no means lose his reward." (*Mark* 9.40-41)
The rewards were to be proportionate to the amount of service.
"Truly, I say to you, there is no one who has left house or brothers or sisters or mother or father or children or lands, for my sake and for the gospel, who will not receive a hundred fold in this time, houses and brothers and sisters and mothers and children and lands, with persecutions, and in the age to come eternal life. But many that are first will be last, and the last first." (*Mark* 10.29-31)

Despite the certainty of the reward, the investment of oneself would be too high a price for most people to pay. In Jesus' case, the price was the willingness to die, to take some risk of staying dead. In the case of others, some of the prices specified by Jesus were absolute marital fidelity (as *Malachi* had insisted), yielding to God's rule as innocently as children do, obeying all the commandments and exceeding them by giving away all one's possessions, enduring persecutions, and refraining from causing anyone who belives in Jesus to sin. Such a list went far beyond the present capacity of Peter-of-the-Rocky-Soil and the Sons of Thunder, to say nothing of the rest of the twelve and the crowds.

The passion prediction section is well sprinkled with accounts of the failure of the twelve. Nine of them were unable to cast an unclean spirit out of a boy. All twelve debated with each other as to which of them was the greatest. John had spoken for all of them in forbidding another man to cast out demons in Jesus' name. They had failed to understand Jesus' teachings about marital fidelity and had to ask him privately. They had forbidden little children to come to Jesus. And, as the crushing blow, Jacob (James) and John concluded the passion prediction unit by asking Jesus for reserved seats in his glory without having to go through the ordeal of persecution to earn the privilege. In a preliminary symbolic way Jesus introduced to them the concept of the cup, all that he could promise them, as the opportunity for persecution without any certainty of reward.

In the passion prediction unit, the definition of resurrection was essentially different from the definition in the pericopes of Jairus' daughter and Herod's belief in the reincarnation of John the Baptizer. Jairus' daughter had been resurrected in the sense of being brought back of life by the miraculous intervention of a healer. She herself played no role in the incident except to have been ill and dead. In the Herod-type belief in the reincarnation of the deceased hero, the return to life was likewise without effort on the part of the resurrected one. If Jesus actually was Elijah, or John, or any other of the prophets he had become so by birth and not by merit. But now in the passion predictions, resurrection was conceived as reward for willingness to suffer and die. Resurrection was not to be a gift to a passive recipient; it was to be a miracle under the active control of the recipient. It was to be a guaranteed result purchased with a specified price, the trade of a present value for a greater value later on.

Note that in such a transaction, death is essentially a non-death. Death as preliminary to guaranteed revivification loses the principal characteristic of death: permanence. It takes on more of the nature of a long nap from which one confidently expects to awaken, a lost weekend followed by restored activity. In this sense, the resurrection predictions designated the death predictions as Elijah-type of non-death, and made appropriate the special role of Elijah in the transfiguration.

THE SPECIAL ROLE OF THE TRANSFIGURATION SYMBOL

The entire passion prediction unit was symbolically crystallized in the incident of the transfiguration. In the surface story, Jesus took the Big Three (Peter, Jacob, John) alone with him up a high mountain and appeared to them there in garments of unearthly whiteness. The Big Three saw Elijah "with Moses" speaking to Jesus. The Big Three wanted to stay there permanently in such company, but the voice of God interrupted to inform them that Jesus was God's son and that they should listen to him. Elijah and Moses disappeared and the four men returned to the other nine disciples, meanwhile discussing Elijah on the way.

The heart of the story is in the Elijah-Elisha imagery. The fact that Elijah appeared "with Moses" must have been Mark's way of calling attention to a peculiar relationship between the two. In *Malachi,* the sentence preceding the only reference to Elijah's name called attention to the statutes and ordinances of Moses (*Mal.* 4.4), implying that it was Elijah's task to see to it that Moses' laws were obeyed. In a resurrection context, there is an interesting parallelism between Moses and Elijah. The story of Moses' death reads as follows.

> "So Moses the servant of the Lord died there in the land of Moab..., and the Lord buried him in the valley in the land of Moab opposite Beth-peor; but no man knows the place of his burial to this day. Moses was a hundred and twenty years old when he died; his eye was not dim, nor his natural force abated......And Joshua the son of Nun was full of the spirit of wisdom, for Moses had laid his hands on him; so the people of Israel obeyed him, and did as the Lord had commanded Moses." (*Deut.* 34.5-9)

Such a death was sufficiently close to being a non-death that the tradition arose that Moses, like Elijah, would return from the grave. It seems likely that the Elijah story itself was rooted in such a tradition, although I know of no concrete evidence to support such a supposition. The relationship between Moses and Joshua was certainly comparable to the relationship between Elijah and Elisha, with the spirit of the master falling on the disciple. To further complicate the parallelism, the meaning of the name Joshua was exactly the same as that of Jesus and Elisha: God is Salvation.

A minor detail of the transfiguration, in typical Markan fashion, came from the Elisha stories. In *II Kings* 6.1 ff., the sons of the prophets said to Elisha, "Let us go to the Jordan and each of us get there a log, and let us make a place for us to dwell there." This was comparable to the Big Three wanting to make dwelling places on the mountain to house them and the heroes.

When John the Baptizer had wanted people to accept him as Elijah, he had costumed himself in Elijah's garb. The result was instant recognition. Jesus had never resorted to such an identification gimmick. His role as Elijah had always been implicit, and thereby recognizable only to the eyes of faith. Recognition had come but always ambiguously—symbolized by scources such as Satan, his unclean spirits, and Peter, each of whom saw something in the Elijah-Jesus identity which was temptative to Jesus. Now, at the transfiguration, the Big Three saw the proof they had been looking for. Elijah-Jesus was dressed not in the hair garments of the wilderness but in celestial garments such as the messianic Son of man coming on the clouds of heaven would wear. They were not alone in such a temptation.

92

Just as it had been the spirit of holiness which had led Jesus from his baptism to the symbolic wilderness in which he first confronted Satan, so now it was Jesus who led the Big Three to the high mountain to see his heavenliness. It was his own temptation which had culminated in theirs. It was he who had predicted that miraculousness would lead him to easy victory. It was he who had told them that the Son of man would come "in the glory of his Father with the holy angels." It was he who had spoken already of automatic reward for willingness to lose one's life. No wonder they saw him transfigured—not just on the symbolic mountain occasion, but daily in their dealings with him.

The Big Three were overawed on the mountain by the experience of being simultaneously in the presence of three heroes such as Moses, Elijah, and Jesus. They proposed to stay there forever. Then, from the voice of God Himself, came a rebuke. The disciples were not to look toward Elijah and Moses in connection with Jesus. They were to listen only to Jesus who was God's beloved son. At the surface level the voice was addressing the three.

At a deeper level, God's warning was addressed to Jesus. It was he who had been "seeing" himself in the company of Elijah with Moses throughout his public career. It was he who had consistently day after day failed to see himself as son of God the Father. In the very events of the passion prediction unit, Jesus had been titling himself son of man, not son of God. Even when he referred to God as Father, God was Father of the Son of man.

"For whoever is ashamed of me and my words in this adulterous and sinful generation, of him will the Son of man also be ashamed, when he comes in the glory of his Father with the holy angels." (*Mark* 8.38)

This was the only occasion between Jesus' baptism and Gethsemane in which he referred to God as Father. Even though the reference was to the Father of the wrong concept of son, the use of the word for the first time indicated that Jesus had discovered the right answer to his quest even though it was still couched in the half-blind, Satanic quality of Peter's confession and Jesus' own transfiguration of suffering sonship into non-earthly resurrected Sonship. The fact that Jesus was not to refer to God as Father again until Gethsemane was an indication that some of the-as-yet-to-be-explored possibilities were not as close to the final truth.

The symbolic disappearance of Elijah on the mountaintop was reinforced by the conversation between Jesus and the three on their way back down. Jesus asked them to keep the event a secret, a standard Markan indication that he had exposed his inner self to them in a way which he knew to be temptative. It was then that the Big Three raised aloud for the first time the question of the relationship between Jesus and Elijah. Specifically they asked why the scribes say that Elijah must come first. He did not reply to the question about the scribes. His answer must have seemed cryptic to them.

"Elijah does come first to restore all things and how is it written of the son of man, that he should suffer many things and be treated with contempt? But I tell you that Elijah has come, and they did to him whatever they pleased, as it is written of him." (*Mark* 9.12-13)

In those words, Elijah seemed to become past tense in Jesus' life, to be succeeded by the Son of man. Elijah-Jesus seemed to die just as Elijah-John had died in the symbol of the beheading by Herod. Jesus' words seemed to indicate that all Elijah motifs had failed because men had treated Elijah-John and Elijah-Jesus according to their will. There was no regret in Jesus' backward look. It had been necessary for him to plumb the depths of the Elijah tradition. It had been in the power of that tradition that he had originally responded to Elijah-John and had subsequently exposed the inadequacies of so much of that tradition still accepted by other Jews.

In the Elijah traditions previously cited by Jesus there was no hint that Elijah would suffer. In the statement by Jesus on the way down the mountain, Jesus specified Elijah's mistreatment, "As it is written of him." By those words Jesus announced that he had in mind a specific passage in scripture. By making the reference explicit, he may have been suggesting that the scriptural reference was much less obvious than many others which, according to *Mark*, the listener or reader was supposed to supply automatically.

The most likely candidate for the passage Jesus had in mind is *Zechariah* 13.4-6.

"On that day every prophet will be ashamed of his vision when he prophesies; he will not put on a hairy mantle in order to deceive, but he will say, 'I am no prophet, I am a tiller of the soil; for the land has been my possession since my youth.' And if one asks him, 'What are these wounds on your back?' He will say, 'The wounds I received in the house of my friends'."

The "hairy mantle" seemed to be an obvious reference to Elijah's identifying garb, the mark of a prophet. The prophet who wore Elijah's mantle without deceit would be pierced by his parents, wounded by his friends. Such a passage would justify Jesus' assertion that Elijah had suffered, "as it is written of him."

If the answer about Elijah's suffering had been limited to Elijah alone there would be no problem. However, Jesus also said that it was written in scripture that the Son of man must suffer and be treated with contempt. I am not aware of any explicit reference to suffering of anyone in Jewish Bible who bore the title son of man. Certainly suffering would be inconsistent with the Danielic vision of the supernatural Son of man on the clouds of heaven. The only possibilities of which I know are the references to the suffering of the sons of Jacob in *Psalm* 22 and the suffering of the "suffering servant" more than other sons of men in *Isaiah* 53. Jesus was to repeat during passion week the claim that the son of man would suffer according to scripture.

It was a fact of considerable importance in *The Gospel of Mark* that Jesus both abandoned the Elijah imagery and arrived at its highest significance (Elijah as sufferer) at the same time. Jesus' own reconciliation to the Father was to come through his suffering. That was not yet fully known to Jesus on the mountain of transfiguration, but the Markan shift in that direction was to be fairly rapid thereafter.

The Shift to Davidic Imagery

It was at this point in his book that Mark began a subtle but dramatic shift away from Elijah and toward David as the messiah figure. Most of the components of the shift were scripturally grounded. *Zechariah's* prophet wearing the hairy mantle without deceit was to do so on that day when "there shall be a fountain opened for the house of David and the inhabitants of Jerusalem to cleanse them from sin and uncleanness." (*Zech.* 13.1) Earlier in *Zechariah* it was Joshua the priest who was to be cleansed in the presence of "my servant the Branch." (*Zech.* 3.8) The "Branch" was a traditional messianic title. Remember that Joshua and Jesus were Hebrew and Greek names with identical meanings: God Is Salvation; and that Mark would have read the name Jesus in his version of *Zechariah.*

> "Take from the exiles silver and gold, and make a crown, and set it upon the head of Joshua (Jesus), the son of Jehozadak, the high priest; and say to him, 'Thus says the Lord of hosts, "Behold, the man whose name is the Branch: for he shall grow up in his place, and he shall build the temple of the Lord" '." (*Zech.* 3.8)

All of that was to happen in connection with the rule of David or his son. It was originally Solomon, David's son, who was to build the temple. Furthermore, according to *Zechariah,* the results of the role of the Branch were to be like those traditionally associated with Solomon's reign.

> "In that day. . . ., every one of you will invite his neighbor under his vine and under his fig tree." (*Zech.* 3.10)
> "And Judah and Israel dwelt in safety, from Dan even to Beer-sheba, every man under his vine and under his fig tree, all the days of Solomon." (*I Kings* 4.25)

The shift from Elijah to David stemmed primarily from the two books in Jewish Bible in which there was strong connections between Elijah imagery and David imagery. In *Ezekiel,* the son of man motif, derived from Elijah, culminated in a vision of a resurrected Israel to be governed by David. In *Zechariah,* Davidic themes were related to messiahship. These emphases on David were enough to insure that Jesus could not have completed his investigation of the adequacy of Elijah patterns without also exploring the Davidic possibilities.

Another Davidic scriptural possibility to be considered was that the predictions of Jesus' suffering found their strongest scriptural justification in *Psalms,* traditionally associated with David. There is no direct quotation in the passion predictions from *Psalms,* but the final passion prediction in *Mark* 10 did introduce the theme of mocking, one of the details from *Psalm* 22 which is the psalm most influential in *Mark's* crucifixion narrative. Thus, in several ways the concern for Elijah's death led Jesus to turn his attention toward discovering what there was in the David material in scripture which could help him find reconciliation with his Father.

In the two final passion predictions Jesus recognized that, as Elijah-Jesus, his opponents had not been only the Jerusalem hierarchy. They had also been the crowds of Galilee, those who would have crushed him. When Jesus had occasion to utter a second passion prediction, in Galilee, he corrected it to indicate that the son of man would be killed by ordinary human beings. In the third, he specified the Gentiles in addition to the Jews.

THE LAST SYMBOLIC TEMPTATION

At the base of the mountain of transfiguration, the other nine disciples were arguing with the scribes about an unspecified topic in the midst of a great crowd. Seeing Jesus the crowd ran up to him, and one person in the crowd told Jesus of his deaf and dumb son whom the nine disciples had been unable to heal. The father was not sure that his son could be helped, but pled with Jesus to help, "if you can."

"If you can! All things are possible to him who believes!"

That reply of Jesus put into a single sentence all the temptations of his public career. In the immediate situation it promised the reconciliation of a father and son on the basis of miraculous power alone. In the long run, it made power the answer to everything.

Jesus knew that the entire setting was temptational. The boy's deafness and dumbness was caused by an unclean spirit, the symbol of temptation. The crowd which had already run up to Jesus (9.15) was seen by Jesus to come running together (9.25) as soon as he expressed the power thought aloud. The 9.15 crowd was physical, but the 9.25 crowd was psychological, the crowd's attraction to power. Jesus resisted the crowd's psychological approach by his most decisive resistance to symbolic temptation.

"You dumb and deaf spirit, I command you, come out of him, and never enter him again." (*Mark* 9.25)

The words had a tone of permanence: "never enter him again." In all previous confrontations with temptation, Jesus had somehow or another left the door open for the spirits to return. Jesus knew that the crowds could crush him, but he had entered into crowd settings again and again. He knew that the disciples were unable to bear fruit, but he had postponed cutting himself off from them again and again. He knew that his miraculous power kept him from becoming God's son and being reconciled to his father, but he had returned to its use again and again. This time, symbolically at least, the decision was final. The unclean spirits were never to return again. In the symbolic form of unclean spirits they never did.

96

In actual fact, temptations continued for Jesus until the very end. One of them occurred immediately. When Jesus exorcised the unclean spirit from the boy, the lad appeared to die. Jesus proceeded to "resurrect" him, thus publicly displaying his power almost in the same breath that he used to struggle against displaying it.

Why such an apparent contradiction? Why did Mark describe Jesus as having overcome his final symbolic temptation in chapter nine when temptations were to continue through chapter fifteen? One possible answer is rooted in the fact that the passion predictions were so remarkably like the passion events. Jesus had discovered the exact truth, the truth which would ultimately triumph over temptation. Overcoming the last symbolic temptation was predictive as part of the passion prediction section.

A more adequate explanation is that the "spirit" theme disappears from Mark when Jesus exorcises the unclear spirit from the boy and tells it never to return. It is not only unclean spirits which disappear, but holy spirit also. Spirit had been introduced in *Mark* when Elish-Jesus explored the model of receiving from John-Elijha a double portion of his spirit, as in the original Elijah-Elisha story. It disappeared from the narrative in conjunction with Elijah's disappearance from the Mount of Transfiguration and from any subsequent role in Jesus' exploration of sonship. Both the spirits of uncleanness and the spirit of holiness were integral to the Elijah-Elisha motifs and apparently unrelated to the David and Daniel motifs which were to follow. This further heightens the impression that all references to spirit were intended by Mark in the sense of spirituality rather than in the trinitarian sense of a separate Spirit person.

The problem for Jesus at the chapter nine stage of the book was somewhat the problem that Peter had. Jesus was the half-healed blind man of the acted parable, seeing the truth, but seeing it as temptation. He saw in the Elijah imagery and its extensions the concepts of voluntary death and bodily resurrection, which were to be true, but he saw them as sub-topics under power, which was to be false.

According to *The Gospel of Mark,* Jesus was to pray once more during his life in the Garden of Gethsemane on the occasion when he submitted himself to a proper view of death and resurrection. In chapter nine, when the disciples asked him why they could not cast out the unclean spirit, Jesus explained to them that "this kind cannot be driven out by anything but prayer." As a prediction it was in an important sense a more accurate harbinger of the cross than all three of the passion predictions. In chapter nine, he did not pray even though he talked about prayer; he merely used miracle. But in the Garden of Gethsemane his use of prayer excluded the possibility of miraculous escape. Even when the Big Three disappointed him there again, he was voluntarily powerless to do anything about it.

The healed boy was Jesus himself. He was Jesus as Ezekiel's son of man who had been plagued by the spirit of dumbness. He was Jesus as son of man who had been unable to speak other than in riddling parables as long as others could not hear or see. He was Jesus as son of man who had tried to speak plainly about his death and resurrecion and who had received only a satanic response. He was thus Jesus who suffered from the spirit of dumbness, the son whose Father yearned for his healing in order that Father and Son might be reconciled to each other. He was Jesus who would have to die and be resurrected in a manner other than miraculous power in order for that reconciliation to occur. He was Jesus from whom temptation could be exorcised only by prayer at Gethsemane.

The number of references to sonship and its cognates in the passion prediction section is quite remarkable. We have already noted the son of man title (used six times), the voice of God on the mountain of transfiguration, and the healing of the dumb son. In addition, Jesus used a child to refute the claims of the twelve to greatness (9.33-37), threatened those who "cause one of these little ones to sin" (9.42), forbade the twelve to hinder children coming to him (10.13-16), quoted the commandment "Honor your father and your mother" and heard the response that a rich man had obeyed all the commandments since his youth (10.17-22), addressed the twelve as "Children" (10.24, and used family imagery in his promise of great rewards (10.23-31). The cumulative effect of such references was to underscore the tightening relationship between sonship and the passion prediction section.

Note the number of times in the passion prediction section that reference to sonship was singular rather than plural. The key passage was the voice out of the cloud at the transfiguration: "This is my beloved son; listen to him." Unlike the original promise of God's love at the baptism which included Jesus without necessarily excluding other sons of God, the transfiguration announcement seemed to say in effect, "Jesus is My son, but you others on the mountain are not; therefore, listen to him and not to them." The response of the Big Three was to see "Jesus only."

Following the transfiguration there was the single son from whom the unclean spirit could be exorcised only by prayer and who was resurrected from the dead. After a second prediction of the death and resurrection of the Son of man, Jesus placed a child in the midst of the twelve in order to teach them that "whoever receives one such child in my name, receives me. . . ." Later he said, "Whoever does not receive the kingdom of God like a child shall not enter it." Finally he addressed the disciples as children when he said "There is no one who has left house or brothers. . .for my sake and for the gospel, who will not receive a hundredfold now in this time. . . ." The emphasis on oneness was further underscored by Jesus' use of the example of the rich man who had obeyed all the Mosaic laws but would not give to the poor, and by his definition of marriage as "no longer two but one."

The apparent Markan point of all that is that the solo nature of the gospel had now begun to become obvious. Jesus was no longer seeking to reconcile all Jews to God, nor even an elite minority. He was now working on the models of reconciliation which were one-to-one

98

relationships between a particular person and the Father.

Another interesting Markan motif highlighted in the section is the reference to "cup". In the account of a stranger casting out demons in Jesus' name, the conclusion was that anyone giving a cup of water to one who bears the name of the messiah would be rewarded. However, in the concluding pericope of the section, the request by Jacob (James) and John for seats in glory, the cup turned into a symbol of being a servant, slave of all, and one who serves and gives his life as ransom for many.

The only pericope in the entire passion prediction section which did not involve either the symbolism of cup or sonship is the argument with the Pharisees about marriage and divorce (10.1-12). It represented an interesting reversal of previous roles. Heretofore, it seemed that the Pharisees had been defending old laws and Jesus had been opposing them in the interests of human privilege. Now, however, Jesus insisted upon the rigorous law, no divorce or remarriage after divorce, and the Pharisees sought to justify divorce by a Mosaic exception to the law. Jesus defended his disagreement with Moses by asserting the Moses' ruling was intended only to be temporary because of the hardness of men's hearts at that stage of history. This was another way of saying that Moses was no longer an authority for Jesus' time; the Moses who had disappeared from Jesus' life on the mount of transfiguration was no longer relevant. The same motif was repeated in the instance of the rich man who had obeyed all the commandments. His obedience to commandments was not sufficient to be called obedience to the sovereignty of God.

Thus the passion prediction section, both symbolically and really, widened the gap between Jesus and significant Jewish tradition.

CHAPTER SEVEN
EASY VICTORY: POLITICAL LEADERSHIP

At the end of the passion prediction unit, Jesus had finally predicted that his killers would be Gentiles. He then described Gentile rulers in these words.

"You know that those who are supposed to rule over the Gentiles lord it over them, and their great men exercise authority over them." (*Mark* 10.42)

He explained that it should not be so for his followers, but even in his act of explaining, the concept of easy victory shone through.

"But it shall not be so among you; but whoever would be great among you must be your servant, and whoever would be first among you must be slave of all." (*Mark* 10.43-44)

In such a saying, servanthood is a role played for the purpose of gaining greatness; slavery is a pretense in order to become first. The distinction is between goal and method. If the goal is to be great or to be first, and the method is to be servant or a slave, there is very little genuineness to the servanthood. Jesus at that time explored the possibility that it was in that manner that the son of man, like *Isaiah's* suffering servant, had come "to give his life as a ransom for many." It was a political strategy, an investment, not an act of self-giving.

As noted earlier, in *Ezekiel* the son of man's prediction of the resurrection of Israel included the expectation that David would rule again in a united, powerful kingdom. It thus seemed a natural transition for Jesus as son of man to move from a stage of exploring resurrection motifs to a stage focussed on the possibility of political messiahship.

In the surface story, a blind man named Son of Timaeus (Bartimaeus) was sitting by the road from Jericho to Jerusalem. Despite the fact that Jesus was surrounded by a great crowd of people, he heard Bartimaeus' voice above the crowd, calling him by the political-military messianic title, Son of David. He approved of that title, healed the blind man's sight, received him as a follower in his entourage, and proceeded to make conscious plans for a hero's welcome parade in Jerusalem.

The name Timaeus is likely to have been derived from an Aramaic root meaning "unclean." Thus Bartimaeus would be Son of the Unclean. That name, plus his blindness, virtually guarantees that Mark considered this narrative as another temptation for Jesus. In addition, the word "immediately" was used, as was the recognition that it was the man's own faith which had healed him, both traditional marks of temptation in this Gospel. The event may well have been an acted parable in relationship to the triumphal entry story which follows it, just as the half-healed blind man pericope had been to the story of

Peter's confession which followed it. Mark must have noted the ironic humor in having Jesus tempted by "Son of the Unclean" soon after Jesus had a final victory over the unclean spirit and had then resurrected the resultant corpse. It must have been the temptation which was resurrected.

The title Son of David needs careful scrutiny. In Jewish Bible, much of the career of King David concerned his sons. They included Absalom who rebelled against him, Amnon who raped his half-sister, Adonijah who expected to succeed David as King, and Solomon the son of Bathsheba who did succeed his father. The father's anguish at the death of a son who had sought to murder him probes much more deeply into the meaning of father-son reconciliation than anything in the Elijah-Elisha tradition.

> "O my son Absalom, my son, my son Absalom! Would I had died instead of you. O Absalom, my son, my son!" (*II Samuel* 18.33)

The son of David who was David's actual successor was Solomon, son of David and Bathsheba. The son who, by age, should have ascended to the throne and who sought to do so, was Adonijah. The choice of Solomon by David was consistent with that long tradition in Israel in which an elder brother is supplanted by a chosen brother. The sign of Solomon had been chosen was that Solomon rode into Jerusalem on David's own mule (ass, donkey). When Solomon became king, his intentions were honorable. He promised his father that he would obey the laws of Moses; he promoised Adonijah that his life would be spared. But shortly after David's death, Solomon killed Adonijah and others, and used a murder as a primary method of making the throne secure. It was Solomon who David trusted to have wisdom in dealing with his opponents, a wisdom symbolized by his decision as to which of two harlots was the rightful mother of an infant. It was Solomon who was given the task of constructing the temple in Jerusalem. It was Solomon whose kingdom was once described as follows.

> "And Judah and Israel dwelt in safety, from Dan even to Beersheba, every man under his vine and under his fig tree, all the days of Solomon." (*I Kings* 4.25)

It was Solomon who had a surname, or perhaps a second name: Jeridiah, Beloved of the Lord. Each of those details has a counterpart in the Markan story. One other possibility needs to be considered. Solomon had somewhat the same relationship to David which Elisha had to Elijah and which Joshua had to Moses. Each of the three successors in those pairs did more than follow their masters; they repeated major motifs from their career. In Solomon's case, according to Jewish Bible, the geographical boundaries of his empire remained exactly as they had been under David, although the empire disintegrated almost immediately after this death. It was Solomon who was assigned the task of constructing the temple which David wanted to erect. It was Solomon of whom God spoke to David, saying:

"When your days are fulfilled and you lie down with your fathers, I will raise up your son after you, who shall come forth from your body, and I shall establish his kingdom. He shall build a house for my name, and I will establish the throne of his kingdom forever. I will be his father, and he shall be my son." (*II Samuel* 7.12-14)

Jesus must have read such evidence with mounting excitement. Solomon, like Jesus himself, had once been designated as God's son and named as Beloved of God. It was Solomon who had fulfilled the Elijah-Elisha rhythm by repeating and fulfilling David's rule, and who had fulfilled the Jacob rhythm by supplanting his brother on the throne. It was Solomon whose father David had taught Israel a meaning of father-son relationship which went far deeper than the possibilities inherent in all of the Elijah and Elisha stories. David had demonstrated that a father is willing to give his life for his son. He would not even permit an enemy to be harmed so long as David's own son sought David's life.

Thus to be the son of David was not primarily to be a military-political ruler. To be David's son was to be the son of the father who had most deeply lived in the rhythm of love. Even though in the predictions of *Ezekiel* and *Zechariah,* the son of David was to be a military-political figure, the root reason why Jesus responded positively to the blind man's assertion that Jesus was the son of David was the opportunity which that title provided for investigating father-son reconciliation.

THE TRIUMPHAL ENTRY

Mark's narrative of Jesus' entry into Jerusalem stressed the fact that Jesus intentionally sought to be greeted there as the Davidic messiah, and that he succeeded in doing so. He sent two disciples to procure a colt so that he could fulfill a prophecy from *Zechariah.*

"Lo, your king comes to you;

Triumphant and victorious is he,

Humble and riding on an ass,

On a colt the foal of an ass." (*Zechariah* 9.9)

Either the colt was one kept ready by zealous Jews who were hoping for a messianic claimant, or it was one for whose use Jesus had made prior private arrangements. In either case the two disciples announced only that "the Lord" had need of it, apparently in this context a messianic announcement to the owners of the colt. Note that, as in the original mission of the twelve, Jesus sent disciples to perform a task as a pair. This time the pair succeeded in doing exactly what he asked them to do.

Jesus' messianic intention was also made obvious by the fact that he entered Jerusalem from the Mount of Olives, a location mentioned only twice in Jewish Bible, both times in connection with David. King

David himself went to the Mount of Olives weeping because of the rebellion of his son Absalom and made arrangements there to put down the rebellion without harming his son. *Zechariah* predicted that at the coming of the Davidic messiah

> "The Lord will go forth and fight against those nations as when he fights on a day of battle. On that day his feet shall stand on the Mount of Olives which lies before Jerusalem on the east; and the Mount of Olives shall be split in two from east to west by a very wide valley...." (*Zechariah* 14.3-4)

Two other passages from Jewish Bible provide messianic parallels for the triumphal entry narrative. The most interesting concerns the line, "on which no one has sat." In *I Samuel* 6, the story is told of the Philistines seeking to send the Ark back to Israel. "Two milk cows upon which there has never come a yoke" drew the cart straight to the field of Joshua. The name Joshua was associated with the messiah in both *Haggai* and *Zechariah*. Mark, reading in Greek, would have read it in his copies of Bible as Jesus. Thus, by identifying one Joshua (Jesus) with another, he could have read the Ark story as messianic in its intention. A second parallel concerns the leafy branches spread before Jesus in the parade.

> "Bind the festal procession with branches, up to the horns of the altar." (*Psalms* 118.27)

Psalms 118 is not necessarily messianic, but *Mark* 12.10 quotes from it in a context which makes it clear that Mark considered it to be so.

Mark's interpretation of *Zechariah* 9.9 teaches us something about the author and his book. Hebrew poetry in the Jewish Bible was most often written so that a second line repeated and modified each first line. Thus, for example, in the second couplet of 9.9, the colt in the second line is the same animal as the ass in the first. Mark understood that and properly described Jesus as riding on one animal. Matthew in his Gospel, by contrast, misunderstood it and portrayed Jesus as entering Jerusalem on two animals. Mark must therefore have had more accurate information about Jewish poetry than Matthew despite the long Western tradition that Mark was written for Gentiles, and Matthew for Jews. The dominant outline of *The Gospel of Mark* thus far indicates that its author was primarily interested in the relationship between Jesus and Jewish tradition. The correct use of Hebrew poetry significantly underscores that fact.

ENTERING AND LEAVING JERUSALEM

An intriguing fact about the triumphal entry is that Jesus had no apparent purpose for coming to Jerusalem other than to use the occasion as a messianic announcement. All he did after coming to the city was to go to the temple, look around, and then leave the city again to return to Bethany. The singularity of purpose in the entry calls attention to the possibility that other days might have different purposes.

Jesus entered Jerusalem five times during passion week, although only once in triumph. His entries and departures were described by

Mark is such a rhythmic pattern that he must have intended it as important to his flow of thought. Note the outline of that rhythm by days.

First Day

He *entered Jerusalem* in triumph from Bethany and Mount of Olives.

He looked at everything in the *temple*.

He returned to *Bethany*.

Second Day

He *entered Jerusalem* by way of the Bethany fig tree.

He cleansed the *temple*.

He returned to *Bethany*.

Third Day

He *entered Jerusalem* by way of the Bethany fig tree, now withered.

He argued in the *temple* with opponents and saw a widow put her whole living into the *temple* treasury.

He left Jerusalem to go to the *Mount of Olives* (and then implicitly to *Bethany* because he started from Bethany the next day).

Fourth Day

He *entered Jerusalem* to prepare for his passover supper after being anointed for burial in Bethany.

He shared a *ritual supper* with the twelve.

He left Jerusalem to go to the *Mount of Olives* where he prayed and was arrested. The twelve fled.

Fifth Day

He *entered Jerusalem* under arrest.

He was tried by *Jewish officials,* by Peter's denials, and by Gentile rulers.

He left Jerusalem to be executed at *Golgotha,* The Skull. The *temple* curtain was torn in two.

In Mark's passion week narratives there were seven recurring elements: Jerusalem, Bethany, Mount of Olives, the temple, and references to three kinds of fruit: figs, olive oil, and wine. Each is important in Mark's flow of thought.

The two closest to the heart of Mark's narrative are the references to entering Jerusalem and doing something in relationship to the temple. Note the interesting pattern when those two alone are separated out.

First Day	Entry in triumph	Observation of temple
Second Day	Entry with twelve only	Cleansed temple
Third Day	Entry with twelve only	Condemned temple leaders
Fourth Day	Entry with twelve only	Instituted his own rituals
Fifth Day	Entry under arrest	Temple curtain ripped in two

As Jesus' entries into Jerusalem shifted from popular triumph to ignoble arrest, his criticism of the temple and its role increased in intensity. His death resulted in the destruction of a sacred temple symbol.

Mark's rhythmic patterns of dealing with the whole of passion must be kept in mind as we study each of the separate days.

FIG TREES, OLIVE OIL, AND VINES

Careful scrutiny of the fruits and fruit trees referred to in the passion narratives calls attention to some remarkable coincidences. Only three fruits are referred to: figs, olives in the form of oil, and grapes in the form of wine. Jewish Bible often connected these fruits or their trees in patterns which Mark found significant for his messianic purpose.

Olive Trees and the Oil of Anointing.—Jesus began his messianic entry into Jerusalem from the Mount of Olives. The root meaning of the word messiah is "anointing," from the ancient Hebrew custom of anointing each new king with oil as a ceremony of investiture. Symbolically, Jesus came from the place of oil, the Mount of Olives, to be anointed with oil, to be invested as the messiah. A king anointed with the olive oil of the Mount of Olives would stand in the tradition of David. Later during passion week, Jesus went to Gethsemane on the Mount of Olives, where he made his firm decision to submit voluntarily to death and where he first acknowledged himself as God's son and God as his father. Gethsemane means, in English, The Oil Vat. At Gethsemane he was anointed as messiah-of-death rather than as the triumphal-entry-messiah of the first part of the week. Meanwhile, at Bethany, a woman had anointed him with expensive perfume in preparation for his death and burial.

Fig Trees and Figs.—On each of Jesus' first four entries into Jerusalem he came from the town of Bethany. The second and third trips involved a fig tree. The derivation of the name Bethany is ambiguous. It may stem from the House of Ananiah and thus mean either House of the Poor or House of the Afflicted; or it may, as suggested in the *Talmud,* mean the same as Bethphage: House of Late Season Green Figs or House of Unripe Figs. All three are possible in Mark's context. He associated Bethany with Bethphage at the beginning of Jesus' first trip into Jerusalem. It was near Bethany that Jesus withered a fig tree for not producing fruit out of season. It was in the house of Simon the Leper (thus House of the Afflicted) that Jesus was anointed for burial. He replied to criticism of that act with the statement, "You will always have the poor with you" (thus House of the Poor). In the apocalyptic section of passion week material (*Mark* 13) Jesus instructed four of his followers to learn the lesson of the fig tree: produce leaves in the proper season.

Vines and Wine.—When Jesus began to act authoritatively as befitted the triumphant messiah, he argued with his opponents. His first argument, with the chief priests, culminated in the messianic parable of the vineyard. At the Last Supper, Jesus used wine as a double symbol. It was his own blood poured out for others. It was a symbol of obedience which he would not drink again until he had actually submitted to God's rule. On the cross Jesus was given vinegar (sour wine) to drink. The specific references to wine in the passion week narratives are consistent with Jesus' earlier reply to Jacob (James) and John that he could promise them only the cup of suffering.

Jewish Bible often referred to figs, olives, and grapes (or their trees) together, especially fig trees and vines. From the vantage point of Mark, the most remarkable parallel is Jotham's Fable, found in *Judges* 9.7-15.

"Listen to me, you men of Shechem, that God may listen to you. The trees once went forth to anoint a king over them; and they said to the olive tree, 'Reign over us.' But the olive tree said to them, 'Shall I leave my fatness, by which gods and men are honored, and go to sway over the trees?'

"And the trees said to the fig tree, 'Come you, and reign over us.' But the fig tree said to them, 'Shall I leave my sweetness and my good fruit, and go to sway over the trees?'

"And the trees said to the vine, 'Come you, and reign over us.' But the vine said to them, 'Shall I leave my wine which cheers gods and men, and go to sway over the trees?'

"Then all the trees said to the bramble, 'Come you, and reign over us.' And the bramble said to the trees, 'If in good faith you are anointing me king over you, then come and take refuge in my shade; but if not, let fire come out of the bramble and devour the cedars of Lebanon'."

If one understands brambles as parallel to the crown of thorns in Mark's account of Jesus being mocked by his Gentile captors, it would seem virtually inconceivable that Mark would not have been conscious of it in his detailing of passion week.

The combination of figs and vines was a traditional symbol of peace and prosperity in Israel. Apart from the fact that both were vital to the economy of the region, the symbol was firmly established in Jewish Bible when Solomon's empire was described as one in which every man would dwell under his vine and under his fig tree. It was used as a picture of peace in *Joel* 2.22; *Micah* 4.1-4; *Haggai* 2.19; and *Zechariah* 3.10. It was used in connection with God's anger against Israel for its unfaithfulness in *Jeremiah* 5.17; 8.13; *Amos* 4.9; and *Joel* 1.7-12.

Many of the references to fig trees and vines were in messianic contexts. *Zechariah* and *Haggai* were both predicting the messianic day of Zerubbabel and Joshua, "the two anointed who stand by the Lord of the whole earth." (*Zech.* 4.14) Recall again that Mark, reading his Bible in Greek, would have read the name Jesus in place of Joshua and would thus have known that *Zechariah* and *Haggai* were referring to the messiahship of Jesus. *Joel* pictured a messianic age without specifying the name of a particular messiah.

I conclude from the foregoing data that Jesus, according to Mark, studied the Davidic messianic material from Jewish Bible and consciously applied to his own situation whatever details he could find which were relevant. In the process of doing so the traditional meanings of many of the symbols were transformed, as the passion week material indicates.

SECOND ENTRY INTO JERUSALEM

The account of Jesus' second entry into Jerusalem consists of two pericopes, the blasting of the fig tree and the cleansing of the temple. The first is one half of a Markan sandwich and depends for its interpretation upon the second half, which occurs on the day of the third entry.

The narrative of the cleansing of the temple has three significant precedents in Jewish Bible. In *Zechariah's* vision of the day of the messiah, the concluding paragraph conceives of a time when no separate temple would be necessary. Every pot and pan in all Judah would be a sacred vessel for sacrifices to God. Even the bells of the horses would have "holy to the Lord" inscribed on them.

"And there shall no longer be a trader in the house of the Lord
of hosts on that day." (*Zechariah* 14.21)

In *Isaiah's* vision of the day when God's salvation would come, the temple would be open to foreigners (Gentiles) as well as to Jews.

"And the foreigners who join themselves to the Lord . . . ,
These will I bring to my holy mountain,
And make them joyful in my house of prayer;
Their burnt offerings and their sacrifices
Will be accepted on my altar;
For my house shall be called a house of prayer
For all peoples." (*Isaiah* 56.6-7)

In Jeremiah's early career, he was instructed to stand in the doorway of the temple and proclaim a warning.

"Do not trust in these deceptive words: 'This is the temple of the
Lord, the temple of the Lord, the temple of the Lord.' . . . . Has
this house, which is called by my name, become a den of robbers
in your eyes?" (*Jeremiah* 7.4-11)

The details of Mark's narrative of Jesus driving the temple merchants from their stalls in the temple area seem to have been built from those three passages in Jewish Bible, the two from *Isaiah* and *Jeremiah* having been directly quoted by Jesus.

By placing the disruption of the temple enterprise immediately after the political-military triumphal entry, Mark created for his readers a major interpretative problem. It is virtually inconceivable for a man who wanted to be king in the tradition of David and his son Solomon to oppose the operation of the temple for which David and Solomon were responsible. Even though the actual building erected by Solomon had long since been destroyed and replaced by another, the tradition of offerings and gifts which Jesus was disrupting was still distinctly Solomonic.

The incident covered two entirely separate issues. The most obvious was Jesus' opposition to the mercantile enterprise which was essential to the proper functioning of the temple as a place of biblically acceptable offerings. Jews came to the temple on pilgrimages from many foreign lands, needing to exchange their native coins for Jewish coins and clean animals. Jesus' objection seems to have been against the entire process, not merely against some misuse of it. That fits the prophetic tradition which opted for justice and mercy rather than burnt offerings, but it is much more difficult to reconcile to the tradition of King David. It comes closest to fitting the passage from *Zechariah* which envisioned a day when there would be no more temple. Worship would stem from every home. That, however, was not Jesus' intention on this occasion. He was cleansing the temple, not abolishing it in favor of a more spiritual worship.

The other issue concerned opening temple worship to foreigners. Jesus' quotation from *Isaiah* clearly justified such a possibility. Nevertheless, it would have been a distinctly impolitic act for a messianic claimant to follow his triumphal parade with the announcement that the temple should be a house of prayer for foreigners. After all, the purpose of a Davidic messiah was to drive the foreign rulers out of the country and to re-establish Jewish hegemony in the Jewish homeland. According to *Acts*, Paul's arrest in Jerusalem stemmed from a mob's resentment of the presumed fact that Paul had "brought Greeks into the temple." The *Acts* story substantiates what seems to have been the general position of Jewish tradition. A messiah in the tradition of David's son Solomon would have built an additional temple for each group of foreigners rather than inviting them to worship in the Jewish temple.

The strange response to the disruption of the temple was that only the chief priests and scribes opposed it. The multitude greeted it with enthusiasm, astonished at Jesus' teachings as the crowds in Galilee had been earlier. The popular reaction would be understandable only if Jesus as messiah was a Robin Hood ousting greedy, cheating priest-tax-collectors. In that case the common people would benefit from getting rid of the merchants even though they had nothing to gain from opening their temple to Gentiles.

There was strong scriptural precedent for excluding Gentiles. "Thus says the Lord God: 'O house of Israel, let there be an end to all your abominations, in admitting foreigners, uncircumcised in heart and flesh, to be in my sanctuary, profaning it, when you offer me my food, the fat and the blood . . . . . No foreigner, uncircumcised in heart and flesh, of all the foreigners who are among the people of Israel, shall enter my sanctuary'." (*Ezekiel* 44.6-9)

Mark provides two clues for comprehending his flow of thought in the connection between the triumphal entry and the temple cleansing.

The first is the introductory half of the acted parable of the blasting of the fig tree; the second, the sequential nature of the entries into Jerusalem. The Markan sandwich of the fig tree encloses the pericope of cleansing the temple and thus calls attention to the relationship between the withered fig tree and disrupted temple. The point was the same in both events: Jesus performed an unreasonable act. It was out of season for figs, even on a tree known to produce late season fruit. There is no call for the reader to try to understand or justify Jesus' reason for doing so. The only point of the incident was to serve as an acted parable for the subsequent episode in the temple.

According to scripture, Jesus' disruption of the temple was out of season. *Zechariah, Isaiah,* and *Jeremiah* were all agreed on the standard for making such a judgment. *Zechariah's* prediction of a time when there would be no more traders in the temple envisioned the messianic age having already come. Not only would a son of David be on the throne, but the people of Israel would have internalized their devotion to God to the extent that each could conduct the appropriate worship rituals in his own home. Even in Jesus' exploration of the possibility of his being the son of David, he certainly should have known that the people were unprepared for a step of such magnitude.

Isaiah's prediction of a time when the temple would be a house of prayer for all people assumed that God's salvation would already have come, that men would be able to "buy wine and milk without money and without price." (*Isaiah* 55.1) It would be an age of justice and righteousness. Even in Jesus' exploration of the possibility of his being Salvation of God, as his name suggested, he certainly should have known that the people were unprepared to live in justice and righteousness.

In *Jeremiah,* the opposite of the temple being a den of robbers was described in these terms.

"For if you truly amend your ways and your doings, if you truly execute justice one with another, if you do not oppress the alien, the fatherless or the widow, or shed innocent blood in this place, and if you do not go after other gods to your own hurt, then I will let you dwell in this place, in the land that I gave of old to your fathers forever." (*Jeremiah* 7.5-7)

Jesus knew that Israel was unprepared for such a life. He had to have known that the temple-as-a-den-of-robbers would be only temporarily disrupted by his violence. On the next day it would be back in business again as the symbolic expression of man's injustice, his oppression, and his shedding of innocent blood.

Jesus' violence in the temple was thus an unreasonable act. It expected to achieve by simple force what three sources in Jewish Bible thought could be achieved only by a dramatic transformation of the spirituality of the people and the dawning of a new rule. At the end of passion week, Jesus knew that he had been tempted and that he had to resist his inclination to substitute physical force for a type of messiahship more consistent with being the son of God. Mark does not make explicit that this was temptation at the moment other than to label the act as unreasonable by enclosing it in the sandwich of the acted parable of unreasonableness.

The other clue for understanding the sequence from triumphal entry to temple cleasing was the rhythm of the entries into Jerusalem. It is likely that Mark intended the narratives of passion week to be read as five separate answers to a single question: what was the proper manner for God's son to enter Jerusalem? Each of the five entries gave a different answer, thus symbolizing the complexity of what Jerusalem stood for in Jewish tradition. From the standpoint of the crowds, Jesus would have been the same person throughout the week. But from the standpoint of Jesus and Mark, Jesus would have been a different person each day, inwardly imagining himself as related to a different segment of Jewish tradition and exploring it to discover its relevance to his overall quest for father-son reconciliation.

Thus his first entry and his second entry would not have necessitated any consistency with each other. The first legitimately experimented with the *Zechariah* tradition of a Solomonic messiah identifying himself with a publicly recognizable sign of political leadership and receiving the plaudits of an expectant populace. The second equally as legitimately tried on for size the prophetic hopes for purified worship which *Zechariah* had given a messianic dimension by his dream of worship in every home. Both were Jewish; both were traditional. Beyond that, they were not connected. The concept of messiah in one differed from that in the other.

It is now apparent why only the chief priests and the scribes objected to the cleansing of the temple. The primary issue was not the disruption of temple mercantile activity. The primary issue was the interpretation of Jewish scripture. The scribes were the authoritative experts in scripture interpretation; the priests were the authoritative experts in conducting worship as prescribed by scripture. Jesus' acts in the temple challenged the authority of both groups.

THIRD ENTRY INTO JERUSALEM

The main theme of the fig tree episode was authority expressed as violence. In the first part of the sandwiched story the violence was unreasonable. Jesus condemned a fig tree and then the temple for not bearing fruit out of season. In the second part of the sandwich, Jesus announced in an authoritative manner reminiscent of his early career that anyone could do anything, providing that he "does not doubt in his heart, but believes that what he says will come to pass." He gave as an example the highly improbable feat of throwing a montain into the ocean, the only necessary power being one's conviction that he could do it.

In the background of Jesus' third day in Jerusalem were the exciting events of the preceding two centruies of Jewish history. Rebelling against the oppression of the Syrian Greek Empire, the Jews had first won political independence and then later lost it to the Romans. During that era, religious writing turned toward apocalyptic and messianic hope. Two major sects were born: the Sadducees who were aligned primarily with the priests and who usually managed to ingratiate themselves with the foreign rulers, and the Pharisees who stood in the prophetic tradition of scriptural law and high morality. The Pharisees were at times as willing as the Sadducees to connive with the foreign rulers, but they more often lost and were then cast in the role of opposing foreign rule. The priestly leanings of the Sadducees led them to be conservative and legalistic in scripture interpretation, whereas the Pharisees' concern for morality led them toward liberalism and modernism. They were willing to bring the regulations of scripture up to date and make them relevant to contemporary living. By a strange quirk of fate, it was this up-dating procedure which led Jesus to condemn them as legalists because some of their new rules were even more picayune than those which they changed. Both the Sadducees and the Pharisees developed their own corps of official interpreters, the scribes. The scribes of the Pharisees tended to be laymen; those of the Sadducees, professionals. Unless otherwise specified it is fair to assume that scribes belong to the Sadducees. During this same period, there developed a Jewish ruling body known as the Sanhedrin, a council of seventy (or seventy-one) elders, also usually dominated by the Sadducees.

On the day of Jesus' third entry into Jerusalem, he debated with representatives of all of the major groups which had originated during that two century era: the chief priests, the elders of the Sanhedrin, the scribes, the Sadducees, and the Pharisees. He also applied to himself the apocalyptic hopes which had arisen.

The chief priests, scribes, and elders first approached Jesus with a trap concerning his authority. Recall that it was Jerusalem scribes who had earlier accused Jesus of casting out demons under the authority of a pagan god, and that the chief priests, scribes, and elders were later to condemn Jesus to death because of blasphemy. They now wanted Jesus to confess to blasphemy by claiming that his authority was from God, or to ruin his popularity with the crowds which had greeted him so enthusiastically by denying that his authority was from God.

Jesus dodged the issue. He refused to put himself in their power by choosing either option. Instead he ricocheted their attack back at them by offering them the same trap options in regard to their acceptance of John the Baptizer. He went on to hint broadly that the parable of the vineyard applied to them. They were those who killed both God's servants and God's son in order to steal God's vineyard for themselves. He referred to *Psalms* 118.22-232, implying that he himself was the rejected cornerstone which had become the messianic head of that corner.

The Pharisees with the support of Herodians then pressed Jesus with an anti-Sadducee, anti-Roman issue. The Saducess had cooperated willingly with the Romans to rule Israel; the Pharisees had opposed such rule and therefore opposed paying taxes to Caesar—probably a popular point of view. Recall that it had been the Pharisees who had earlier condemned Jesus for eating with tax collectors, whose occupation was synonymous with sinfulness.

Jesus again dodged the issue. He refused to put himself in the power of the Pharisees by either advocating or opposing the payment of Roman taxes. His answer was the epitome of the office-seeker's art: he made a positive, high-sounding proclamation which would offend no one.

The Sadducees then approached Jesus with an anti-Pharisee question. The modernizing Pharisees believed in resurrection from the dead and an after life. The Sadducees asked a question based legalistically on scripture rules about brothers who were required by law to marry the widow of a deceased older brother. The question implied that Jesus agreed with the Pharisees and would thus be embarrassed by his inability to solve the dilemma.

Jesus did not dodge the issue, but it must have seemed to his audience that he did. On one hand, he affirmed his belief in resurrection. But on the other hand, he denied that it had anything to do with the dead or with resuscitated bodies. Resurrected people, he indicated, are like heavenly angels, probably in the sense of messengers. More important, the God of Jewish scripture had never been the God of the dead. He had always been the God of the living, as had been demonstrated by the incident in which Moses had spoken to God at the burning bush.

Both the Pharisees and Sadducees had queried Jesus hypocritically. They had each sought to advance a case against the other at the expense of Jesus. The Pharisees pretended to believe that, like Jesus, they were concerned only about the way of God. The Sadducees pretended to believe in resurrection in order to express their puzzlement over a resurrection-based dilemma. In each case, Jesus cut through the hypocrisy.

Despite the fact that the opponents were wrong all the way through, Jesus was tempted by them. Taken as a whole, the three controversies were like the blasting of the fig tree. Jesus relied on his authority and his cleverness. He destroyed the arguments and reputations of his opponents as he had destroyed the tree. There was in his manner none of the charity, love, and forgiveness which had characterized King David's reaction to many of his opponents, to say nothing of the charity which the New Testament general associates with Jesus himself.

Given the Markan context, Jesus' reference to casting mountains into the sea, in the acted parable of the fig tree, is likely to have been related to a passage in *Zechariah*. The passage referred to a predicted messiah named Zerubbabel.

"This is the word of the Lord to Zerubbabel: 'Not by might, nor by power, but by my spirit,' says the Lord of hosts. What are you, O great mountain? Before Zerubbabel you shall become a plain; and he shall bring forward the top stone amid shouts of 'Grace, grace to it.' Moreover the word of the Lord came to me, saying, 'The hands of Zerubbabel have laid the foundation of this house; his hands shall also complete it'." (*Zechariah* 4.6-9)

Throughout the first three days in Jerusalem Jesus had sought by power and by offices of power to move the mountains of opposition and install himself as the top stone. But the messianic dream of *Zechariah* was antithetical to power; it was rooted in spirituality. The son of David tradition included tears at the excessive use of power. Subsequent events were to make it clear that God was calling Jesus away from the power and violence alternative and that he had been tempted in exploring it.

Calling to a More Adequate Sonship

At midpoint of the third day, God began to call Jesus to a more legitimate messiahship. The calling occurred in three steps. It began by bringing Jesus into confrontation with the very best in the scribal tradition: the recognition that *Deuteronomy* 6.4 and *Leviticus* 19.18 were the highest expressions of law. These were the commandments to love God and neighbor. The problem was, as Jesus was aware, that these commandments were not sufficient. One who believed in them was not far from submitting to the sovereignty of God, but he had not yet arrived. The implicit question for Jesus was: what was needed to fill the gap between where the commandments left off and where actual obedience to God began. The implicit question for the scribes was: what was there in the nature of being a scribe which prevented one from bridging that gap.

Jesus' second step in his calling to a higher messiahship was his recognition that the scribes had two problems, one scriptural, and the other personal. At the level of scripture interpretation, they were mistaken. They read David as a man of power, a power which would extend to his son who would put his enemies under his feet. Jesus noted that, according to *Psalms* 110.1, David himself, inspired by a spirit of holiness, had made such an interpretation impossible. David was referring to a messiah who could not be a son of David. How could David ever have called his son his Lord?

At the personal level, the scribes were too much in love with public honor to submit to God's rule. They wore their academic gowns and their prerogatives without concern for the poor upon whose resources they feasted as parasites.

This was a key insight for Jesus. Throughout his career to this point he had functioned somewhat as a lay scribe. He had been avidly interpreting scripture, seeking to find in scripture the clue which would unlock for him the secret of father-son reconciliation. In Capernaum Jesus had intuited that the scribes were his accusers, and he was right.

On the way down from the mountain of transfiguration the Big Three had inquired about the position of the scribes, and at the base the other nine were arguing with the scribes. Now he was warned that the process of scribal interpretation was inadequate at its best and parasitic at its worst. It had led him throughout his career to inadequaate goods. It had led him most recently to contrive a great parade in his own honor and to resort to physical and psychological violence against his opponents.

Jesus was thus prepared for the third and climactic stage of God's calling to him. It was a poignant event. Jesus watched from within the temple area, either with his eyes or his imagination, the affluent bringing their gifts. He then saw a poor widow give everything she owned, two copper coins. He recognized in her act what all scripture interpretation lacked, the essential act of obedience to God. To obey is to give all.

When Jesus left the temple, he knew that the temple was done for. In his mind it no longer had any positive function. His disciples saw it as a marvel of architecture. Jesus saw it spiritually as a pile of rubble, assigned religiously to demolition because it could not engender actual obedience to the rule of God.

The Special Role of Bethany

Thus ended Jesus' experiences in Jerusalem on the day of the third entry. The day itself was not over. Still on the third day he left the city for the nearby Mount of Olives for an apocalyptic conversation with four of the twelve disciples. This was the first time that Jesus had not returned directly to Bethany. That fact, breaking the Markan rhythm, calls attention to the unique role of Bethany in the events of these three days.

Bethany was originally the town of the acted parable of the fig tree. It was the launching site of the unseasonable dream of purifying Israel by the physical and psychological violence of political leadership. It was from Bethany that Jesus came intentionally to receive a military hero's welcome, as David himself had been accustomed to receive. It was from Bethany that Jesus came to overturn the temple mercantile enterprise and to impose an embargo on carrying anything within the temple precincts. It was from Bethany that Jesus came to dispute and confound all of his opponents, catching them in their own traps and embarrassing them before the public. In all of that, Bethany was the City of Unseasonal Fruit.

But Bethany was also the House of the Poor. When Jesus was called away from his violence-prone vision of messiahship, he was called by a woman of poverty. He had previously recognized that scribes devour the living of poor widows. When Jesus returned to Bethany he was found in the house of Simon the Leper, House of the Afflicted, where he recognized that the poor will always be present, and where he was anointed as the messiah of death. Thus, the delayed return home can be expected in Mark's context to have a transitional quality between

Jesus' calling by a woman of poverty and his anointing in the House of the Poor.

As Jesus left Jerusalem this time, the son of David traidition died for him. The son of David had been loved by his father, and thus provided an attractive model for Jesus in his own quest for a proper response to his Father's love. But each of David's sons had responded violently. Jesus had discovered for himself that the attitudes of violence are inherent in political dominance. They prevented genuine reconciliation with the Father.

CHAPTER EIGHT
APOCALYPTIC EASY VICTORY: END OF THE THIRD DAY

Jesus' stay in Jerusalem on the day of his third entry had ended with his prediction of the destruction of the temple. On his way back to Bethany he sat on the Mount of Olives with his original four disciples. The inclusion of Andrew, Manly, along with the Big Three, signaled a shift away from the pro-Jewish themes which the twelve and the Big Three alone had symbolized and toward the broader humanness symbolized by Andrew as part of the original four. This was consistent with the context which involved a question about the destruction of the Jewish temple.

On the surface, Jesus answered for the four a simple question. They wanted to know what were the signs they should look for to warn them that the demolition of the temple was near. Jesus' reply was a jumble of contradictions which make little sense without the interpretative assistance of *Mark's* broader context and biblical allusions.

Beneath the surface of Jesus' reply was a mosaic of biblical references, largely from the apocalyptic sections of *Ezekiel* and *Daniel*. According to Ezekiel 11.23-25, God stood on the Mount of Olives to call the son of man to his prophetic career. In *Mark* Jesus was on the Mount of Olives on this occasion to predict the coming of the Son of man on the clouds of heaven. It was in *Ezekiel* that rumor followed rumor (7.26), that famine followed famine (5.12-17; 14.13; 12.16), and that sword, pestilence, and famine would strike at once.

> "He that is in the field dies by the sword; and him that is in the city famine and pestilence devour. And if any survivors escape, they will be on the mountains." (*Ezekiel* 7.14-16)

It was in *Ezekiel* that the breath of God would come from the four winds to resurrect the faithful (37.9) and that the heavenly lights would be extinguished in sun, moon, and stars (32.7). The parallels to specifics in Jesus' reply are so exact that there must have been conscious awareness of them.

Three additional parallels came from *Daniel*. One of them Mark quoted in modified form.

> "I saw in the night visions, and behold, with the clouds of heaven there came one like a Son of man, and he came to the Ancient of Days and was presented before him." (7.13)

Daniel's concluding sentence was much like *Mark* 13.13: "He who endures to the end will be saved."

> "But go your allotted way till the end; and you shall rest, and shall stand in your allotted place at the end of days."

The third parallel was the reference to the desolating sacrilege, usually translated in Jewish Bible as "the abomination that makes desolate" and referred to in both *Ezekiel* and *Daniel*. In both books it is clear that the phrase was intended to refer to idol worship in the Jerusalem temple. In *Daniel* a historical reconstruction of the setting of the book makes virtually certain the assumption that the abomination which makes desolate was the enshrinement of a statue of Zeus on the Jerusalem temple altar, as ordered by the Syrian Greek emperor, Antiochus Epiphanes.

Most scholars of *Mark* have used the reference to desolating sacrilege as the key to dating the authorship of the book. The logic of their argument has been that because Mark added the parenthetical comment "let the reader understand" to the already obvious parallelism with *Daniel* and *Ezekiel,* the author must have been calling attention to some act of desecration of the Jerusalem temple which had already occurred prior to the time of the writing of the book. Some have thought that this referred to an attempt by the Emperor Caligula to have his own statue placed in the temple in the year 40; others have decided that the reference was to the destruction of the temple by the Romans during the 69-70 rebellion. The majority have used the latter explanation and have thus insisted that *Mark* had to be written in the year 70 or later. Otherwise, argue the majority, the reader would not have understood what Mark was pointing at with his parenthetical comment.

There are at least three reasons why *Mark's* internal context does not permit such a reconstruction of the meaning of desolating sacrilege. The first is its improbability in light of the intended audience. The Gospel, as interpreted in its own literary context, absolutely requires a readership thoroughly acquainted with Jewish Bible. In virtually every pericope it assumes that readers will understand the implicit relationship between an event in the life of Jesus and a parallel in scripture. Therefore, a warning flag such as "let the reader understand" would have to call attention to something out of the ordinary, to a type of desolating sacrilege which would not be a close parallel to the original scripture references.

The second reason is that the apocalyptic utterances of Jesus in *Mark* 13 occurred in the context of an already disrupted temple and opposition to temple ritualism. Jesus himself had recently impeded temple worship by ousting the merchants. He had predicted that the temple would be dismantled stone by stone as a consequence of the inadequacy of temple worship and priestly scriptural interpretation. He stood in the traditions of the prophets who had opposed temple rituals and burnt offerings. Therefore, for Jesus and his followers a desecration of the temple building would not have been a desolating sacrilege, however disastrous it might have been for temple-oriented Jews. Nor would the destruction of the temple have introduced a persecution aimed especially at followers of Jesus as a portion of the apocalyptic sayings envisions.

The third and most important reason why the reference to

desolating sacrilege ought not to be read as a prediction of the destruction of the temple is that the entire set of apocalyptic utterances in *Mark* 13 has a strong predictive function internally within *Mark*. The predictive function of the passion predictions has already been noted (the order of the trials, the identity of the killers, the connection between crucifixion and resurrection, the third day, etc.). The triumphal entry on the Sunday of passion week was the first of a series of patterned entries into Jerusalem and thus a prediction of the climactic entry on Gethsemane Thursday. The woman who gave her all to the temple treasury was predictive of Jesus' own act of giving his all by the crucifixion. Many other details in the easy victory sections of *Mark* have had similar foreshadowing functions. Thus it is consistent with *Mark's* developing pattern to look at Chapter 13 for its relevance to the coming crucifixion.

Barabbas was a false messianic claimant. The darkness at the crucifixion from the sixth hour to the ninth hour was an example of the extinction of the light of sun, moon, and stars. The fig tree parable would accentuate again the lesson which Jesus was to learn the next morning in Bethany, the City of Unripe Figs, where he was to be anointed for death. The emphasis upon the importance of faithfulness in the face of suffering pointed to the very attitude which was to characterize Jesus on the cross. The ambiguity about the issue of signs (variously no signs, false signs, true signs) was prophetic of one temptation on the cross: the invitation from Jewish officialdom to come down from the Roman cross as a sign of his Davidic messiahship.

In light of all that, the most adequate interpretation of the desolating sacrilege must be the death of Jesus. "Let the reader understand" that the abomination which desecrates is not something which happens to a building but something which has happened to the son of God and messiah Jesus whose body was set up where it ought not to have been, on a cross. As far as using that reference itself as a way of dating the composition of *Mark,* all that could be argued from it is that the book had to have been written after the crucifixion of Jesus. A much later date is required by the necessity of the book having been written at a time when the Jesus community was sufficiently separated from the Jewish community that it was no longer temple-oriented and when the followers of Jesus could refer to the Jews as members of a religion different from their own. *Mark* gives no indication whatsoever as to when such an awareness of separateness occurred.

The apparent confusion of Jesus' reply is considerably diminished by noting its relationship to persistent Markan themes. The reply is best understood when broken into three sections. The section from 13.5-13 is dominated by Jesus' inculcating a manly courage in the face of suffering, a courage appropriate to Andrew's presence. The themes of Holy Spirit and preaching the gospel, which had been largely absent from Jesus' career, since the four had been replaced by the twelve and the Big Three, were now reintroduced. Under conditions of persecution it was to be the Holy Spirit which would enable people to speak rightly even though in the world of the persecutors all hope of reconciliation between parents and children had evaporated.

"And brother will deliver up brother to death, and the father his child, and children will rise against parents and have them put to death...." (*Mark* 13.12)

It is difficult to say for sure that Jesus intended his reply to be relevant only to the two sets of brothers, but the 13.5-13 segment of it was addressed only to them in second person pronouns. Not only would parents and children turn against each other, but brother would also turn against brother. Their task was to be what it had been when they were originally called from their nets: to preach the good news. It was a task which had been central in Jesus' career during the time when he had been most aware of the Holy Spirit's message of the Father's love, which was also the time of the original calling of the four.

However, in the chapter thirteen context the task took on two different dimensions. Preaching the good news of love was to be aimed at the Gentiles, "all the nations," and it was to be done in expectation of failure rather than victory. The trend toward universality had been developing throughout Jesus' career and was in fact consistent with the nature of love itself since it could not be arbitrarily limited to any one group or religion. Only in the passion predictions had suffering been conceived as a significant answer to Jesus' quest for the meaning of Father-son reconciliation. There, the suffering had been foreseen in temporary terms: a three-day death followed by resurrection. Now suffering was thought of as a virtually permanent condition and equally as universal as the preaching of good news. Many nations would war against each other; famines and earthquakes would occur in Gentile nations as well as in Israel; and persecutions would take place both in Jewish councils and synagogues and before Gentile governors and kings. Even such spectacular events would not foreshadow the end about which four disciples asked; such events would be only the beginning of sufferings, and the four would still have to be faithful through it all.

Such an answer was thoroughly humanistic. It envisioned the replacement of the Jewish temple with human ability to withstand persecution, an ability which needed no temple, no ritual, no traditions. It envisioned that men imbued with the spirit of holiness would find in every conceivable situation the right words to say whatever the pressures brought to bear upon them.

As in every other humanistic insight of Jesus earlier in his career, there was embodied in this one ambiguity which led him into temptation. The second segment of Jesus' reply, 13.14-31, demonstrated that in several ways. The title "Son of Man" in its Danielic form was now openly adopted. Jesus' death was to signal the beginning of a virtually universal persecution. Supernatural signs would be abundant and their fulfillment scheduled for the immediate future.

The general thrust of the second part of his reply was to elevate his own significance and to diminish that of others. No longer was suffering to be the consequence of courage in the face of uncontrollable disaster and cruel persecution. Rather now it was to be the altogether indiscriminate calamity visited upon those who happened to be alive at the time of Jesus' death, the abomination of desolation. It was to include pregnant women, farmers working their fields, and people seeking respite from the heat by sitting on their rooftops at evening. Their suffering would result from the coincidence that they were alive when the abomination which makes desolate was set up where it ought not to be. In such a setting, God would function as the rescuer of those whom He had arbitrarily chosen in advance as His elect. It would not be possible for any human being to endure to the end without supernatural assistance.

Jesus conceived his role to be changed. He was not now to be the courageous man among courageous disciples. Rather he was to be the supernatural Son of man among mere humans. Whereas in the humanistic section of his reply, the "others" who came in Jesus' name provided natural signs (war, earthquake, famine) to lead people astray, the "others" were now to be messianic claimants who themselves would perform miraculous signs and wonders to lead people astray. Taken out of context the reader could subsume Jesus' condemnation of them under the rule proposed in *Deut.* 13.1-3:

> "If a prophet arises among you, or a dreamer of dreams, and gives you a sign or a wonder, and the sign or wonder which he tells you comes to pass, and if he says, 'Let us go after other gods,' which you have not known, 'and let us serve them' you shall not listen to the words of that prophet or that dreamer of dreams; for the Lord your God is testing you, to know whether you love the Lord your God with all your heart and with all your soul."

In context, however, the Deuteronomy rule could not be applied to the false messiahs any more than to Jesus himself. In the second section of his reply Jesus made the issue to be one of "true" signs versus "false" ones, not signs versus no signs as in the first section. Jesus now promised that after his death, the abomination of desolation, he would reappear on the clouds of heaven as the Son of man in conjunction with a true set of signs as prophecied by *Daniel* and *Ezekiel*. The Son of man himself, in his godly role, would complete the rescue of the elect from the troubles of earth.

In further contradiction to the first section of Jesus' reply, all this was to occur in the immediate future, before the present generation should have passed away.

It is questionable as to whether the parable of the fig tree in *Mark* 13 belongs to the second section of Jesus' reply or to the third, or to both ambiguously. Its thrust is that "all these things" will take place before the present generation passes away. Which things? The supernatural signs spoken of in the second section? Or the fulfillment of the internal predictions by the crucifixion itself? On the surface it would appear that the supernatural interpretation is most plausible. It would be consistent with the desolating effect of the judicial murder of the true messiah for such signs to occur immediately.

Beneath the surface, the grammar and the context argues for the opposite answer. The first section of Jesus' reply was spoken in the second person to the four alone; the second section was spoken largely in third person pronouns: "Let those flee," "no human being would be saved," and "they will see the Son of man." But the parable of the fig tree returns to second person address: "When you see". The implication may have been that Jesus intended a distinction between what the four would see (abomination of desolation as suffering) and what others would see (supernatural signs in the heavens). This was a distinction which Mark was to use with great effect in his account of what the priests would see when they misconstrued the meaning of Jesus' confession.at this trial.

The fact that the tree was a fig tree, as distinct from an oak or an apple, was important in Mark's context. The name of Bethany and the earlier acted parable of the withering away of the fig tree had obviously been built around the name of Bethany as The House of Unseasonal Green Figs (Unripe Figs). Now Jesus was using a fig tree as an object lesson in seasonal fruit, a distinct reversal of the earlier motif. When he was to return to Bethany it was to be to the Bethany which was the House of the Poor and the House of the Afflicted. He was to return to Bethany to be anointed for death and to make preparations for a Passover meal in which death would not pass over.

Finally, in the third section of Jesus' reply to the four disciples about the signs for the destruction of the temple, Jesus concluded that no one other than God could know about such dates. To be a son was only to be ready for opportunities when they appeared. The key words were to be "watch" and "pray", the combination of words which were to have their fulfillment in Jesus' life in Gethsemane.

The rhythm of Chapter Thirteen was thus shown to be identical to that of so many other sub-stages of Jesus' career. A possible answer to the question of how the son should respond to the love of the Father was discovered to contain a miraculous counterpart which Jesus was first tempted to adopt for himself and which he later resisted. Having done so he was ready to pass on to a different alternative.

In this case, the good which was proposed was associated with the spirit of holiness, and was thus symbolically announced as the true answer to Jesus' quest if it could be disentangled from the temptation associated with it. That was the problem for Jesus as he returned from the Mount of Olives vision of supernatural messianic intervention to find in Bethany the more accuate content of the lesson of the fig tree. Bethany was to send him back to the Mount of Olives again, but not to the easy victory of *Daniel's* cloud-borne Son of man. Bethany was to send him the next time to Gethsemane where suffering would be correctly identified with the son's proper response to the Father.

CHAPTER NINE
CRUCIFIXION: THE PASSOVER REVERSAL

From the time of Jesus' return from his short, self-imposed exile near Tyre and Sidon, Jesus' experiences and his search for scriptural clues about father-son reconciliation were more and more dominated by failure and death. In each instance the failure and death were easily overcome by miracle or expectation of resurrection or triumphal entry or by apocalyptic hope. Each of those victory themes faded away, and a new form of failure and death emerged in the forefront of Jesus' vision of his own life. Although some were more explicit than others, all these events were passion predictions in the sense that they suggested the ultimate direction which his reconciliation with his Father was to take:

1. Jesus' failure to heal the spiritual blindness of the twelve.
2. Jesus' explicit predictions of his death in 8, 9, 10.
3. The collapse of the Elijah and Moses themes on the Mount of Transfiguration.
4. The failure of the twelve to cast out the unclean spirit at the base of the mountain.
5. The almost continuous failure of the twelve thereafter.
6. The violence inherent in Jesus' attempt at political messianism.
7. David's recognition that the death of the father would be preferable to the death of the beloved son.
8. The necessity of David's death before his second beloved son could come to the throne and fulfill David's dreams.
9. The apocalyptic predictions of suffering and death.
10. The internally predictive nature of the apocalyptic utterances, foreshadowing the actual passion events.

As Mark viewed Jesus, all those events were paradoxical. Both in Jesus' immediate experiences and in the scriptural sources they had seemed to point to victory. But when Jesus came to the end of his quest he discovered that God's will was exactly the opposite of what he had previously thought. That reversal was for Mark the heart of the gospel. The gospel had begun in *Isaiah* as that kind of glad tidings which the world applauds. It ended in Jesus' life with the good news of a judicial murder which the world abhors.

The reversal reached its climax at Passover. It was no accident or coincidence that the story of Jesus' actual death began "two days before the Passover and the feast of Unleavened Bread." By modern calendars it was Wednesday before sundown. On that day, *Mark* relates, the chief priests and scribes decided to arrest and execute Jesus secretly. They feared public reaction from the thousands of Passover pilgrims if a messianic claimant were killed during the Passover celebration. Their decision made the last three days of the week significantly different from the first three. Jesus and his opponents had previously been content to argue with each other, seeking largely to best each other at the scribal art of biblical interpretation. Now, at the beginning of a new three-day sequence, the opponents' intent changed to murder.

Jesus simultaneously made a corresponding shift. Bethany, the city which had been for him only the place of unseasonal fruit, suddenly became the Bethany of the apocalyptic fig tree parable, the fig tree which puts forth tender branches and leaves in season. The season of death was at hand. Jesus entered the house of Simon the Leper, the Bethany which was the House of the Afflicted, and was there anointed for his death. Jesus could not have known that on that same day the priestly group had ordered his death because of his messianic claims. Nor could the priests have known that Jesus had now been anointed as the messiah whose goal could be achieved by death. Both decisions meshed perfectly.

Jesus' saying about poverty, spoken in Bethany, The House of the Poor, has been difficult for most Christians to live with. Some who were present in the house of Simon the Leper objected to the waste of precious nard when there were poor people who could have been benefited by a gift of the money for which the ointment could have been sold. Jesus argued that because he was soon to die it was better to do something beautiful for him than to do good to the poor. After all, in the House of the Poor there would always be poor to help. The saying probably originated because of the pun on the meaning of the name Bethany.

Mark probably intended the entire pericope to be symbolic. It conveys the impression that Jesus had already made a firm decision to surrender himself to death in the very near future. The Gethsemane story was to make it obvious that Jesus had not made a firm decision in Bethany. Furthermore, the concluding sentence referring to "wherever the gospel is preached in the whole world" implies that Jesus would have known that there was to be a widespread preaching movement after his death. The confident tone of that prediction is inconsistent with the development of the passion narratives. The puns on the name of Bethany added to the symbolic quality of the event. The fact that the leper's name was Simon and that still another Simon (of Cyrene) was to carry Jesus' cross raises a question as to whether Mark intended some play on the name of Simon Peter. The conclusion that the pericope was intended to be symbolic is buttressed by the breaking of Jesus' rhythm of leaving Bethany each day, entering Jerusalem, going to the temple, and returning to Bethany. On this occasion Jesus stayed in Bethany the entire day. Only Judas Iscariot left town, to go to Jerusalem to make his deal with the priests.

It has already been noted that at each previous stage of development during Passion Week Jesus had explored the adequacy of some good which turned out to be temptative. There is a tendency among scholars to treat the material beginning with the fourteenth chapter as if the remainder of the book was all of one piece, dedicated to the crucifixion. The anointing in the house of Simon the Leper makes clear that such was not the case.

Contrast the poor woman who gave her all to the temple treasury and the rich woman who brought expensive ointment to perfume Jesus' hair. The one was seen by Jesus as an example of one who gives all. The other was seen as one "who has done a beautiful thing to me." In the latter incident the needs of the poor were in fact ignored; Jesus did construe the situation in such a way so that he and he alone would be honored by it. He assumed that the good news which would be preached would be consistent with such acts. This was not at all the temptation to convert sonship into miraculousness with which he had earlier been confronted. Apparently Jesus had put that allurement behind him. What he now found facing him was the desire to be honored by his own act of giving himself in death, and for that honoring to go on beyond his death.

BETRAYAL BY JUDAS

The first actual step toward the crucifixion was the betrayal by Judas. Jesus knew from scripture that Judas (the Hellenized version of the Hebrew original name Judah) was the name of the betrayer and that betrayal was an ambiguous event. In the Joseph story, most of Joseph's brothers were simply willing to let him die; they were murderers. Reuben, the oldest brother, sought to save his life, even though unsuccessfully. It was Judah who both saved Joseph's life and sold him into slavery. That was the betrayal, an act of mixed good and evil.

The ambiguity of Judah continued in subsequent events. He betrayed his daughter-in-law Tamar by not giving her his third son as a husband. She retaliated by trapping Judah into siring for her a pair of twins, the second of whom supplanted his brother as the first born. It was that supplanting brother through whom a major genealogical line was continued from Jacob. Still later, when Joseph sought to retain Benjamin with him in Egypt, it was Judah who offered to remain in Egypt as a slave to Jospeh in order to prevent his father Jacob from dying of a broken heart at the loss of Benjamin. In that strange manner, the most evil of Jacob's sons became the most righteous.

It was from Judah the betrayer that Jesus learned the secret of father-son reconciliation. David had pointed in that direction but inadequately. After the death of his son Absalom, David said that he would have preferred to have died for his son, but he did not do so. He stayed alive until all his vital powers were spent. He talked voluntary death but he did not practice it. Judah, on the other hand, actually offered to become a slave. It was that act of compassion which led Joseph to weep and reveal himself to his brothers, and ultimately to be reunited with his father.

One of the enduring problems of Gospel interpretation has been the lack of any obvious motivation for Judas' betrayal. In *Mark*, the betrayal followed psychologically from Jesus' acceptance of the anointing in Bethany. There, for the first time, Judas presumably heard Jesus announce his willingness to die without being miraculously resurrected. For a messianic claimant, that was heresy. Only in *Isaiah*'s suffering servant poetry (53-54) had messianism been linked with death. Otherwise, Jesus' penetrations into scripture had led him only to models for overcoming death. From the point of view of Judas and the Jews gathered for Passover, Jesus would have to be prevented from dying or to be resurrected from death if he was to fulfill the messianic dreams.

It made little sense for Judas to seek Jesus' death. His motivation must have been to prevent Jesus from dying. That was the pattern established by Judah: Joseph had to be kept alive. Only by saving Joseph's life had the victories occurred, the miraculous transformation of the man-at-death's-door into the ruler who was like Paraoh himself.

Judah-Judas must have wanted the new Joseph miracle. He must have hoped for a new Pharaoh Jesus, a new Caesar Jesus, a new David Jesus, a new man of power in place of the Bethany weakling willing to die. It is highly likely that Judas planned to take advantage of the Passover occasion with its thousands of Jewish pilgrims present to trap Jesus into using his miraculous power. Either he would back Jesus into death's corner and force him to fight back to save his life; or he would force Jesus to claim the miraculous resurrection which he had so freely predicted earlier. In either case, Jesus and Israel would emerge as victors over Rome, and Judas would have been an instrument for the saving of Israel.

The betrayal by Judas thus followed exactly the same path that Jesus' own temptations had followed throughout his career. He had persistently struggled with the issue of his own power and how to handle it. The precise form of Judas' betrayal would not have been possible had not Jesus entered Jerusalem as the political messianic claimant. Judas never dreamed that Jesus had changed so rapidly and that he would have the courage to go through with his announced intention of voluntary death.

THE DAY OF DECISION

Jesus' fourth entry into Jerusalem was for the specific purpose of eating the Passover meal. According to the generally accepted ritual rules, it was to be eaten on Thursday evening before sundown, the eve of the seven day Feast of Unleavened Bread. Mark does not seem to have made any distinction between the Passover Feast itself and the seven day feast to follow.

Passover was a ritual meal eaten to commemorate the night in Egypt when God's death angel passed over the land, killing the first born in each Egyptian family and flock, but sparing the Hebrew families and flock. The result of that night was the Hebrew exodus from slavery. The ritual meal included unleavened bread as a reminder of the haste in leaving Egypt, bitter herbs as a reminder of the bitterness of slavery, wine as a symbol of the joy of freedom (known to have been used in Jesus' day, but not required by scripture), and a ritually slain lamb whose blood had been thrown against the temple altar as a symbol of God's redemption of his people and a reminder of God's protection of the Hebrew first born.

The parallelism between Jesus' preparations for his triumphal entry into Jerusalem and for his Passover entry is very strong. On both occasions he sent two disciples to perform a task. I do not understand why he sent exactly two, but he had done the same when he had earlier sent the twelve out on missions by pairs. In each of the two planned entries, the pair were to find something, a colt tied up or a man carrying a jar of water. They were given a message to deliver, and it was expected that the recipient of the message would automatically accede to the demand. The first man was to trust the two strangers with his colt; the second was to offer his house for thirteen strangers to use for eating supper. Or, it may have been the case that Jesus cleverly contrived each of the events to make it appear that the owner of the colt and the owner of the house were strangers to Jesus when in fact they may have been collaborators with his messianic claims.

If collaboration occurred, it would appear that there should be some biblical justification for the Passover supper to match that for the triumphal entry. Recall that Solomon had ridden into Jerusalem on David's colt to symbolize the legitimacy of his kingship, and that *Zechariah* had predicted that the messiah would do so again. There seems to be no scriptural justification for the advance preparation for the Passover meal; the likelihood of collaboration is thus diminished.

Why then should Jesus have instructed his pair of disciples to follow a man carrying a jar of water? I have the general impression that water carrying was woman's work in biblical times. If so, a man carrying water would perhaps be some special type of person, perhaps a member of an all-male religious sect, perhaps a low status male reduced to woman's work. Mark does not seem to have provided the internal clues for answering that question.

Conversation at the meal made it obvious that the purpose of the occasion was to institute a new Passover tradition rather than continue an old one. Jesus began by announcing that one of the twelve would betray him, probably alluding to *Psalms* 41.9 in doing so.

"Even my bosom friend in whom I trusted
Who ate of my bread, has lifted up his heel against me."

It should not be too quickly taken for granted that he was referring to Judas. All twelve of them were saddened; all twelve asked, "Is it I?" All twelve dipped bread in the same dish with Jesus. If "lifting up one's heel against me" means running away or deserting, all twelve were eventually guilty. Simon Peter was most likely to be a bosom friend trusted by Jesus, and it was he who most spectacularly deserted Jesus by denying acquaintance with him. In this respect, all of the twelve were Judah-Judas; all twelve were betrayers; all twelve were living embodiments of *Psalms* 41.9.

During the meal Jesus instituted a new understanding of the occasion. He broke bread, not the unleavened bread required for Passover but ordinary leavened bread. He blessed it, not a table grace before meal but a special blessing of some kind for this special act. He distributed it to the twelve, telling them that he was giving them his body. He then took a cup of wine, expressed thanks for it, and asked each of the twelve to drink part of it. He told them that it was his own blood of the covenant, an obvious reference to *Exodus* 24. There, Moses took the blood of sacrificial animals, threw half of it on the altar and then read to the assemblage the words of God's covenant.

"And they said, 'All that the Lord has spoken we will do, and we will be obedient.' And Moses took the blood and threw it upon the people and said, 'Behold the blood of the covenant which the Lord has made with you in accordance with all these words'."

Zechariah understood the blood of the covenant to have messianic significance. It would be upon the occasion of the messiah's entrance into Jerusalem that God would set his captives free "because of the blood of my covenant with you." (*Zech.* 9.11) Jesus' full statement has most often been understood in *Zechariah*'s terms.

"This is my blood of the covenant which is poured out for many. Truly, I say to you, I shall not drink again of the fruit of the vine until that day when I drink it new in the kingdom of God."

The interpretation hinges upon the meaning of kingdom of God. As always in *Mark* it means obedience to God's sovereignty. It does not refer to an apocalyptic transformation of the world, God's supernatural intervention into human affairs, or anything of that kind. It would read most understandably if put in these English words:

"I shall not drink again of the blood of the covenant until that day when I truly obey what the covenant of God demands and thus drink a new wine."

Not only does such a translation fit both the letter and the spirit of the words themselves, it also fits the context of Jesus' emerging decision to yield himself to voluntary death as an act of obedience to God.

The meal concluded with a hymn. If it was the hymn traditionally sung at the end of a Passover meal, its text came from *Psalms* 115-118, called the Hallel. The recurrent theme of the Hallel is God's rescue of his people; the concluding psalm emphasized the line: "His steadfast love endures forever!" It was an appropriate psalm for Jesus the son who was searching for an adequate response to the Father's love. Mark had already emphasized its appropriateness by quoting on Jesus' lips its passage about the rejected stone becoming the head of the corner and by alluding to its "festal procession with branches" as part of Jesus' triumphal entry.

THE IDENTITY OF THE SON OF MAN

A major problem in the interpretation of the Passover meal event was Jesus' assertion that the "son of man" was to go "as it is written of him" in scripture. In the Markan context, Jesus must have been referring to his own death as son of man. The difficulty is that nowhere in scripture that scholars have been able to identify is there a passage containing a literal prediction of betrayal or death for a figure bearing the title of son of man. To indicate the complexity of that problem for Markan interpretation, it is helpful to gather in one place all of the son of man passages referring to suffering, death, betrayal.

"And he began to teach them that the Son of man must suffer many things, and be rejected by the elders and the chief priests and the chief priests and the scribes, and be killed, and after three days rise again." (8.31)

"For what can a man give in return for his life? For whoever is ashamed of me and of my words in this adulterous and sinful generation, of him will the Son of man also be ashamed, when he comes in the glory of his Father with the holy angels." (8.37-38)

"Elijah does come first to restore all things; and how is it written of the Son of man, that he should suffer many things and be treated with contempt? But I tell you that Elijah has come, and they did to him whatever they pleased, as it is written of him." (9.12-13)

"The Son of man will be delivered into the hands of men, and they will kill him; and when he is killed, after three days he will rise." (9.31)

"Behold, we are going up to Jerusalem; and the Son of man will be delivered to the chief priests and the scribes, and they will condemn him to death, and deliver him to the Gentiles; and they will mock him, and spit upon him, and scourge him, and kill him; and after three days he will rise." (10.33-34)

"For the Son of man also came not to be served but to serve, and to give his life as a ransom for many." (10.45)

"For the Son of man goes, as it is written of him, but woe to that man by whom the Son of man is betrayed!" (14.21)

"It is enough; the hour has come; the Son of man is betrayed into the hands of sinners." (14.41)

"Day after day I was with you in the temple teaching, and you did not seize me. But let the scriptures be fulfilled. And they all forsook him, and fled." (14.49-50)

"Again the high priest asked him, 'Are you the Christ, the Son of the Blessed?' and Jesus said, 'I am; and you will see the Son of man sitting at the right hand of Power, and coming with the clouds of heaven.'" (14.61-62)

Several possibilities for patterns from tradition emerge from such a list. *Mark* 8.37-38 may have its roots in a popular apocalyptic Jewish book which did not find its way into the canon, *Enoch*, where the Son of man is distinctly a messianic figure seated at the right hand of glory. The *Enoch* passage might also account for the request of Jacob (James) and John to be seated next to Jesus when he came into his glory. It could be that Mark was influenced by other non-biblical books which I have not considered in my own attempt to reconstruct Mark's logic.

A second possibility is that *Mark* 10.45 was intended to be patterned after *Isaiah* 53.12.

"Therefore will I divide him a portion with the great, and he shall divide the spoil with the strong; because he poured out his soul unto death, and was numbered with the transgressors; yet he bare the sin of many, and made intercession for the transgressors."

The logic of the easy victory section of *Mark*, in which being last was the method for getting to be first, was a temptative perversion of the poem about the Suffering Servant in *Isaiah*, but was clearly built upon it.

Could it be that the general model of the Suffering Servant was the basis for Jesus' predictions of his own suffering and death? The identification between Jesus and the Suffering Servant has been strong in Christian writings. There are at least four reasons for supporting such a hypothesis. One is the general willingness of both Jesus and the Servant to suffer voluntarily. A second is the fact that the *Isaiah* poem compares the Servant with the "sons of men" thus providing a possible link with Mark's concern for the son of man. A third reason is the possibility that *Isaiah*'s image of the Servant as a "lamb that is led to the slaughter" might relate to the lamb slain for the Passover meal. This would be more plausible if Jesus had referred to himself as the slain lamb rather than as broken bread and shed blood. The fourth reason for associating *Isaiah*'s poem with Jesus' reference to himself as the suffering and slain son of man is that the poem began by referring to the gospel. By far the strangest literary fact in *Mark* is the absence of any reference to the gospel in *Isaiah* after the opening assertion that the gospel began in *Isaiah*. The Suffering Servant poem began as follows:

"How beautiful upon the mountain are the feet of him who brings glad tidings (the gospel), who publishes peace, who brings good tidings (the gospel) of good, who publishes salvation, who says to Zion, 'Your God reigns'."

If Mark intended Jesus' words, "as it is written," to refer to the Suffering Servant as the one who brings the gospel, it would make sense out of all the intervening silence on the subject of gospel in *Isaiah*.

Unfortunately tnere are two overwhelming reasons for rejecting such a conjecture. The first is that it would make *Isaiah* an adequate interpreter of gospel. It would provide in the imagery of the Suffering Servant a sufficient Jewish answer to the question of what it means to be a beloved son of God. That possibility would be inconsistent with the conclusion at which Jesus and Mark ultimately arrived, namely that no Jewish model was good enough for reconciling son to Father.

An even more compelling reason against the Servant hypothesis is that Mark passed up the opporutnity to pattern the events of the Passion Week after the details of *Isaiah* 52-53 as he did after the details of *Psalm* 22. Mark's style seems to have been to exhaust each model of which he made use. Virtually every pericope from the Elijah-Elisha cycle has a counterpart in Jesus' career. So does every major motif from *Malachi*, plus much of *Ezekiel, Zechariah, Daniel,* the Jacob-

Joseph stories, and several of the *Psalms*. It is virtually inconceivable that Mark would have used the Suffering Servant as a pattern for the suffering of the son of man and then have taken no explicit details from the poem. Mark apparently was content to refer to *Isaiah* and *Nahum* for the purpose of describing the beginning of the gospel without any carry-over for the development of the gospel.

The most fruitful possibility for discovering the biblical referent for the predictions of the suffering, betrayal, and death of the son of man stems from the fact that Mark increasingly used details from one or another of the *Psalms*. A key one is in the account of the Passover meal.

"And as they were at table eating, Jesus said, 'Truly, I say to you, one of you will betray me, one who is eating with me.' They began to be sorrowful, and to say to him one after another, 'Is it I?' He said to them, 'It is one of the twelve, one who is dipping bread in the same dish with me. For the Son of man goes, as it is written of him....'."

Psalm 41 described the betrayal of the psalmist by "mine own familiar friend, in whom I trusted, who did eat of my bread...." *Psalm* 41 does not refer to the son of man, but it is apparent that Mark interpreted the psalm as a reference to the son of man. That fact is the key clue for unlocking the secret of the whole series of son of man passages which refer to suffering, betrayal, and death.

It is likely that Mark understood the *Psalms* as a single book rather than as a collection of separate poems. He apparently reasoned that what applied to one part of the book applied to all of it. Thus Mark could build on sonship references such as these.

"I will tell of the decree of the Lord. He said to me, "You are my son; today I have begotten you." (*Ps.* 2.7)

"What is man that thou art mindful of him, and the son of man that thou dost care for him?" (*Ps.* 8.4)

Even though such passages did not refer to the suffering or death of a son of man they could be combined with other passages from *Psalms* to justify the Markan assertion that the son of man went to suffering and death "as it is written of him". Once having made such an identification, virtually every detail of the crucifixion could come from a reference in a psalm which did not explicitly refer to a son of man. Jesus explored such psalmic possibilities in great detail.

It was also in the *Psalms* that Jesus discovered the models for the relation of the son to the Father. In poem after poem, the psalmists described the persecution they were undergoing at the hands of their enemies. In poem after poem they asked for God's help, and in all cases ended their poems by indicating that such help had been given. Occasionally the final confidence was preceded by a time of doubt, by a question as to whether God was abandoning the psalmist. Jesus showed particular interest in that issue: was the suffering of the son of man to be climaxed by abandonment or by rescue? The two sides of the son of man motif, the humanistic side and the supernatural rescue side, were involved in that question as they had been in every other son of man passage in *Mark*.

When son of man is viewed as an idiomatic way of saying human being, as is often the case in *Psalms*, the scriptural possibilities for interpreting Jesus' reference to the predictions of the suffering of the son of man are considerably broadened. They could then include the sufferings of the Suffering Servant, the prophet Jeremiah whose life may have been used as a model by the poet who wrote the Suffering Servant poem, Job, and the other materials in scripture which are interrelated with *Isaiah, Jeremiah,* and *Job.*

The use of son of man as a general designation also calls attention to one of the most important senses of sonship in the Jewish Bible, the sons of Adam. The genealogical passages in *Genesis* were given great emphasis by their author. In the Greek language there were two ways of writing "son of man". One of them, "son of anair," was intended generically to refer to the son of all mankind. The latter word for man in Greek was the equivalent of the Hebrew word for Adam, he whose name literally meant Mankind. In a strictly legalistic literary sense all sons of man were sons of Adam.

Jesus explored many meanings of sonship. He had during his career related himself to the sons of Jacob, the sons of David, the sons of the prophets, the son of man as portrayed variously in *Ezekiel* and *Daniel*, the general notion of Israel as a young man, the son of Mary, the son of whoever would do the will of God, the only Holy Son of God, and probably some other concepts which I have missed. I am convinced that in his willingness to be betrayed to death Jesus transformed the meaning of sonship. For him to be a son of man was no longer to adopt a messianic title which necessitated a particular historical justification. It now took on for him the meaning of all sonship. the son of humanity, the son of every generation, all the sons of scripture, the recurring son. By his death he was to become what any son should be who wished properly to respond to the father's love. He was in that sense son of man.

The crucifixion was to be not only an instance of unjust capital punishment. It was also to be the final confrontation between son and father, in which the son's love would be tested by his conviction that the father had abandoned him. In Jewish scripture, the betrayal turned out in each case to be a false alarm; God rescued the psalmist from his difficulties. In *Mark* the betrayal turned out to be for real; there was to be no rescue.

HOW COULD JESUS HAVE KNOWN THAT HE WOULD BE BETRAYED?

On the surface, Jesus' prediction that one of the twelve would betray him gave the impression that he had some inside knowledge. It appeared either that the news that one of the twelve was to betray him was leaked to him, or that he knew by miracle what Judas was planning.

A different possibility arises from interpreting the betrayal as a psychological event in Jesus' own inner development. Previously Jesus had intuited what others would do or think because of what was happening to him. So it was when he accused the scribes of condemning him for blasphemy, and when he labeled Peter (Rocky) as satanic for calling him messiah. Major surface events in the careers of both John the Baptizer and Jesus had their greater significance as expressions of the internal development of each man. John's arrest and death were more events of his spiritual failure than they were physical occurrences. Jesus was in danger of being crushed by the crowd only in the sense that he was lured by the enticement of popularity. His self-imposed exile to foreign territory was the outward expression of his mental rejection of Jewish models. His journey to the mount of transfiguration need not have involved a mountain; it was essentially a temptation event in the imagination of Jesus and the Big Three.

Betrayal was of a similar nature for Jesus. The record of the twelve indicated that all of them, not just Judas, had their sights set on greatness, glory, victory, unearthly brightness. They basked in the glory of their successful master, so much that they were willing to protect him equally from little children and miraculous competitors. They had emulated him by both preaching and healing as they had seen him do. For Jesus to abandon his dreams of greatness and voluntarily give himself to death was virtually to demand that all of the twelve, singly or in combination, betray him. They could not have done otherwise.

That is to say, betrayal was an act which grew naturally out of Jesus' own decisions. It was he who had fired the Judean flames of desire for freedom from Roman rule by riding into Jerusalem in the manner of a Davidic messiah. It was he who had roused the Capernaum hope for a compassion which would abolish both sickness and death in a single generation. It was he who had at every turn undercut the incipient efforts of the twelve by showing them how to perform difficult tasks easily by means of miracle. It was he who had combed the scriptures and found in them many pious but Satanic alternatives to a proper response to God's love. It was Jesus who constructed the situation out of which betrayal was the natural and normal consequence. To have prevented betrayal, all of Israel would have had to change simultaneously with his own transformation from easy victory to voluntary death.

To say that betrayal was a natural consequence of the situation which Jesus had constructed around himself does not answer the question as to how he knew specifically that he would be betrayed. That question is followed in the *Mark* text by two similar ones: how could Jesus have known that he was to go to Galilee after his death and resurrection, and how could he have known that Peter was to deny him exactly three times after the crowing of dawn's rooster? None of the questions admit of exact answers, but all of them have a similar general answer.

Jesus knew that he was to be betrayed because he decided to explore the meaning of betrayal. This does not mean that he arranged to be betrayed, but it does mean that he decided to cease his intervention into the failure-proneness of the twelve. Heretofore, he had always rescued them from their own weaknesses—in the boat, at the feeding of the crowd, in the miracles of restored understanding. Now he had decided to stop functioning as a rescuer. The consequences were predictable. Symbolically the betrayal would be performed by a Judah, for Judah was the biblical name for betrayal. Factually, all of the twelve would desert him; all of the twelve were his trusted friends who would "turn their heels against him" as *Psalm* 41 suggested. Symbolically the Big Three went to sleep in Gethsemane and would not watch with Jesus during his hour of decision. Symbolically Rocky would exemplify his surname by falling away under conditions of persecution as the parable of the soils had suggested. All such acts were Judah acts, summarized in the betrayal by Judas Iscariot.

For Jesus to stop functioning as a rescuer was a decision with a reverse side. In *Psalms*, God was the rescuer. For Jesus to abandon rescue as a career activity implied that he would also no longer expect God so to function. Thus Jesus was involved not only in decision about himself but also in a fundamental redefinition of the nature of God.

HOW COULD JESUS HAVE KNOWN THAT HE WAS TO GO TO GALILEE?

Immediately after the supper, Jesus and the twelve (probably only the eleven, without Judas who had to leave sometime during the evening to be able to lead the arresting crowd back later) went to the Mount of Olives. The first event to occur there was a conversation in which Jesus predicted that all of the twelve would abandon him and would be scattered, but that he later would be resurrected and precede the twelve (or eleven) to Galilee. What had there been in Jesus' internal development which would justify such a prediction?

Galilee was home for both Jesus and the twelve. It was Jewish borderland. In Mark's geography, South of Judea there was nothing, but North of Galilee was Gentile territory. Galilee was ideologically the only place where Judaism bordered on foreignness. Galilee was Hellenized Judaism, the locale for Hellenized Hebrew names and Greek names. Galilee was Elijah country, the arena in which Jesus had worked through most of the temptations inherent in following Elijah's path to being God's beloved son. In short, the Galilee of Jesus' career was not primarily a geographical area. It was essentially a state of mind, a type of existence.

Judea, by contrast, was David country. It was politically oriented according to the politics of the time: extremist, cruel, abrupt, violent. Within six days of Jesus' arrival in Judea's capital, Jerusalem, he had been both celebrated as a national liberator and executed as a betrayer of the national hope of liberation. It was in Judea that John the Baptizer had found unanimous response to his ritual demands and unanimous rejection of his plea for repentance. It was those same

Judeans who unanimously chose the insurrectionist Barabbas in place of the Jesus who would not fight back against Pilate.

The difference between Galilee and Judea was one of degrees. Both were violence prone. Galilee had its Herod who murdered John, just as Judea had its Pilate for Jesus. Both were subject to mass psychology. Galilee's crowds alternately surrounded Jesus and abandoned him according to his willingness to bend to the crowd's whim, just as Judea's crowds rose and fell in their opinion of John and Jesus. But Galilee provided time. Its leaders did not immediately state the issues in terms of life and death. Even Herod in all his cruelty had to be duped into the execution of John by the good act of keeping a promise the consequences of which he had not foreseen.

Judea was Judas country. Judea was named for Judah, the betrayer of Jospeh. From the viewpoint of Judeans, Judah was not remembered primarily as a betrayer. He was the lion of his father's blessing (Gen. 49.8-12), the chief among his brothers. From Mark's viewpoint, Judah was the betrayer. As namesake for Judea, he made all Judea the land of betrayal. Thus it was in *Mark* that Jesus' career brought him to Judea only once after his original calling, and that trip culminated in the conscious expectation that he would be betrayed and executed on the initiative of Judean leadership.

Galilee was the opportunity for growth; Judea the time of harvest. For any Jew seeking a relationship to God based on love between father and son, Galilee was the only acceptable site at which to begin. Gentile territory did not have the resources for the quest; Judea would not provide the time for it.

Jesus knew, without any necessity of miraculous foretelling of the future, what would happen if his disciples would continue the father-son relationship quest after his death. They had already launched themselves on the path by adopting the strategies of preaching and healing which had been his own starting points. That is to say, they had become twelve more new Elijahs, functioning in a new Galilee. Once started and continued, the rhythm of the search for father-son reconciliation was inevitable. It would lead by virtue of the resources in scripture and life to all of those son-related positions in Galilee which Jesus had explored along his way, and ultimately back to Judah's Jerusalem and death. In such a rhythm, Galilee was not necessarily a geographical area at all. It was the borderland between tradition and love, between the old answers and the new.

Jesus envisioned that his death would scatter the disciples like sheep without a shepherd, but that his resurrection would send them back to Galilee on the same paths which he had trod. It was not at all clear what kind of a resurrection that would be. Negatively, it could not be a simple physical miracle because a miracle of that kind would produce the opposite result. Instead of inducing the twelve to follow him on their own Galilean Elijah trail it would leave them permanently in the state of mind they experienced at the transfiguration, content to live forever in the reflected glory of others. Positively, it had to be a resurrection which would create in each of the twelve a sense of being loved somewhat comparable to Jesus' own spirit baptism in John's wilderness.

HOW COULD JESUS HAVE KNOWN THAT PETER WOULD DENY HIM THREE TIMES DURING THAT SAME NIGHT?

When Peter (Rocky) responded that he would not fall away even if all the others did, Jesus predicted explicitly that Peter (Rocky) would deny him three times during that very night. As David Breed puts it, "Before the rooster crows you will be chicken three times."

Jesus could easily have predicted that Peter would deny him some time. He would have needed no other information than his knowledge of Rocky's character which he had recognized at the time when he bestowed the surname upon him: one who would fall away "when tribulation or persecution arises on account of the word." (*Mark* 4.17) But to predict that there would be exactly three denials during a particular night seems to demand of Jesus some kind of superhuman knowledge since even Peter did not know in advance what he would do.

Gethsemane

The question as to how Jesus knew that Peter was to deny him exactly three times during the coming night can be answered only in the broad context of the role of Gethsemane in Jesus' total career. Between the baptism and the crucifixion, the event in Gethsemane was the single most important one in Jesus' career. It provides the definitive clues for the interpretation of *Mark*.

Several preliminary observations are necessary in order to view the contextual relationship of Gethsemane to Jesus' total career. First, the name Gethsemane means Oil Vat, hence idiomatically the place of anointing with the oil of the messanic Mount of Olives, on which Gethsemane was located. It was here that Jesus first fully accepted the right answer to this long quest and was thus properly anointed as the messiah.

Second, it was at Gethsemane that Jesus first accepted God as his father and himself as God's son. Heretofore he had explored many other designations of sonship, but had never admitted, even privately to himself according to *Mark*, that he was really the son of God. In doing so, he addressed God by both the formal title, "Father" and by the more affectionate "Abba" (Papa, Daddy, etc.).

Third, just as there were exact parallels between the first "triumphal" entry into Jerusalem and the preparations for the Passover meal, so there were equally exact parallels between Gethsemane and the events connected with the Mount of Transfiguration. Both events occurred on a mountain. The response of the Big Three was similar on both occasions. At the transfiguration, "he (Peter) did not know what to say, for they were exceedingly afraid." In Gethsemane, "he (Jesus) came and found them sleeping, for their eyes were heavy; and they did not know what to answer him." On both occasions their failure was linked to inability to speak. In *Mark*'s symbolism such failure undoubtedly refers to their spiritual blindness and deafness which was accompanied by spiritual muteness. At the transfiguration they did not listen; in Gethsemane they did not watch.

In both events Jesus confronted God. At the transfiguration, while being tempted to see himself as a leader clothed in unearthly brightness he was reminded of God's love for him as a son. In Gethsemane he submitted to God's will by acknowledging himself as a son. The only other occasions in *Mark* in which God and Jesus were mentioned in the Father-son relationship, other than by tempting spirits, was at the baptism and crucifixion.

The sequence of those four events, standing out thematically as they do from the rest of the book, compel us to re-examine their flow of thought. At the baptism Jesus saw the spirit of holiness descend upon himself and heard an unspecified voice which presumably was the voice of God. Mark, however, did not identify the voice as being that of God. Between the baptism and the transfiguration, unclean spirits sought over and over to provide for Jesus a temptative interpretation of that voice and its message.

At the transfiguration another voice, also presumably the voice of God but unidentified by Mark, reiterated the announcement that Jesus was the beloved son. This time, however, the information was intended for the Big Three rather than for Jesus. The three missed its significance entirely and never mentioned it thereafter according to *Mark*. Perhaps there was some thematic connection between their inability to speak and the possibility that they had not really heard when they were told to listen to God's son.

At the base of the mountain, when Jesus rejoined the rest of the twelve, he cast out an unclean spirit for the final time and ordered it never to return. The entire Markan motif of the conflict between the spirit of holiness and the unclean spirits occurred between the baptism and the transfiguration. At Gethsemane the spirit motif was reintroduced in the saying about spirit and flesh, thus raising the interpretative probability that temptations had a different content before and after both the transfiguration and Gethsemane. I will return to that point. Meantime, note that Jesus said of his act of ridding himself forever of the unclean spirit temptation that such a result could be achieved only by prayer, and not by the miracle of exorcism which the disciples were ineffectually trying to use. At that time, however, Jesus did not pray. He seemed to exorcise the demon, thus establishing the probability that the act was symbolic and that prayer would later figure in a decisive act of overcoming temptation.

At Gethsemane, Jesus prayed three times. In his prayers he privately accepted voluntary death as his son of God role. This was the only occasion since the transfiguration in which it was reported by Mark that Jesus prayed. It was also the occasion at which Jesus overcame the long series of temptations which had kept him from discovering the adequate content of sonship. There can thus be little doubt that Mark intended Gethsemane as the fulfillment of the predictive qualities of the transfiguration event.

Mark designated only three times at which Jesus prayed, each involving a major decision in his quest for sonship. There were three other incidents in which Jesus pronounced the blessing for food, but Mark did not label those as acts of praying. It may be that Mark conceived of prayer itself as a father-son relationship involving major decision-making. If so, the exorcism of the demons and other forces of temptation which kept Jesus from an adequate response to sonship could happen only in prayer. To seek to achieve the same end by miracle would be to succumb to the demons. Only in direct confrontation with the Father could the son discover his proper relationship.

With Jesus during his prayer were the Big Three who had been told at the transfiguration that Jesus was the son of God. Jesus' request that the three watch seems to make sense only in the context of their knowledge that he was son of God but had not yet been confronted with the moment in which he had finally to claim or reject such sonship. On their last previous visit to the Mount of Olives they had asked him about signs of the future, and his final word on that subject had been that the only guideline for the future was to be alert for such an occasion.

If, as seems most likely, Jesus' Big Three were the symbolic counterparts of Judaism's Big Three patriarchs, the Gethsemane incident demanded a universalistic definition of sonship. Abraham was known as father of the Jews. The relationships among Abraham, Isaac, and Jacob were father-son relationships. Together, the three men stood for the entire history of Jewish origins. Both the transfiguration and Gethsemane experiences left the patriarchs with nothing to say. It was they who finally failed Jesus in his hour of greatest need. It was their children, symbolized by Judas and embodied in the Judean Jews, who were to betray Jesus and arrange for his execution. To be a son of Abraham, Isaac, and Jacob was not sufficient for being a child of God.

The sonship motif, as described in the above paragraph, may give a clue as to why Jesus addressed Peter as Simon at Gethsemane. Mark called him Peter; Jesus called him Simon. As Peter he was the disciple who accepted the word with eagerness but would fall away equally soon under conditions of persecution. As Simon he was a son of Jacob and a symbolic representative of Judaism.

The sequence from the transfiguration to Gethsemane also helps put the relationship between son of God and son of man into proper focus. At the transfiguration, the son of man title was still for Jesus a contradiction between the manliness of voluntary death and the godliness of supernatural glorification. At Gethsemane the contradiction was resolved. Jesus accepted voluntary death as his duty as son of God and went forward to be betrayed as son of man. For the first time in his career, son of man and son of God had the same meaning for Jesus.

138

At Jesus' trial before the chief priests, he was asked if he was the son of God. He acknowledged publicly that he was, thus completing the rhythm of the four father-son confrontations.

Baptism	Private announcement to Jesus only
Transfiguration	Public announcement to Big Three
Gethsemane	Private acceptance by Jesus
Trial	Public acceptance by Jesus

Even in accepting the role of son of God privately Jesus knew that death was already its consequence. When he accepted it publicly the officials of Judaism declared that the death penalty was the appropriate consequence. Their rationale, the defense of monotheism, is easy to comprehend. Jesus' reason for connecting sonship and death is much more difficult to comprehend and will demand a thorough analysis.

Denial and Betrayal During This Same Night

If one starts with the assumption that Jesus did not have advance information about what would happen later that night after the Passover meal and Gethsemane, one must conclude that there are necessary logical and scriptural connections between the commitment to voluntary death and the inevitability of immediate denial and betrayal.

The first night of Passover was the night of death. On that night the eldest son and first born of the cattle of each family in Egypt died. When that night was celebrated the idea of death was in the air.

Fathers were instructed to teach their sons the meaning of that night. The ritual of the meal had been built around that relationship of father and son. The very purpose of the celebration was to pass on to the sons the meaning of Passover. The success of that ritual is still obvious today in that it is a major unifying factor among otherwise discordant divisions of Judaism.

Jesus' problem was that at the Passover meal and in Gethsemane he chose to reject the Passover tradition. It held that on this night Jewish sons would be saved, and only Egyptian sons killed. Now, Jesus was committing himself to voluntary death. Whoever followed him on that route could not longer be Jewish insofar as God's deliverance from Egypt was definitive of Judaism.

In that respect, everyone who wished to remain Jewish would have to dissociate himself from Jesus immediately, i.e. during the night in which he refused to be a son according to the tradition. Denial and betrayal during that particular night were thus necessary according to the logical requirements of the scriptural instructions about Passover.

Denial Exactly Three Times

In point of fact, Peter (Rocky) denied Jesus seven times during the Passover night, three times while Jesus was at prayer, once at the arrest, and three times in the courtyard of the high priests. The two groups of three call attention to the significance of threeness as a clue to the meaning of the night's events.

In Gethsemane, Jesus prayed three times. He took with him for that occasion only three of the twelve disciples, the Big Three. Before he separated himself from them, he told them that he was suffering great internal distress and that he was troubled about the immanence of his death. He suggested to them that they could somehow share with him the import of that hour by watching, by being alert, while he went to pray. He prayed; the three went to sleep. Jesus returned, awakened them, repeated the instructions along with a warning and went again to pray. A second time they slept; Jesus returned, reiterated his warning, and left a third time. A third time they went to sleep. Jesus interpreted their sleepiness as providing the occasion on which he was to be betrayed.

The narrative raises a host of problems, few of which have satisfactory answers. To begin with, there was nothing in Jesus prayer which demanded that it be prayed three times. The language of the prayer implied that Jesus had accepted God as his father for the first time in his entire career. Jesus addressed God as "abba" (daddy or papa) in addition to the more formal "father". He requested that the cup of death be taken from him, but pledged himself to submit to the will of the father rather than following his own desire. For Jesus to have said all that once would have been as effective as saying it three times.

It would be inconsistent with Mark's style to picture Jesus as having prayed three times merely in order to give the disciples three opportunities to fall asleep, and thus prove that he was right in predicting that Peter would deny him three times during that night. Nowhere else does Mark indicate that Jesus had such a picayune attitude.

The Gethsemane story appears to be too stylized to be accepted as simple reporting of an event. It seems inconceivable that Jesus would pray the same words three times, that all three men would go to sleep three times and that Jesus would twice speak identical words to them, all in the immediate context of a prediction that Peter would deny Jesus three times and just prior to another occasion on which he did so.

The same three men were present who had participated in the companion event on the Mount of Transfiguration. The parallels between those events are precise in other respects, but there was little reason for three people only to be there unless their threeness was in itself significant. Add to this the three passion predictions and the persistent fact of resurrection on the third day, and there are far too many threes in the transfiguration-Gethsemane cycle for coincidence or accident.

I have earlier noted the mysterious connections between the number three and the reports of resurrections in the Elijah-Elisha cycle, and the possibility that the Big Three were representative of the three patriarchs of Judaism. Another significant instance of threeness is found in *Exodus* 19, just before Moses went up to Mt. Sinai to receive the tablets of the law in the direct presence of God. That event happened, according to God's directions, on the third day of the third new moon after the departure from Egypt. The central details of mountain, confrontation with God, and emphasis on the number three are probably enough to tie together the transfiguration, Gethsemane, and the incident on Mt. Sinai. Assuming that to be so, Jesus' transfiguration would have been in the presence of Moses, Elijah, and the three symbolic patriarchs. At that time, Jesus had dissociated himself from the Moses and Elijah traditions, but not from the patriarchal tradition, i.e. original Judaism.

Prior to the original Passover night, the Egyptians had suffered from three days of darkness whereas the Hebrews were in light. It is hard to imagine what the author of *Exodus* had in mind in picturing the relationship of Egyptians and Hebrews by such imagery, unless what was for the Egyptians darkness was for the Hebrews light. At the end of the third day, the Egyptian misery became deep darkness in the death of their eldest sons and cattle. That darkness was the source of freedom for the Hebrews, their light.

It is likely that there were two diametrically opposite but closely related meanings in threeness at this stage of Jesus' career. One was the scriptural sense of expectation about the third day and the three patriarchs, probably rooted in numerological origins no longer known, but abundantly evidenced in Jewish Bible. The other was the clarity of Jesus' conviction that all the Jewish expectations had failed. Everything about threeness was now involved in Jewish going to sleep, denial, accusation, trials, etc. The Big Three had to go to sleep three times; Peter had to deny Jesus' three times; there had to be three trials; the sun would not shine at the crucifixion for three hours—all to demonstrate that the failure was that of Judaism in general and not just Peter in particular. Peter was merely its spokesman.

SPIRIT VERSUS FLESH

Prior to the transfiguration, Jesus' career conflicts were symbolized by the tensions between two spirits, holy and unclean. Both sets of spirit voices called Jesus to self definitions based on patterns which were external to himself. The spirit issues questioned whether it was better to be a preacher or a physician, whether to emphasize forgiveness or ritual, whether to be associated with one's biological family or a new family of like-minded people, and whether to demand of others that they live proper lives without assistance or to rescue them when they failed. The spirit issues juxtaposed the kind of messianic leadership which Jesus wanted to provide with the kind the Jews were willing to accept. But in all cases the spirit conflicts concerned leadership styles which made more difference to the followers than to the leader. It was they who were to obey preaching, receive healing, be forgiven, etc.

After the transfiguration, when there were no longer any unclean spirits in Jesus' experience, leadership gave way to personal accomplishment. The same rhythm of temptation, inadequacy in the midst of good, continued, but the conflicts were now between images of personal self-giving and personal glorification. There was a remarkable consistency between the leadership styles desired earlier by the crowds and the opportunities for personal glorification explored by Jesus. Even though the latter did not depend upon the loyalty of the crowds for their success, the crowds were totally willing to follow in the train of the glorified one, thus bestowing upon him the role of leader whether he intended it or not.

Only at Gethsemane did the meaning of this shift become apparent to Jesus. He recognized that his personal problem was not a conflict of good and bad spirits, but a much more deeply rooted tension between all spirit willing to do the good and the flesh's opposition to pain and death. Even the unclean spirits had advocated goods of great excellence. They too were in conflict with the unadulterated self-centeredness of flesh.

Note that Jesus recognized that this conflict was as relevant to the Big Three of Judaism as it was to himself.

> "Simon, are you asleep? Could you not watch one hour? Watch and pray that you may not enter into temptation; the spirit indeed is willing, but the flesh is weak." (*Mark* 14.37-38)

When Jesus found the three taking their ease in sleep after his third period of prayer, he knew that flesh had won its battle with spirit in their case.

Another Look At Peter's Denials

In the instant that Jesus took his stand firmly for spirit and the Big Three were content with flesh, the relationship between them underwent a qualitative change. Recall that when Jesus sent the twelve out on a mission, they imitated his previous behavior. He had preached, they preached. He had healed; they healed. He had cast out demons; they cast out demons. They were Junior models of the messianic leader.

After Gethsemane this was no longer the case. He had entered fully into the realm of spirit which their devotion to flesh could not comprehend. By that act he became fully a stranger to them, one whom they could not recognize even though he continued to have the same physical characteristics they had been familiar with. This was exactly the problem at the heart of the resurrection narratives in *Matthew, Luke, John,* and *Acts,* although in different settings.

In an important sense, the gospel which began in *Isaiah* predicted such a result. Both the crowds and the twelve had been unable to see with the inner eye of understanding. Peter, suffering from the half-healed blindness of the acted parable, had been able to recognize Jesus only as a heavenly figure and not as the son of God and son of man en route to the cross.

So it was that when Peter was asked by the maid in the courtyard of the high priest if Peter was acquainted with Jesus, he had to say "No!"

He was in fact unacquainted with him; he had never really seen him or listened to him. In a simple physical sense, Peter was lying for he had often been with the body of the man who had opted for spirit rather than flesh. But Peter had made the opposite choice and could thus see only with the eyes of flesh. The man of spirit he never knew.

THE BETRAYAL BY JUDAS

Jesus could not be God's son in the truest meaning of that term until all men had abandoned him. That is, he could not go voluntarily to the cross until he went alone. According to the passion predictions he had to be murdered by everyone, by Jews, by mankind, by foreigners. Symbolically, the loyalty of the Big Three and particularly the loyalty of their spokesman, Simon, was the last barrier between Jesus and the fulfillment of his quest. When the weakness of Simon's flesh was stronger than the willingness of his spirit of loyalty, the conditions for the crucifixion were completed. The betrayal could then occur.

The aloneness of crucifixion was primarily a thematic necessity which had little to do with the decisions of the particular people around Jesus. The voluntariness of the crucifixion had less to do with Jesus' rejection by others than it had with the intensity of his own internal decision. That decision had to be made utterly alone. No one else would or could have made it for him. Betrayal was thus the thematic counterpart of aloneness.

While Jesus and the eleven were still on the Mount of Olives, Judas came from the chief priests, scribes, and elders, accompanied by an armed crowd. He performed three acts. First, he asked that Jesus be lead away in safety. Second, he addressed Jesus as "Master". Finally, he kissed him. These were the acts of betrayal by a friend rather than a foe. It was apparent that Judas, out of loyalty to Jesus as master, was doing that he thought best for Jesus.

Another one of the twelve used his sword to defend Jesus by cutting off the ear of the servant of the high priest. It is highly probable, with all of Mark's interest in the symbolism of seeing and hearing, that Mark intended this account to be read symbolically. If so, it would probably imply that in a subsequent event the high priest would be unable to hear spiritually. In any case, it is important in Jesus' development that he did not respond to the incident by an act of healing. His voluntary crucifixion depended absolutely upon his willingness to yield all power and especially the power to use miracle. He was also beyond the point of seeking to heal the sight and hearing of others. The act of defending Jesus with a sword was a different kind of betrayal, equally as well intentioned as that of Judas, equally as concerned about Jesus' physical safety, equally as oblivious to the decision he had made to submit himself to God's will.

FLIGHT OF THE TWELVE

When Jesus was in the power of the crowd and Judean officialdom, everyone who had previously followed him fled, leaving Jesus without supporters. On this occasion, in physical fact, those who fled were the twelve. They in turn symbolized by a young man who had been clothed only in linen cloth, but who left the linen behind when he fled from the arrest scene.

Some scholars have speculated that this pericope was the disguised signature of the author, his way of intruding himself into the Jesus story by telling of his own involvement. Built from that hypothesis is the further fiction that it was in Mark's mother's home that the last supper was held, and that he arrived at the arrest scene by sneaking out of the house and by following Jesus to Gethsemane after supper.

A more adequate interpretation stems from Mark's counscious use of symbolism. Throughout the book, he had used young people as symbols of Israel, particularly the new Israel which some of the prophets and Jesus had each envisioned. Linen was introduced as a symbol for the first time in this pericope. It was used once again, as the shroud in which Jesus was buried. It fits perfectly into Mark's thesis to say that the twelve and all others who had followed Jesus fled from burial linen. They wanted nothing to do with a messiah who would permit himself to be killed.

CHAPTER TEN
THE CRUCIFIXION: THE THREE TRIALS

When Jesus was arrested he was on the Mount of Olives outside Jerusalem. Immediately afterward he was taken under arrest back to Jerusalem, thus marking his fifth entry into the city. The contrast from his first entry was dramatic. He had then been the triumphant messianic claimant whom everyone welcomed. He was now the lonely son of God from whom everyone had fled.

THE FIRST TRIAL

The first trial occurred before the high priest. Assembled with him were all the chief priests, as well as all the members of the Sanhedrin and some scribes. For such an assemblage to be brought together late at night after the Passover meal must have been a considerable accomplishment on the part of whoever was masterminding the plot against Jesus. Nevertheless, once Jesus had been brought before the group it became apparent that the council was determined in some sense to act justly. Many false charges were brought against Jesus, including the charge that he had threatened to destroy the Jerusalem temple and to build another in its place in three days without using human hands. But those who were testifying to such charges did not agree with each other, and the council did not hold him to be guilty. When the high priests asked Jesus to defend himself against the false charges he refused to do so and kept silent.

The strange fact about the central false charge was that it was both true and false. Jesus had not been quoted by Mark as having said any such thing. Even if Jesus had said it, he would not have intended it as a threat to raze the building or a boast to be able to construct a building miraculously. Still the statement was true. Jesus was a threat to the temple. His death would psychologically destroy it for all who followed him. During those centuries when the Jews have been without a physical building called the temple many of them have still been temple-oriented. In their hopes and prayers and imaginations they have looked back with nostalgia to the temples of yesteryear and looked forward with yearning to a temple yet to come. Jesus' death would end all that for any Jew who became a Jesus follower. And on the third day, on resurrection day, there would be established a new focus for worship in place of the temple.

The high priest then asked Jesus the key question:
"Are you the messiah, the Son of the Blessed?"
Jesus' answer was, in effect, affirmative. The question appears to have two parts but was undoubtedly intended by the high priest to be single. It implied that anyone claiming to be the messiah would also

have to claim to be the divine Son of God. The question was intended to ask if Jesus made that claim? The circumlocution, "Son of the Blessed," was used because an orthodox Jew would not speak the name God directly, but every Jew would understand the intent.

The intent of the question and the actual words of the question were not necessarily the same. The words were neutral and permitted an entirely different interpretation. Jesus responded to them as if they meant that the messiah was a man who properly understood his role as son of God.

Jesus went beyond the simple affirmation which the high priest was asking for. He added the observation that the high priest and the others would see his answer in terms of *Daniel's* supernatural Son of man seated at the right hand of God and coming on the clouds. He did not tell them what he knew, namely that they would be wrong in so doing, that their seeing would be the special kind of blindness from which all suffered who could not see messiahship in the crucifixion.

By virtue of Jesus' affirmative answer to the question which the high priest intended, Jesus was in fact guilty of blasphemy. It is ironic that Jesus was finally found guilty of blasphemy because it was the charge which he first intuited that the scribes would bring against him in Capernaum for offering forgiveness to the crowds. Had the crowds with the unclean spirits had their way, Jesus would long since have been found guilty of this charge, because they wanted him to proclaim himself publicly as the Holy One of God. To do so would have been blasphemy.

The chief priests and scribes had given Jesus an opportunity earlier to confess guilt to the charge of blasphemy. In the controversies following the cleansing of the temple, they had sought to trap him into asserting his divine authority in order to protect his popularity with the crowds. Had he done so, he would have been admittedly guilty of blasphemy. On that occasion he avoided the trap by tossing the hot potato question back to them.

In an entirely different sense, Jesus was innocent of the charge of blasphemy. For him to claim that he was the messiah and that the messiah was a man who had learned properly what it means to respond to the love of God as a son may have been unorthodox Jewish religion but it was not blasphemy. It was a redefinition of traditional theological terms, but it did not claim divine status or serve as an example of impious irreverence. It was a serious attempt to interpret scripture at a level of insight deeper than that attained by the scribes with whom Jesus came into contact. Even had he been mistaken his attempt would not have been properly labeled blasphemous.

Once Jesus had formally confessed his guilt to the charge in the form in which the council understood it, there was no question as to the verdict. According to scripture, he had to be guilty and to be condemned to death. That was not an arbitrary decision by cruel men; it was an essential aspect of the main thread of Jewish scripture: God was One, and nothing was to be permitted to threaten that oneness. It was the sacredness of Jewish monotheism which made it a desolating abomination to house a statue of a pagan deity in the temple. It was the sacredness of Jewish monotheism which made Elijah's murder of hundreds of priests of the Baalim a justifiable act. For the council to hear Jesus' confession of guilt and not assign the death penalty would have been unthinkable in traditional Judaism.

Nevertheless, the decision of the council was clothed in hypocrisy. The words with which the chief priests and scribes mocked Jesus when he was on the cross need to be taken seriously.

"Let the Christ, the King of Israel, come down now from the cross that we may see and believe." (*Mark* 15.32)

Had he done so, had he proclaimed his opposition to Rome by thwarting the decision of the Roman ruler, Pilate, the chief priests and scribes would have joined his movement with all the eagerness of converts. Their hypocrisy was made especially obvious by their support of Barabbas, the insurrectionist against Rome whose name was in fact blasphemous by every Jewish standard. The blasphemy was excusable because it was overshadowed by the willingness of Barabbas to provide what the priests wanted, a messiah in the tradition of King David. Such a messiah would not have been condemned for blasphemy even if he had been guilty of it.

At the first trial itself, some members of the court demeaned themselves by cheap mockery, unworthy of the stature of their religious office even if Jesus had deserved their verdict. They spat on him; they blindfolded him and then demanded that he use his miraculous power to tell them which of them was hitting him. The blindfold over his eyes symbolized the spiritual blindness of theirs.

THE SECOND TRIAL

In the three passion predictions in *Mark* 8, 9, 10, the first and third were quite specific. In the first, Jesus would be killed by Jewish officialdom; in the third, by Gentiles. The second, however, was very general: Jesus would be killed by mankind. So likewise were the trials. The first and third were formal trials before Jewish and Gentile courts. The second was general, in which Jesus was tried by mankind with Peter (Rocky) as its spokesman.

If it were not that the three passion predictions virtually demanded a general trial by mankind between the specific trials before the priests and Gentile rulers, one would never have imagined that Peter's three denials constituted a separate trial. Jesus was not present. This too was consistent with the second passion prediction, for Jesus had spoken it while in hiding in Galilee. The charges were levied against Peter, not against Jesus. It was Peter who knew himself to be guilty when the rooster heralded dawn. In what sense then was this event a trial?

The setting was simple. Peter had followed the arresting party at a distance and had gone into the courtyard of the high priest to warm his body at a fire. While there, he was asked three times to admit that he was a follower of Jesus. Three times he denied it, the third time emphasizing his denial by invoking a curse upon himself. The curse was appropriate.

At daybreak a rooster crowed. Peter was thus reminded that Jesus had predicted his triple failure less than half a day earlier. The impact of that memory was so powerful that Peter broke down and wept. He did not weep because his denials were hurting Jesus. He had not wept when he went to sleep three times in Gethsemane and thus set the final stage for betrayal. The going-to-sleep denials had been really damaging to Jesus, but Peter had not wept. His tears flowed when the crowing cock called Peter's attention to the emptiness of his boast that he would never fall away.

In that moment, Peter knew himself as Peter, as Rocky, as the one who would fall away when tribulation or persecution came. In that moment Peter represented the great percentage of mankind, those who would protect their own personal safety even at the price of denying any acquaintance with the son of man from Galilee. Just as Simon Peter represented Judaism in going to sleep three times in Gethsemane when Jesus spoke to him as Simon, so he now represented all mankind with the Greek name Peter.

The charge against Jesus in his first trial had been blasphemy, and at his final trial it was to be treason. Both were easily definable. But Peter's denials charged Jesus with a more serious and more complex fault, that of being a stranger to the concerns of mankind. It did not break the religious laws of the Jews or the political laws of the Romans, but it was an offense more heinous in the eyes of the multitudes. Jesus was the man no one knew, the alien even to his closest associates, the man of spirit in a world where everyone else in his immediate context preferred the concerns of flesh.

THIRD TRIAL

According to Mark, the Sanhedrin waited till after daybreak to arrive at a final decision about Jesus' fate. Recent historians, using Jewish records as their source material, have cast considerable doubt on the legality or likelihood of the Sanhedrin's procedure during that night. However right or wrong they may be, it does not affect the picture portrayed by Mark. He depicts the council as having met during the night for the purpose of receiving testimony, and then waiting till after daybreak to decide exactly what Jesus' punishment should be. Their decision was to bind Jesus and take him to the Roman governor (technically a procurator) with a request that the death penalty be imposed.

The Jewish officials gave Pilate many reasons for their request. The only one to which Pilate paid much attention was that Jesus had claimed to be the king of the Jews, i.e. their messiah. In a paradoxical way the charge was both true and false. In his guilty plea at the trial before the priests, Jesus had confessed that he claimed to be the messiah. At that trial his accusers defined messiahship in terms of divinity and convicted him of blasphemy. Now they chose to define messiahship in terms of political rule in order to get Jesus convicted of treason against Rome. At the time of the trial Jesus had no interest whatsoever in political rebellion against Rome. On the preceding Sunday, however, he had entered Jerusalem for the first time in a manner which promised Judeans that he would lead them in such an undertaking. Granted that he had never purchased a sword or enlisted a guerrilla warrior, his Davidic entry into Jerusalem constituted an implied public promise to lead the fight to free Israel from foreign rule and re-establish the empire of David.

It tells us something about Mark's style to remember that the issue of loyalty to Rome was the subject of the second controversy after the cleansing of the temple, just as divine authority had been the subject of the first one. A re-examination of the pericopes following the cleansing of the temple indicates that each of the controversy incidents was the counterpart of an event in the trials and crucifixion. Mark skillfully constructed the narrative of the events early in the passion week so that each episode was predictive of an event at the end.

Early in the Week	End of the Week
Messianic entry into Jerusalem	Charge of rebellion against Rome
Cleansing the temple	Charge of destroying the temple
Controversy about authority	Charge of blasphemy
Controversy about paying taxes to Caesar	Charge of rebellion against Rome

To this point each of the predictive events led to a charge levied against Jesus in one or another of his trials. The third controversy concerned resurrection and was thus to become predictive of the resurrection narrative following the report of Jesus' death.

The trial before Pilate served two main purposes for Mark. It enabled him to nail down his sonship theme in a much more definitive way than had been previously possible, and it exposed once and for all the hypocrisy of rulers of Judaism in their request for the death penalty. Both purposes were attained by introduction into the narrative of a prisoner named Barabbas who had been jailed for the crime of sedition against Roman rule. Pilate offered the crowd the choice between freeing Jesus and freeing Barabbas. Historians have been unable to uncover a historical justification for such an offer in Roman Palestine, but Mark took the practice for granted.

The name Barabbas means Son of the Father, or literally Son of Papa. Jesus was called to be son of the Father. In Gethsemane he accepted for the first time his identity as son of Father/Papa. From the Jewish priests' point of view the crime for which he ought to have been put to death was his claim that he was Son of the Father. Jesus intuited early in his career that his exploration of sonship was blasphemous and that the scholarly interpreters of scripture would condemn him for it.

Barabbas was admittedly and openly guilty of each of the two major charges which the priests brought against Jesus. His very name was religiously blasphemous. His intention was to become political king of the Jews, thus committing treason against Rome.

The literary function of Barabbas in Mark's Gospel was to clarify the key issue. The Jews were asked to take their choice between two versions of the Son of the Father. The Barabbas version made an open claim to holiness and accompanied it with military subversion of foreign rule. The Jesus version focussed on being the son of mankind and refused to defend against unjust treatment at the hands of Jews and Romans in particular or people in general. Barabbas was what the crowds had wanted from the beginning. His name was what the unclean spirits had asked Jesus to announce for himself. When Jesus chose another version of Son of the Father the crowds abandoned him.

Thus was the hypocrisy of Judaism, as conceived by Mark, finally exposed. Jesus was not killed because he was guilty of either of the main charges against him. He was killed because he refused to be guilty of them. In his passion he would neither act with divine authority, nor lead the rebellious masses against foreign rule, both of which he could have instituted at once by the miracle of taking himself off the Roman cross.

It should be noted once again that the crowds in Jerusalem which cried for Jesus' crucifixion were the same crowds baptized by John. Their willingness to murder Jesus was the final measure of John's failure and theirs.

As at the trial before the Sanhedrin, so at the trial before Pilate the culmination was mockery. In each instance the mockery was symbolic of the nature of the trial. In the religious trial, Jesus was asked to use his miraculous power to identify those who were striking him while he was blindfolded. In the political trial, Jesus was clothed in purple, crowned with thorns, struck on the head with a reed-scepter, spat upon, and given mock homage. Mark may have intended the crown of thorns to complete the predictive quality of Jotham's fable, in which the brambles ruled in Israel when the other three fruits of passion week refused to be false to their good natures.

CHAPTER ELEVEN
THE CRUCIFIXION

Most of the major details of Mark's crucifixion narrative fall into one of three categories. They are details modelled after a biblical psalm, or after the Elijah motif, or after the number three. Most of them are from the *Psalms*. From *Psalm* 22 Mark took the following models:

"My God, my God, why hast Thou forsaken me?"

They have pierced my hands and my feet.

They divide my garments among them, and for my garments they cast lots.

All who see me mock me; they make mouths at me; they wag their heads.

He committed his cause to the Lord; let him deliver him, let him rescue him.

From *Psalm* 69:

For my thirst they gave me vinegar to drink.

From *Psalm* 38:

My friends and my companions stand aloof from my plague, and my kinsmen stand afar off.

As already noted, from *Psalm* 41:

Even my bosom friend in whom I trusted, who ate of my bread, has lifted his heel against me.

The pattern in both *Psalms* 22 and 69 was the same. The psalmist found himself in great difficulty because of his enemies, prayed to God for rescue, and was rescued, after which he praised the Lord. In each instance the entire responsibility was placed on God. When the enemies were winning, it was God's fault; when the enemies were vanquished, it was to God's credit.

The number three loomed large among the crucifixion details. Jesus was placed on the cross at the third hour (9:00 a.m.); darkness began at the sixth hour (noon) and ended at the ninth hour (3:00 p.m.), at which time Jesus died. During the first three-hour period, passersby taunted him with the charge that he had boasted that he could rebuild the temple in three days but could not save himself. Less explicitly, Jesus' cross was carried by a father whose two sons were named, the threesome of Simon of Cyrene with sons Alexander and Rufus; and there were three people crucified, Jesus plus a robber on each side.

There have been many other triads, groups of three, in *Mark*. The Big Three disciples, the three passion predictions each culminating in a prediction of resurrection after three days, the strange references to threeness in the Elijah-Elisha resurrection materials, the three controversies in which Jesus was involved after the cleansing of the temple, the three crossings of the lake by boat. Archbishop Carrington of Quebec referred to dozens of other triads in a book called *The Primitive Christian Calendar,* but admittedly had to be arbitrary in including or excluding many things in order to make the whole book a collection of three's.

The closest that the Jewish Bible appears to come to a precise literal justification for a resurrection on the third day is *Hosea* 6.2.

"After two days the Lord will revive us;
On the third day he will raise us up,
That we may live before him."

A much more persistent biblical theme involving threeness is the combination of a father and two sons. Adam's first two sons were Cain and Abel, and God favored the second son. Abraham's first two sons were Ishmael and Isaac, and both God and Abraham favored the second son. Isaac had two sons, Esau and Jacob, and both God and Isaac favored the second son. Joseph had two sons, Manasseh and Ephraim, and God favored the second son. *Malachi* used this rhythm as his proof that God loved Israel. Mark used this rhythm in the supplanting of Levi by Jacob (James), and of Mary the mother of Joses by Mary the mother of Jacob (James) in the resurrection narrative. He had a father with two sons carry Jesus' cross. Other than that incident, I am not able to discover any evidence which ties the father-and-two-sons triad to the third day theme or to the three time repetition of events. Yet it is obvious that Mark must have intended his biblically informed readers to find a clear meaning in his repetition of threes.

One important clue to the meaning of the event is the name Simon. Jesus had first been anointed for death in the house of a Simon (the Leper); Simon (Peter), in the company of two others, had brought on the betrayal by sleeping through Jesus' prayers in Gethsemane; now another Simon (of Cyrene) carried the instrument of death. The designations "leper" and "of Cyrene" do not seem to be thematically related to the events other than to indicate some relationship to Judaism. A Simon from Cyrene would undoubtedly have been a Jewish pilgrim from the dispersed Jews at the festival, thus on the borderline between Jewish and Gentile. The name Simon was more Jewish than Greek, but the names of his sons were Greek; Simon of Cyrene was a Hellenized Jew. By carrying the cross, Simon perhaps symbolized by his name that both Jewish and Gentile forces were involved in the crucifixion.

Even more important is the fact that Mark specified that Simon was a father. The manner in which he was referred to, as the father of Alexander and Rufus, was unnecessary for the purpose of designating who carried Jesus' cross unless it was important that a father was the cross bearer. This relates back to a puzzling part of the Gethsemane decision.

In Gethsemane, Jesus' prayer centered around the distinction between the will of the Father and the will of the son. The inference was that the Father was somehow on the same side as spirit, and the son on the side of flesh. The key question to be asked is: why was it the will of the Father that the son die voluntarily? Or, to put the same question differently, how were Father and son to be reconciled only by the voluntary death of the son?

In Gethsemane, Jesus took for granted that the Father willed the death of the son. In the crucifixion narrative a father carried the instrument of death, thus symbolically re-emphasizing the Father's involvement in the son's death. This seeming lack of parental concern was even more dramatically highlighted by the cry of dereliction.

The Cry of Dereliction

The agonizing cry, "My God, my God, why hast Thou forsaken me?", is most often known as the cry of dereliction. It is a quotation of the opening sentence of *Psalm* 22 and the only sentence spoken by Jesus in *Mark's* crucifixion narrative. In *Psalm* 22, as in several other psalms in which the psalmist began by complaining of his great troubles, the poem was climaxed by a description of God coming to the rescue and receiving the poet's praise. It has often been suggested that the same pattern inheres in the crucifixion story. According to that suggestion, Jesus was momentarily tempted to blame God, as the psalmists did, but then realized that he would be rescued by the resurrection, somewhat as the psalmists were, and gave a great cry of victory immediately at the moment of death.

The internal evidence in *Mark* points in the opposite direction. Throughout his entire career Jesus had struggled against miracle as temptation. For him to win his final victory by virtue of the certainty of a miracle would be to dismantle the entire case so laboriously developed in his struggle against being satisfied with inadequate goods. It was part of the failure of Elijah and Elisha, of Moses and Joshua, of the prophets' view of the future and the psalmists' view of God that all of them ultimately took refuge in miracle. Jesus had found that miracle undercuts human effort, prevents repentance, disregards forgiveness, leads to self-centeredness, and in all ways keeps one from understanding the role of a well loved son.

The crowds wanted a miracle. They recalled the miracle of Elijah, who was rescued from death at the moment of apparent death. They heard Jesus' cry as a plea to Elijah and sought to prolong Jesus' life to allow time for Elijah or Elijah's God to arrive for the rescue of Jesus.

It was only in the crucifixion that the Elijah example was proved finally inadequate. God does not rescue from death. His love is for man in his condition as man, and needs not be be shown by violating the human condition, as the Elijah tradition held. Nor is it the case that the human son can respond in love only to the rescuing deity. The son can accept death as the will of the father. Jesus did.

In the act of reversing the Elijah imagery, Jesus also reversed the Passover. Judaism had built itself on the theme that God would deliver the pious man from his difficulties just as He had delivered the Hebrews from slavery in Egypt by causing the death angel to pass over the Hebrew homes while lighting on the homes of the Egyptians. However much it may have called the Jews to unique responsibilities, the Passover imagery was based on the Jews' belief in special privilege and a God of rescue. Burton Leiser even suggests that "Passover" would be better translated as "Protection."

It is the thesis of *Mark* and Mark's Jesus that the reconciliation of Father and son can occur only when the son abandons that position of special privilege and accepts his fully human role without expectation of divine delivery from difficulty. The cry of dereliction symbolized that fact. Like every other good in Jesus' career, it was ambiguously both temptation and high calling. As temptation, it invited Jesus to limit himself to the selfish plea of the psalmist, asking for relief. As high calling it was Jesus' commitment to a Father from whom he no longer expected relief.

THE ADULT SON

The events from Gethsemane to Golgotha brought to a climax Jesus' quest for Father-son reconciliation. In every biblical model he had explored the father had in some manner or other taken care of the son. The general traditional image of sonship imagined a young, dependent son, perhaps in the symbolism of *Mark* a twelve-year-old not yet able fully to care for himself.

Jesus' own age was not specified by Mark, but the inference is clear that he was an adult who was received with adult respect and ultimately put to death with an adult punishment. His question, finally, was what it means to be an adult son as distinguished from a youthful son.

In terms of flesh, the relationship of father and son is quite clear. The father is the biological progenitor; the son the result of the parental creative act. That relationship can never be reversed.

In terms of spirit, the relationships of father and son are constantly shifting. Consider the normal ways in which fathers dominate the lives of their sons at age 6 and 16 and 36. The son at age 6 is almost totally dependent; at age 16 he is well along the way of exploring patterns of independence, with a consequent generation gap between himself and his parents; and at age 36 he is entirely on his own. Not long after that, the father in his old age tends to become dependent on the son, and thus in a sense for which neither English nor Greek have an adequate vocabulary the son tends to become his father's "father" and the father enters into a second childhood of dependency.

The religiously radical proposal of *Mark* is that the Father and the son cannot be reconciled to each other until their spiritual relationship is based on the non-dependency of the adult son. The nondependency is mutual. The Father wills that the son cease functioning as a son; the son no longer expects the Father to function parentally.

The most strange and fascinating fact of Jesus' entire career was that all the time Jesus was exploring the possible meanings of sonship he was also investigating the possible meanings of fatherhood. There seems to be no other way to understand the persistent phenomenon of Jesus' associates seeking to place him in the father role. They wanted him to take care of their sick, their leprous, their paralyzed, and to rescue them from death and imperial subjugation. Jesus was seeking to be a proper son; they demanded of him that he be their father, an incarnate representative of the Fatherliness of God, so that they could forever remain dependent children.

Mark's thesis is that Father-son reconciliation depends upon mutual and simultaneous crucifixion of the filial relationship. The voluntary death of the son implies the voluntary death of the Father. Such death is spiritual. What dies is sonship and fatherhood, not the man and the deity.

To be a biologically adult son is to be spiritually not a son at all. To be the father of a biologically adult son is to cease to function in all fatherly ways. Not only that, but reconciliation occurs only when both Father and son know that their sonship and fatherhood are irrevocably gone.

Thus, the cry of dereliction. Jesus committed himself in Gethsemane to the certainty that God the Father expected him to grow up and break off all reliance upon Him. What he did not sufficiently understand then became obvious on the cross: the Father's response would be to treat the son's commitment to adulthood with utter respect. Jesus' exact words were set by the tradition of *Psalm* 22, but the general thrust was that the newly independent son looked backward nostalgically to the time when the Father came to the rescue. Never again!

That "never again" was the completion of the good news which began in *Isaiah* and Judaism. Nothing was left except for Jesus to die.

The death was a real death in the ordinary biological sense of the term as well as a real death in the dependency relationship of Father and son. Every impulse to preserve the interests of flesh was simultaneously a type of sonship. To die as a son, so that one is no longer dependent upon any kind of father figure, is to die to the concerns of flesh, including the concern for remaining alive. Thus the physical event of the crucifixion was the logical culmination of the end of the dependency relationship and submission to the will of flesh.

THE VICTORIOUS DEATH OF THE SON OF GOD

From the vantage point of the mockers (Jewish officials, scribes, robbers) Jesus' death was ignominious defeat. From the vantage point of the Roman soldier in charge of the crucifixion detachment, Jesus' death revealed that he was truly a son of God. In the psychological space between those two judgments, the curtain of the Jewish temple was symbolically ripped in two, and Jesus' separation from temple Judaism made complete. The Gentile soldier was reacting to the manner in which Jesus died. He apparently saw in Jesus' response to his mockers and his great cry a quality of grandeur which Mark was unable otherwise to depict.

There can be no question but what the centurion spoke for Mark. He alone of all the characters in Jesus' life story recognized in Jesus the quality which for the author was the central fact of importance: that Jesus was God's son and that he accepted this sonship by his act of voluntary death. Unclean spirits and miracle-loving Jews had earlier tempted Jesus to other definitions of sonship, but only the Roman officer responded to the crucifixion as an act of a son of God.

Whether Jesus shared that sense of victory or not cannot be ascertained from Mark's account. He left his reader for evidence only a wordless cry uttered just before Jesus' last breath.

The failure of the Jewish religious leadership was accentuated by the puns of Jesus' name in their concluding mockery. Recall that the name Jesus meant God Is Salvation. They tempted him in such words as these:

"Save yourself and come down from the cross."

"He saved others; he cannot save himself."

They looked at salvation in terms of increasing the number of years of one's physical life.

Jesus opened up the possibility, for which Mark provides no content, that salvation meant something entirely different. Jesus had been saved *from* the temptations of self-orientation which had plagued him as each new good had become available to him. He was saved *from* self-preservation, self-emulation, self-authority, and all other self-centered attitudes. Mark did not indicate what Jesus was saved *for* other than to be reconciled to the Father.

Furthermore, Jesus opened up the possibility, likewise contentless in *Mark,* that God was different from what the Jews assumed. He was not the cosmic intervener in the midst of human difficulty, like the Father of a small son seeking to protect him from error, defeat, and death. Rather he was the Father of a fully adult son, standing by in love, permitting the son-now-become-an-adult-in-his-own-right to pursue his own struggle for meaning. The symbol of Jesus' changed concept of God was the torn curtain in the temple, a curtain which symbolized the mysterious hiddenness of deity. The crucifixion eliminated the mystery. What had previously been hidden was now exposed to view. God was no longer the miraculously benevolent parent whose acts were beyond the comprehension of dependent children. God had become, at least for Jesus, the adult friend with whom Jesus was on the same rank. Christian theologians were consistent with Mark in assuming that one could see God by looking at Jesus, even though Mark did not develop such a hypothesis.

CHAPTER TWELVE
THE RESURRECTION

After the crucifixion, Mark reported that several women were watching the crucifixion from a distance, and that among them were three women not previously mentioned by name in the book: Mary Magdalene, Mary the mother of the younger Jacob (James) and Joses, and Salome. All three of those women had come with him from Galilee; others had apparently joined him in Judea. The three named women were the same ones who were to appear at the tomb on Sunday morning for the purpose of embalming Jesus' body.

Their presence at this juncture of Jesus' career calls special attention to the strange role which women occupied in Mark's version of the Jesus story. Recall each of the following.

1. The first miracle: Peter's mother-in-law
2. His family: a mother, brothers, and sisters, but no father
3. The first resurrection: the daughter of Jairus
4. The first faith healing: the woman with a twelve-year-old hemorrhage
5. Herodias' daughter who caused the death of John the Baptizer
6. Syrophoenician woman with daughter
7. Widow who put two coins into temple treasury
8. Woman who anointed Jesus for burial in Simon the Leper's house
9. The women who watched the crucifixion
10. The woman at the tomb on resurrection Sunday

In most instances the nameless women served a significant symbolic role at a decisive turning point in Jesus' career definition. Early, in Galilee, the women called him toward miraculous techniques which were inconsistent with his program of reconciliation with his Father. Later in Syria and Judea, they called him toward his death, although they were each unconscious of doing so. At the end, they were present at his death and tomb.

It seems most logical to assume that most of the women were intended only as symbols. The women did not seem to count for much in themselves; they were used as stage pieces to illustrate the way in which Jesus' quest was influenced by the most humanly routine events. Subsequent to the symbol of opening skies at his baptism, Jesus never again was given any clear sense of direction by an unequivocally divine communication and probably not even then. He had to find his messages from God in the words and actions of ordinary and largely insignificant people around himself. Women fulfilled that role admirably.

Nothing is known about the three named women. The stereotype about Mary Magdalene that she was a sexually sinful woman, perhaps a harlot, has no standing in *Mark*. (The material from *Mark* 16.8b ff. which includes the reference to Mary's harlotry is commonly considered to have been later added to *Mark* by some other author inasmuch as it is not found in the earliest manuscripts. Its themes are strongly anti-Markan.) Mary the mother of Jacob (James) and Joses may have been Jesus' own biological mother, inasmuch as Jacob (James) and Joses were the names of two of her five sons (the others Jesus, Simon, Judas). This seems strange inasmuch as Jacob (James) was referred to as "the younger", as if the reader should know who Jacob (James) the Older was. In the list of the twelve there were two Jacobs, neither of whom was known to have a brother named Joses. Nothing is known about a Salome.

JOSEPH OF ARIMATHEA

Insofar as Jesus was betrayed by Judas, his biblical counterpart was Joseph. In face of the dominant tradition in the other Gospels that Mary's husband was named Joseph, it is of great note that there is no Joseph in *Mark* other than Joseph of Arimathea.

Mark portrayed Joseph as a respected member of the Sanhedrin, thus one who had voted in favor of Jesus' execution but who was seeking to obey God. His response to the crucifixion was to "take courage" to identify himself publicly with the martyred messianic claimant by offering to provide a tomb for him. There is no evidence to support the fiction of *The Passover Plot* that Joseph was a secret follower of Jesus conspiring with him to make it appear that Jesus was really dead when in fact he was only in a coma. In *Mark's* version of the story, Pilate took pains to ascertain that Jesus was really dead. Witness to that fact was provided by the same Roman centurion who had recognized in Jesus' death the credentials of his sonship to God.

The real problem with the Joseph story is its function in *Mark*. On the surface, Joseph's act was the common human failing of celebrating the virtues of a prophet only after the community had put him to death. Americans know this well in the popular reaction to Lincoln, the brothers Kennedy, and M. L. King. In this sense, the story was Mark's dictum that the highest possible response of official Judaism to Jesus was to honor him after having killed him. That hardly seems like an adequate reason for the narrative's inclusion in a book in which virtually every incident had a clearly identifiable place in a developing flow of thought.

One possibility for a more satisfactory answer stems from the possible pun on the "rock" from which the cave-tomb had been hewn. Recall that the name Peter (Rocky) came from the same root as rock: Petron and petras. The relationship of Rocky to the rocky soil of those who hear the word with joy but fall away in times of persecution and tribulation has already been clearly justified by Mark. Peter lived up to

158

his name both in Gethsemane and in the high priest's courtyard, as well as in his flight at the arrest.

In retrospect, it seems strange that Jesus would give a failure-oriented surname to a man who was to occupy the key position in his group of followers. That strangeness was accentuated by the relative disappearance of the name Peter from the passion narratives and its replacement by the name Simon. Jesus was anointed in the house of Simon the Leper, called Peter Simon in Gethsemane, and had his cross carried by Simon of Cyrene.

From Mark's viewpoint as the author decades later, it would make much sense for Simon to have been given an ambiguous surname, pointing on the one side toward failure and on the other side toward truth. Thus the name Peter would refer both to the rocky soil of flight from persecution and the rock from which the burial tomb was hewn.

The most satisfactory solution to the problem of interpreting the meaning of the Joseph of Arimathea pericope comes from taking seriously the Joseph tradition from Jewish scripture. Joseph was the great rescuer. After being betrayed by his brothers and cut off from his father Jacob, he was reconciled to all of them by a series of acts which matched his power and their need. Immediately afterward Jacob pronounced a blessing upon each of his twelve sons, the two most bountiful ones bestowed upon Judah and Joseph. When Jacob died, Joseph's task was to provide for his burial in a cave tomb in Hebron. Thus the final Joseph task was to bury Jacob, the father whose name was synonymous and whose tradition of preferential treatment was the Jewish proof of God's love.

It was that tradition which was symbolically buried by the Joseph of *The Gospel of Mark.* Joseph wanted very much to do the will of God. When he provided a tomb for Jesus he unwittingly did so in a fashion better than he knew. He buried the father and son relationship of God and those willing to become adult children of God just as the original Joseph had buried father Jacob.

It was fitting for Joseph to do so at Passover time. When the Hebrews fled from Egypt at the original Passover, the only sacred treasure they took with them was the collection of the bones of Joseph. His bones were appropriate relics for the rescue-minded Passover Hebrews then and for their Jewish descendants in Jesus' day.

RESURRECTION SUNDAY

The two Marys observed where Jesus was buried and returned on Sunday morning, after the sabbath, to complete the arrangements for his permanent interment. Their names are mentioned three times, once when they observed the crucifixion from afar, once when they observed the burial, once when they came for the embalming. In all three instances the name of Mary Magdalene is written identically. It is not clear what Magdalene means, or if it refers to a town named Magdala exactly where that town was.

The references to the second Mary differ in each instance. At the crucifixion she was Mary the mother of Jacob (James) the younger and of Joses. At the burial she was Mary the mother of Joses. On resurrection morning she was Mary the mother of Jacob (James). In the incident reported in *Mark* 6.1ff., Jesus' return to his fatherland, his mother was named Mary, and his brothers were Jacob (James) and Joses and Judas and Simon.

Despite the difficulties referred to earlier, there are several indications that Mark intended this second Mary to be the mother of chapter six. Judas and Simon each had their separate roles in the passion narrative: Judas as the tool of betrayal, Simon as the rock of burial. Jacob and Joses were mentioned first to identify them as sons of the same mother, and secondly to bring to the forefront again the persistent biblical theme of God's preference for a second son. By comparing the third reference to Mary with the second, it can be said again that Jacob supplanted his brother Joses.

One must be careful here to distinguish between historical details and literary types. Mark gives no hint as to the chronological age relationship between the five sons of Mary. The crucifixion reference to Jacob as the younger does not specify younger than whom. It is clearly the case that in the literary meaning of Jacob that all Jacobs were younger brothers. Literarily, the oldest brother, the legal heir, the one who should have been the favored son, was always being replaced by a Jacob, a younger brother who was chosen to be loved in place of the official heir. This could very well explain Mark's designation of Jacob as "the younger" without any necessity of answering the unanswerable question: younger than whom?

The women went to the tomb after sunrise on Sunday morning, approximately 39 hours after the death at 3:00 on Friday afternoon. Counting Friday, Sunday would be the third day. The passion predictions in chapters 8, 9, and 10 had specified that the resurrection would be "after three days," which might well be interpreted to mean on the fourth day or later. Scholars have differed in their views on that subject. Mark does not seem to recognize any discrepancy between the prediction and the fulfillment. It seemed to have been his intention to use the passion predictions as providing an accurate order for the three trials of Jesus and as an accurate forecast of the resurrection. Also, just as the first two arguments with Jewish opponents after the cleansing of the temple predicted the two major charges to be levied against Jesus, so the third argument predicted the resurrection. That argument concerned the issue of whose wife a woman would be in the resurrection if she had been married to seven brothers on earth. There can thus be no mistaking the generally predictive intention of Mark throughout his book. It is highly unlikely that he would have intended a difference in time between "after the third day" and "on the third day."

When the women approached the tomb they expected to find a stone across the entrance. To their surprise it had been rolled back, but they were never informed as to how the rolling back had occurred. Inside the tomb, they saw to their right a young man clothed in a white robe. Mark did not specify his identity. Other Gospels suggest that he was an angel. In *Mark,* he was a messenger.

The Greek word for angel is the same as the word for messenger. If transliterated it comes out angel; if translated it becomes messenger. If translated into Hebrew it becomes Malachi. It was from *Malachi,* the messenger, the angel, that the message about father-son reconciliation came which enabled Jesus' quest to begin. Now, at its end, a new Malachi, a messenger, an angel, was present to predict a new quest for others.

"Go, tell his disciples and Peter that he is going before you to Galilee; there you will see him, as he told you."

The reaction of the women, appropriately enough, was trembling, astonishment, fear, and silence. They said nothing to anyone about what they had heard. One must not then ask the obvious historical question: if they didn't tell anyone, how did Mark know about it to write it down in his book? That is to treat a literary phenomenon as a bit of historical data, and to impose the standards of the sciences upon the humanities. An author, who consciously uses literary style to convey meanings, creates in his work a world of its own, not subject to the criterion of truth in some other realm. Mark shared that prerogative with all other authors of literary works.

The meaning of the women's silence was obvious. They were afraid to have the rhythm of events in Galilee start again, that chain of lip service adulation and actual rejection leading to a new Golgotha for others among the Jesus people. It was not for themselves only that they were afraid, but for the men. Only men, according to Mark, pursued the reconciliation road which Jesus showed must lead to voluntary death.

Why then should it be said that Jesus was resurrected? The young man, whose youth had been used as a constant symbol of a new Israel throughout Mark's accounts, had said:

"Do not be amazed; you seek Jesus of Nazareth, who was crucified. He has risen; he is not here; see the place where they laid him."

If those words do not refer to the resuscitation of a corpse, a meaning which would destroy the whole fabric woven by Mark, to what do they refer? That is the final question which the reader must answer in order to comprehend the gospel of Jesus as the messiah, the son of God.

The Gospels of *Luke* and *John* are quite clear in their answer to that question. All physical appearances of Jesus failed to communicate his identity to those who should have recognized him if all that was at issue was a resuscitated corpse. *Luke's* two men on the road to Emmaus experienced the resurrection whey they became courageous enough to feed a stranger with their own bread in their home. *John's* Jesus returned for the purpose of sending the disciples as the heavenly Father had sent him, i.e. to die. It was predicted of Peter that if he genuinely loved even in the ordinary sense of filial love that this would lead him to the self-giving love which would cost him his life. Thus in *John* and *Luke* the resurrection of Jesus was quite clearly an invitation to his followers to repeat the rhythm of his career and come eventually to their own crucifixions.

The same holds true in *Acts*. Only those who were willing to give of themselves participated in the resurrection experiences after Jesus' departure from earth. The twelve, mistakenly, looked for him in a sky-oriented miracle. Stephen saw him in his act of giving his life and forgiving his killers. Saul saw him in the courage of those in Damascus who were willing to trust their lives to a known murderer carrying papers which would have extradited them to Jerusalem for execution.

Unfortunately, Mark did not develop a resurrection section in sufficient detail to provide such clear answers. He only implied what the other writers bluntly stated. The meaning of resurrection was not resuscitation; it was not miracle; it was not a condition of existence in after life which would raise questions about the marital relationship of husbands and wives. The meaning of resurrection was symbolized by the return "home" to Galilee where Jesus had worked out for himself his relationships to his religious heritage and found it inadequate to the dream provided by that heritage, that he would be reconciled to the Father who loved him. He ultimately found that reconciliation only by yielding his whole self. That answer was the good news which Mark wanted to proclaim: the gospel of Jesus, the Christ, the son of God.

The instruction to return to Galilee, the home of the twelve, makes sense out of the otherwise diverse details of the story. Galilee was the place of filial relationships. The instructions were given by a malachi, a messenger in the tradition of concern for father-son reconciliatrion. They were given at the site of an empty tomb where there were no sacred relics of a rescuer named God Is Salvation to call them back to reliance upon him. The frightening question for the women, and inferentially for the men to whom they were to deliver their message, was: by returning to Galilee would the twelve discover eventually the same kind of Father that Jesus had? Would the twelve also have to become adult sons cut off from the parental protection?

Peter was given special mention in the instructions. He was called Peter, not Simon. Perhaps it was especially fitting in his case, for Mark knew of his family only a brother and a mother-in-law, not a father. In a simple legalistic sense, Peter was thus free to discover a new relationship to a father.

One final question. In what sense was Jesus himself resurrected? The logic of the comments thus far have been to the effect that the resurrection was an experience of the disciples who were to return to their own versions of Galilee and repeat each in their own settings the quest for father-son reconciliation which would lead them to a new Jerusalem of voluntary death and judicial execution. Is that all?

The answer lies in the distinction between Jesus as a body and Jesus as the son. For the body to be resuscitated would be to set at nought Mark's carefully constructed fabric of anti-Jewish criticism. It would be to affirm that the right answers were always in Jewish Bible, and that the ultimate heart of the God-man relationship was salvation as rescue. It would be to put flesh above spirit and reduce the crucifixion to a weekend interlude in an otherwise active life.

Jesus as son was resurrected. By his willingness to die to the childhood dependency concept of sonship he entered automatically into a reborn adult sonship of independence. Such a transformation of the spirit occurs *in* the body but is not defined by what happens *to* the body, Other New Testament authors were to make much more of this point, but its logic is implicit in *Mark's* brief reference to resurrection.